MARGAR

Learning to Read

'A person who sets up to teach reading should recognize
that he may be more ambitious than he seems.'

I. A. RICHARDS

THE BODLEY HEAD
LONDON

For
S.E.D.S.
J.E.D.S.

Remembering
U.S.B.
H.M.B.
C.R.

British Library Cataloguing
in Publication Data
Meek, Margaret
Learning to read.
1. Reading   I. Title
428.4   LB1139.R4
ISBN 0–370–30722–4

© Margaret Meek 1982
Printed in Great Britain for
The Bodley Head Ltd
32 Bedford Square, London WC1B 3EL
by Redwood Burn Ltd, Trowbridge
First published 1982
Reprinted 1984
Reprinted and bound in this format 1986
Reprinted 1987

CONTENTS

Introduction: A Way In

Most parents I know are keen to help their children to learn to read, but they are puzzled about where to start. I have written this book in the belief that anyone who wants to encourage a child of any age to read and write should have access to the present state of understanding of these processes, and every possible encouragement to enjoy and share the stages by which a child comes to know what reading and writing are all about. If you like books and reading, you will help your child to learn. Begin by believing that he or she *will* learn if you can find the time and the books. It is as simple as that and as difficult.

Teachers also want your child to be able to read and write, but they are officially responsible for the literacy of all children. Most people think that is what schools are for. Sometimes teachers are so overwhelmed by their awareness of the importance of this task that they give the impression that reading and writing are special kinds of learning and therefore bound to be difficult. It is easy to underestimate the size of the operation that confronts most teachers. (Imagine having to meet thirty five-year-olds knowing that they must all be able to read fluently within the next two years.) But it is also possible to overestimate the problem. Most boys and girls do learn to read. The few who do not are those who attract the attention of the reading 'experts'.

Some children learn to read before they go to school; some never need a single reading lesson; others progress slowly; some isolated people remain illiterate all their lives. The individual differences of children are both perplexing and intriguing, so that researchers into the processes of learning are naturally attracted to reading. Their expertise fills many books, mostly written for teachers and mostly about reading failure. Yet we have still not discovered the best means of helping all children to learn.

A great deal of thoughtful research has concentrated on

ways of teaching reading. Most of it is designed to reassure teachers about the *class* teaching of reading and to offer advice about teaching thirty children in one room. The unhappy effect of the pronouncements of reading experts is to make both teachers and parents uneasy by distinguishing certain kinds of reading failure. Before a child goes to school he doesn't really know he can fail. Parents rarely fail to teach their children what they want them to learn. Their parents have already taught them all the things that make them human—to smile, to walk, to talk and to take part in conversations, to meet people, and to feed and wash themselves. At first, reading seems to be another natural activity. Then, as school approaches, it suddenly becomes strange, something to be learned in a different way, in a different place, so parents quickly forget how many things their children have successfully learned with their help.

Now parents look to the experts, the teachers and the reading specialists, and become anxious in case their child may not 'get on' in school. A 'reader' is no longer a child or a person who reads, but a special kind of reading book. There is also a special jargon for reading progress which is judged not by the books children are able to read and enjoy, but by a stage on a chart or a scale. Before long, parents feel that reading is so special a skill as to be unnatural, like Olympic gymnastics or playing a violin in the Albert Hall at seven. They are often surprised to learn that teachers, faced in their turn by other experts, are equally worried and confused. The victim of all this anxiety is, of course, the child.

For the last twenty years I have been a parent, with children at school, a teacher of reading to both children and adults, and a lecturer involved in research into the nature of the reading process. As a parent I have often been puzzled by my children's reading progress. As a teacher I have confronted stony-faced seven-year-olds, aggressive adolescents, and nervous adults for whom learning to read and write seemed an insurmountable barrier. When I came to be a teacher of reading teachers I discovered that, while much extensive research revealed no more than common sense would assume, it also offered a great deal of help and encouragement from which everyone could profit. I have seen a sensitive student achieve as much in a reading lesson as a seasoned veteran in remedial teaching, and I have observed how delight in a simple story well told can bring more success to a child than the most carefully graded reading scheme. At the same time, I have seen parents show all the signs of distress as they pushed their children towards books. I have watched teachers fail for want of genuine knowledge about reading, including the child's view of what reading is all about. And I have learned, painfully sometimes, that parents, teachers and reading experts can achieve most if they collaborate and co-operate on the child's behalf. A parent needs the teacher's expertise to tell him how the child's progress compares with that of others over a period of time. A teacher who hears a child read every day does it for such a short time that practice at home is always necessary. Both profit from the expert's understanding of what reading is—compared with talking and writing, for instance. Above all, each needs the trust and confidence of the others. So this book is an attempt to build up that confidence, and to direct everyone who is interested to the way by which readers are made, namely, by reading books and enjoying them.

To learn to read, children need the attention of one patient adult, or an older child, for long enough to read something that pleases them both. A book, a person, and shared enjoyment: these are the conditions of success. The process should begin at an early age and continue as a genuine collaborative activity until the child leaves school. Understanding the reading process may help, but there is nothing so special about it that any interested adult cannot easily grasp it by thinking about why he or she enjoys reading.

If this is so, why are there reading problems and problem readers? Adults forget how they learned to read; only unsuccessful readers remember the details of their struggles. Once we have learned to read, we stop worrying about whether we can do it or not. We may even read much less than before. It is possible, even in a literate society, to read and write very little. Being able to read when you have to is one thing: doing a lot of it when you don't have to is another. Reading takes time, and nowadays most people are generally much more sociable than in the past when solitary private reading was more common. We have to understand the difficulty children now have when there are so many demands that their lives should be socially motivated. They will read well and may enjoy the activity, sometimes choosing to do it in preference to many other enjoyable things. They will not enjoy it just because adults tell them reading is important. To be fully convinced, they have to find books they like and to see adults and other children reading for pleasure.

But it is still true that reading is very much bound up with school and the academic performance of the individual. Teachers cannot help favouring good readers; they make classroom life easier. They seem to progress more quickly because they learn for themselves. In the same way, teachers like to think that their teaching method works. A teacher and a child who confirm each other form a creative partnership. In our social system literacy is the way to success. Those rites of initiation into a society—the examinations—favour the literate, and most jobs require special reading skills. Every teacher worth her salt wants her pupils to be competent and sensitive readers. So how can parents, teachers and reading experts meet and make the collaborative job of helping a young reader, especially a beginner, a pleasant and profitable undertaking?

In this book I make four basic assumptions. First, that reading is an important thing to do. Without this conviction nothing can happen. In the following chapters you will have a chance to see how it applies to the child who concerns you most. It is also important to realize that not all the electronic media in the world will replace what happens when a reader meets a writer. Reading is far more than the retrieval of information from a collection of printed records. It is the active encounter of one mind and one imagination with another. Talk happens; the words fly, remembered or not. Writing remains; we read it at our own pace, which is the rate of our *thinking*. Real reading cannot be done without thought. As it is a kind of 'inner speech', it is bound to have a marked effect on the growth of the mind of the reader. When your child is learning, or has learned, to read, his thinking is changing in a remarkable way. We often don't notice, because, like all successful development in children and in ourselves, we take it for granted. Can you really imagine what life would be like if you had never learned to read? The social disadvantages—not being able to read street signs or the notices in the post office—are easy to understand. But what about the encounters with new ideas, and the ways we confront ourselves, and society, and our view of life, even when we seem to be doing nothing more sophisticated than reading a novel? We are at home in the world to the extent that we discover there are other people like ourselves, and reading is one of the most significant ways of doing this.

My second assumption is that reading is learned by reading. This is not so simple as it sounds, but it is absolutely fundamental. Right from the start the learner has to behave as if he meant to become a reader. The helping adult must confirm him in this role by treating the beginner as a serious apprentice. The biggest mistake we make is in giving the five-year-old the notion that you learn to read by a series of exercises, like scales in music, and then you are rewarded with a 'real' book or 'real' reading in another form. The children who teach themselves to read do it by turning the pages of books and looking at the pictures long before they tackle the print. When they focus their attention on the print it is because they want to know the story and to tell it to themselves.

The third assumption is the crucial one: that what the beginning reader reads makes all the difference to his view of reading. For very young beginners, reading is a kind of play, something you do because you like it. Gradually you discover it's a specially good kind of play, less trouble than dressing up, but just as exciting for imagining you are someone else and somewhere else. Real readers discover how to be more than themselves. The natural way to do this is to sink into a story. Ask yourself where you *are* when you read a novel and you will see what I mean. Much of what I shall say about reading will be bound up with children's books.

Then, because I am aware that my writing style bears the stamp of a long habit of didacticism (old teachers never die), I must say here that teaching and learning, to be successful, must be genuinely shared. In the early stages of helping children to learn anything, the adult has to do a great deal. You see this clearly as children learn to talk, when, right from the start, the learner takes part in real conversation— even by making noises in response to something said to him. Gradually the nature of the sharing changes and becomes more a matter of taking turns. So with reading and writing. A mother looking at a picture book with a four-year-old who is telling her a story about it is doing something essentially the same as a university tutor discussing a text with a student.

The chief prompting to write this book has come from meeting parents in schools where the subject of reading is kept as a closely guarded secret by the teachers, thereby provoking the same kind of anxiety that comes when doctors on hospital rounds speak in special tones about the fatally ill. There is nothing about reading that parents cannot know and understand. Indeed, the subject is endlessly fascinating for anyone who wants to be informed. I am also concerned that, when there is clearly less money for books in schools, parents should have some help in choosing books for their children that can help them to become readers. The impetus to get involved is strongest when, as often happens, I am browsing through the shelves in a bookshop and I come across a scene such as this:

In a corner, a man on his own is taking books off the shelves and putting them back with barely a glance. Two young assistants try to help, but can't get into contact. A third, more steadfast, asks him the age of the child he is choosing a book for.

'Ten,' says the man, 'but he's not a good reader. I'm looking for something to help him.'

The assistant selects *The Lion, the Witch and the Wardrobe* from a shelf of paperbacks.

'All ten-year-olds seem to like this.'

The man looks at a few pages.

'Isn't it a bit long and old-fashioned?'

'Well this then?' The assistant offers *Silver's Revenge*.

'I don't think he's even read *Treasure Island*. Anyway, he couldn't manage that!'

'Oh, I thought you were going to read to him.'

'Not really. I want him to *learn* to read. They don't seem to be doing much about it at school and he never brings a book home. Have you got a book that would tell me what to do to help him?'

'You mean a *reader*? Or a book about learning to read?'

The assistant and the customer pass on to a shelf marked 'reading schemes'. A small volume is chosen, approved and bought.

When I see this happen, I want to bring together the father, the teacher, the child and a quite different book, and lots more. What I want to do then you have to read on to find out.

HOW TO USE THIS BOOK

Each chapter of the book deals with children learning to read at different stages. Each stage depends on what has gone before and leads on to what comes next. You can begin by looking under the heading of the age of the child you are concerned about. There you will find: an account of what reading seems to involve for a learner at that stage; suggestions for the kind of help a parent or interested adult can give; an account of how some difficulties arise. There are also some examples of the kinds of questions that people ask about children's reading. Some questions may seem strange or unlikely. You have to take my word for it that they all began as genuine enquiries, although in some cases I have made them more general to apply to a wider range of children. Above all, don't worry if you think none of the questions is relevant to your child. Do not ignore the book-lists at the end of the book. What a child reads makes a difference to his reading competence, so begin to help him by looking for books you can read together. Even if you have tried everything that is suggested and your child is already expert, go on enjoying the pleasure and privilege of sharing a book with him in a way that pleases you both. The time for doing this is all too short.

If you have a problem which you think I have ignored, do write to me. If you do that, please begin by telling me all that your child *can* do when he or she tries to read. Real help begins by strengthening confidence rather than by emphasizing failure.

When I teach a child to read and to write I know that no other experience is quite like it. No one need fail for lack of assurance that he will succeed or for want of books that make reading worthwhile. We owe our young people a share of our reading pleasure, good books to make a reading dialogue a real experience and something we can talk about together. I shall also suggest that reading is inseparable from talking and writing and that everyone has the right to find his own voice in writing, for, today, this is what children need to know above all. In all these ways we use our greatest asset, language, to become the people that we are.

English pronouns offer special difficulties to anyone who writes about reading. At each stage in their development, boys and girls show noticeable differences, but these are not my first concern here. Using the non-discriminating plural forms 'children', 'young people' or 'teen-agers' so that I can say 'they' goes against my argument that readers have different individual styles. So I have said 'he' in the first part of each chapter and 'she' in the questions that follow. Consistently and realistically I have used 'she' for the teacher.

I

Literacy

The most appealing reasons for teaching children to read and write seem to be practical ones. In our waking lives we are surrounded by print, much of it in public places—like posters and notices—some of it dropping through our letter-boxes as official letters and forms. We are told in different ways what to do, what to buy and how to take care of things. We are urged to choose special kinds of cigarettes, then the writing on the packet warns us that smoking damages our health. We read advertisements for cars, the Highway Code and the licence application. Newspapers want our readership and political parties our vote. Our names are recorded on insurance certificates, medical cards and mortgages, which, even when computerized, have to be read. All of this is related to a commercial network of buying and selling, and we have an elaborate system of writing notes to each other about our rights and obligations. Just think of all the kinds of reading and writing that come together in something as common as a newspaper.

We take all of this so much for granted that we scarcely notice how we have extended the meaning of 'to read' beyond an encounter with print on paper into the world of advanced technology. Where once people 'read' the stars, teacups, and palms, we now have doctors who 'read' X-rays, and scientists who interpret flashes on radar screens and scanners. We talk of reading meters, dials and radio signals from outer space. Some critics read films, as others do poems. Specialists read the age of the earth in rocks, the tracks of animals in the wild, the signs of prehistory in archaeological finds. Children playing at cops and robbers dash about in imaginary radio-cars calling, 'Do you read me—over'. Modern literacy includes a whole range of special abilities, and children now in school will be expected to acquire some of them in order to be at home in the world we have made.

We put so much emphasis on the usefulness of literacy that we often fail to see that it has always involved more than learning how to read and write. Historically it is associated with human worth and dignity; it has exalted poor men above princes, or, more simply, guaranteed one man a job when another had none. In developing countries literacy always has a high priority so that the privilege of the few can become the right of all. Universal literacy is now the ideal, so that the power that comes with clerical skills may be extended to all classes of people. We accept this idea gladly because we instinctively know that reading and writing are strong means of enlarging our humanity, and this makes them something more than a traditional, basic technology.

This we know, but we seem confused about how much and what kinds of literacy we want. We have not decided if, because life is so complicated nowadays, everyone has to be better at reading and writing than ever before, or whether we want to give everyone the powerful privileges of the literary élite, the professional readers and writers who shape and mould public opinion. Perhaps we want both. The debate is sharpened by the presence of the media that make it less necessary to read as much as people once did. We want everyone to be given a chance to take on at will the wide range of what exists to be read, and to make known their opinions and ambitions in writing, if they want to. But we know that many people may today actually read less. Our failure to solve the problem of illiteracy comes from our vagueness about the implications of these questions.

I believe that every child now in school, or about to go there, should have the opportunity and the help to become as fully literate as he can. By this I mean several things that extend our understanding of learning to read and write far beyond the idea that these are basically useful skills. We all need the kind of literacy that makes us un-worried by the notices at a bus stop, the instructions on a packet or even the writing on an airline ticket. No one should be victimized by our print-dominated world, obliged to believe all he reads or to buy everything he sees advertised. To be literate, in the civic or material sense of belonging to a literate society, is to be able not only to read but also to question the authority of even the most official-looking document that makes demands on us. It is as important to understand the notice about the rates as it is to pay the bill.

But literacy doesn't begin and end in the official sphere of social contracts. It concerns us as people who create our culture, in all its variety and complexity. Good readers are more than successful print-scanners and retrievers of factual information. They find in books the depth and breadth of human experience. Think of all that you would never have experienced if you had not learned to read. Readers are at home in the life of the mind; they live with ideas as well as events and facts. They understand a wider range of feelings by entering into those of other people. They are free to choose one kind of existence rather than another. They can travel over the universe without moving from a chair, or read simply for the delights of idleness.

If you ask habitual readers what reading is for, they will say that it is a special kind of pleasure, or that it has purposes so distinctive that it cannot be replaced by anything else. Reading is so closely linked with their growth as individuals that often they cannot distinguish in memory what actually happened to them from what they have read about. Reading may not necessarily have made them better people, but it certainly has given them access to more experience than anyone can encompass in a single lifetime. Good readers say that they discovered all of this (without knowing until later that they had discovered it) in childhood.

My main contention is that we must offer all our children the possibility of this kind of reading, right from the start. They should also have the means of making themselves understood in writing as well as in speech. Writing begins with having something to say, something important enough to last longer than conversation, and the writer is his own first reader. Although writing is no longer the only way of recording important information—the computer does that now—it is still our best means of making our opinions known beyond the circles of those we talk to. When we wrestle with language to produce a text that matches our thinking we can inspect our thoughts in our own time, there, on the page. The written word not only records what is known, it also creates knowledge. The writer examines the relation of one idea to another. He expresses thoughts and feelings in such a way that a reader can say: 'I see what you mean', or 'I know how you feel'. The literate understand this. Children have to come to know it. When they begin to write they draw on the resources of knowledge and feeling within themselves so that their understandings deepen and clarify. Reading, writing, thinking, knowing and feeling are all bound up in each other.

Although this book is mainly about reading, when we encourage children to read we also have to consider ways of helping them to say what they want to say in writing. In this way we give them the tools of thought and the means of developing their understanding of what they know and feel.

To do this, we have to see literacy as something more than learning to read in a 'basic' or 'functional' manner, to fill in the form about the voters' register or to read a simple manual of instruction about 'How to get a mortgage'. If we want our children to read more competently and sensitively in order to live more richly and to contribute to what is to be read, then we have to move beyond a utilitarian view of literacy, especially in the early days of introducing children to books. The way children are taught to read tells them what adults think literacy is. If we want our children to read well, they must themselves have good and compelling reasons for doing so.

This is where the difficulty lies. We know why reading and writing are important, but our reasoning about good jobs, for instance, cannot impress a beginner. You can't tell a five-year-old about the importance of literacy; you can only help him to discover the fun of it. We know children learn by watching adults; yet many literate parents, even those whose work demands specialized reading skills, are never seen to open a book. A striking paradox of present-day literacy in advanced societies is that, although the standards of competence for everyone are expected to rise, the amount and the kind of reading that most people do may actually be less than the abundance of printed matter and books makes it seem. We are no longer sure what a 'well-read' person is like, except to say that he can read what he wants to without worrying about it. The most curious thing about a fully literate person is that he knows what he needn't read. Good readers are secure in the knowledge that no one reads everything.

This distinguishes the literate from the illiterate. For many different social and intellectual reasons there are still adults in our society who have never discovered how to read. They teach us many things about reading and about how people learn to do it. They also have a different view of literacy. They know its power, its extent, the way it influences every situation, from catching a bus to ordering a meal. Their isolation from the common life persuades them not only that they cannot read, but also that they are somehow a different kind of person. Worst of all, they have a deep and curious fear that, if they *could* read, they would have to read all they see. They have no vision of themselves as readers. So the illiterate in our day become outcasts who are insecure in a way that they would not have been when illiteracy was common. Most adult illiterates blame their schooldays for what has happened to them. They believe their teachers failed them. If they begin to learn to read when they are older, their greatest problem is not with the words on the page, but in understanding how to behave like a reader, in adopting a different view of themselves as people. So when we help children to read, we are also telling them about literacy and society, about the reasons for reading and about themselves as learners. The view of reading a child accepts is the one his first teacher gives him.

Before you start helping your child to read, spend some

time thinking about what you believe literacy is. If you can, try to discover how many of the people you know think reading and writing are simply useful, and how many consider these skills to be pleasurable or important for other reasons. Some will blame television or the telephone for what they imagine to be the decline in standards of reading and writing, but these are also humanizing and helpful things. Consider your own reading. What would you like to read if you gave up doing something else? If you want to help your child, remember that he will take on your view of reading first of all. If you enjoy it, he will too.

When reading experts describe the reading process, it seems very complicated, so that when a four-year-old reads successfully we are rightly astonished. Clearly, there is something special about beginning to read that makes the start important. 'Getting the hang of it' is still a mysterious business, which is why reading experts spend a great deal of time with the small number of children who, despite careful teaching, don't seem to be able to make reading work for them. We now know that, although reading may seem to be the same for everyone, it clearly is not. One of the greatest problems for the beginner is that he cannot tell by watching them what readers are actually doing. He depends a great deal on what he is told to do and this may confuse him because, at first, he has to read aloud, something that skilled readers rarely do. Whereas the child learning to speak enters directly into dialogue with those who encourage him to learn, the beginning reader has two teachers: the one who tells him what to do and 'hears' him read, and the writer whose text he has to understand. Hitherto we have given great prominence to the teacher; now we are beginning to understand the teaching role of the text and its writer.

In the act of reading what someone has written, we enter into a kind of social relationship with the writer who has something to tell us or something to make with words and language. The reader takes on this relationship, which may feel like listening, but is in fact different in that it is more active. He recreates the meaning by processing the text at his own speed and in his own way. As he brings the text to life, he casts back and forth in his head for connections between what he is reading and what he already knows. His eyes scan forward or jump backwards. He pauses, rushes on, selects from his memory whatever relates the meaning to his experience or his earlier reading, in a rich and complex system of to-ing and fro-ing in his head, storing, reworking, understanding or being puzzled. Some successful readers say that they feel they are helping to create the work *with* the author. Children talk about being *in* a book, as if that were a place. We know we can possess a book in our heads after the actual volume has been returned to the library. Sometimes we carry phrases and characters about with us for the rest of our lives. Later we read significant things that illumine texts we had read before we left school. We gain more lives than one, more memories than we could ever have from what happened to us: in fact, a whole alternative existence, in our own culture or that of others. This is what the learner has to learn to do, and what we expect teachers to teach. Literacy has powerful consequences; not the least is that it changes one's view of oneself and the world.

Suppose you ask yourself, 'What does the learner have to learn?' about a child beginning to talk. Can you imagine sitting a two-year-old on your knee and giving him lessons in grammar? But, in fact, this is what you do, among a host of other things, by talking to him from his earliest days. Gradually he begins to talk back, and because you want him to join in a dialogue with you and the rest of the family you don't mind if you do most of the talking and he answers with only one or two words that no one but you can understand. That is a good start. You help him by adding words gradually to his repertoire, telling him the names of things, and letting him take over a bigger share of the conversation. You encourage him by responding and he learns to talk by talking.

In something of the same way, young fluent readers learn by being invited to become co-readers. If a child is shown print as something distinctive in the world around him, to be looked at, both in the street and in books, he will find that the same things appear over and over again. Gradually he pays attention to print he chooses to look at and he says words aloud or to himself. What he looks at and distinguishes increases, until he can match a fair amount of seeing with saying. He recites a notice, perhaps, such as 'Get in lane' or 'Box junction: do not enter box until your exit is clear' every time he meets it. He next comes to know what a book is, and to associate it with the stories his mother or father tells, or the reading they do when they sit down with him.

By this time he also hears rhymes, songs and special family phrases, even swearing. He discovers that when someone reads to him, there is a book voice that accompanies the story. So when he looks at a picture book on his own, he also practises this tone; he gives sounds to the page. Try repeating 'This little pig went to market' and you will see how the intonations mark the stages in the tale so that the beginning and the end are distinguished as much by the way you say the words as by the meaning. The reader has to discover that every story, every book, has its own voice, what I shall call 'the tune on the page'.

The beginner has to learn this and all the other things that we take for granted. He can take time to think about what a writer says. He controls the input, and gradually makes sense of the way the author has linked things together, especially in stories. The interweaving of the reader's meanings and the author's meanings are what we call understanding.

Have you ever seen a child playing at reading, pretending to do it by holding the book (upside down, even) and telling a story he is making up? If you can believe that this child is doing what readers do, getting the hang of reading *as a whole*, then you will have no difficulty with the ideas that follow in the next chapter. The child who plays at reading by imitating what readers seem to do is in a better position to begin to read than those whose first step is instruction in the alphabet. He is discovering what is in this activity that attracts and pleases him, and he is showing that he is prepared to try it for himself. At this point, the question of how he should be taught does not arise, any more than it does when a mother talks to her baby.

The learner has to learn that the stories in books bring pleasure and delight, a way of looking at the world. All else in literacy will follow because he will want to be part of the process so as to prolong what he enjoys. Once he has found how stories work he will know that print on a page unfolds as a living event.

Many children read exceptionally well without a single school reading lesson. They become skilled by discovering for themselves what reading is all about and how to do it. Often their parents help, and the pleasure is shared. Many more could do so if they were not so aware of the part played in reading lessons by teachers in school and hesitant about usurping the teacher's role. Reading teachers seem to be expert, so parents are naturally inclined to look to them as the source of reading wisdom.

A reading teacher's expertise comes from what she learned during her training, and from her classroom experience and the books she reads or the courses she attends. She feels the winds of change as they blow through reading theory and practice. She adheres to the ideas that work for her, and gives her support to those whose books seem to reflect her own practical common sense. Because they are in the classroom where the research evidence has to be gathered, teachers have expertise that cannot be gainsaid. Too often, however, they are given inadequate models or explanations of the reading process and then they trade their own good insights for the doubtful expertise of others.

Knowledge, in the form of theories, information from tests, and practical experience from other teachers, reaches teachers from many sources. Medical science offers details about seeing and hearing. The sciences of perception and neurology are called on to explain what the eyes do and why some children reverse letters when they write. Psychologists have always been interested in reading because it is an excellent example of school learning. A child of five may arrive in school with no ability to read and become quite fluent by the time he is seven. Clearly, teaching made a difference. What did the teaching and the teacher do so that the child could learn? Why do some children fail? How can we test success so that we can diagnose failure and anticipate it? What motivates a child to read? To these and other questions about how learning works psychologists have devoted enough time, attention and money to ensure that they are now the dominant reading experts, and teachers have come to believe that psychological models of reading are the best for their purposes. Therefore they tend to break reading up into stages and to teach each stage in turn. On the whole they want parents to support but not to supplant their teaching, so they tend to suggest that instruction is best left to those who know about the sequence of learning and the materials best suited to each stage. You can see how the situation appears to the child. His parents want to help but tend to be deferential to his teacher. His teacher wants him to do special kinds of reading activities which may not, especially at first, look like the kind of reading his parents hope he will do.

An alternative viewpoint, that reading is too important to be left to the experts, is presented in this book. Reading is whole-task learning, right from the start. From first to last the child should be invited to behave like a reader, and those who want to help him should assume that he can learn, and will learn, just as happened when be began to talk. Once a child knows that print has meaning and that he can make it mean something, he will learn to read. The adult's job is to read with him what both can enjoy, to let him see how the story goes, to help him to observe what is there to be read, and to tell him what he needs to know when he finds it difficult. Learning to read in the early stages, like everything else a child has come to know, is an approximation of adult behaviour with a genuine, meaningful function. The child's guarantee that he will be successful is that he has already mastered an even greater task, that of talking and making speech express his meanings. Again, the adult's role is to respond to what the child is trying to do as he uses his knowledge of language and of the world to discover what happens when he looks at pictures and print.

This view of reading draws its support from two sources. First, from a belief, enhanced by researchers and studies into the development of language in children, that beginning readers know how language functions in use. They expect it to make sense. The second source is our understanding of how vital stories and rhymes are to children, and how early in life they respond to the rhythm of repeated verses as a special kind of play, and how, once they know how a story works, they use its form to help them to predict its sense as it is being told or read. A story is an experience a child can carry in his head. He soon learns that, if it is also in a book, it can be read again and again. When we hear a child reciting a well-rehearsed often-read tale as he looks at pictures it is tempting to believe he has 'just memorized' the words on the page from hearing them often. He is, in fact, behaving like a reader, discovering the satisfaction of a *known* text—we always want the author's words to be the same—having become fluent and understanding how stories work. Because nowadays we judge literacy by a reader's response to *new* text, something he has never seen before, we tend to forget that most of us learned to read by recognizing on the page what we could already repeat to ourselves.

So, when we talk of beginners behaving like readers we also mean that they will recognize what they remember, and guess their way through a text in order to make sense because they know that print carries a message. The kind of teaching that follows on this assumption is that children should be encouraged to use whatever clues they can distinguish to discover what the text means. In the early days there are two main sources of help: the illustrations in the book and a supporting adult to answer the questions the reader asks.

Every year I ask my new class of teachers what they remember about learning to read. Most of them have no recollection of the process; they think it just happened, and that this was unusual. They are always sure that they could read before they came to school. None of them believe that it is quite common and that you can expect this of most children. The teachers who remember their early lessons clearly are those who also experienced some difficulty in matching what they were told to do with their idea of what reading was about. There is always someone who recalls being scolded for 'guessing' instead of 'sounding out' the letters and the words and who read slowly for years as the result of reading one word at a time. The most difficult thing to persuade these new teachers about is that every good reader learns in his own way, *whatever* the teacher tells him to do, by taking the task in hand for himself.

This is not to imply that teachers and others cannot teach a child to read. They can, and do, help him to learn. In addition, the teacher's responsibility is to understand, as fully and as well as she can, what the process actually is, so far as this can be revealed by good research.

The parents' role is different; it is to encourage the child to believe that reading is a worthwhile and pleasurable thing to do, that literacy is within his grasp, and to provide the means for his enjoyment and success. Don't think you have to take a whole course on reading before you start; and don't worry if you think you do not read enough. When you begin with a child the amount you read will increase before you realize it, and you will rediscover the pleasure with him. As you read together, he will learn to read, and you will learn about reading. Remember, you have one special advantage: you know your child as an individual. At home he isn't a pupil, 'a new starter', but someone you know better than anyone else does. You are the first person ever to help him make his way in the world, and the most powerful model for what he wants to be able to do.

The invitation extended to readers of this book, the supporting adults who care about their children's literacy, is to learn about reading and writing as the children you want to help learn to read and write. It involves entering into an equal partnership with the teachers in school and with the children themselves. No child learns to read by reading only in school; he needs lessons, but he also needs supported practice. Parents know best how to tolerate a child's gradual approach to what adults actually do. They understand how a child puzzles things out, how he doesn't mind being perplexed so long as he isn't made anxious. The instinctive expertise of parents lies in their patience and the time they are prepared to devote to what they see as important. Because they think this is ordinary, they tend to underrate it in something as crucial as learning to read, just as they take storytelling for granted, and gossip, and the day's news, and answering questions. Yet all of these things are at the heart of mastery of the written word.

If you want to start at once, or to solve a problem, you can now turn to the section that deals with the age group you are interested in. There you will find an explanation of how reading fits into the other kinds of learning your child is doing at that stage, some answers to questions people ask about it, advice about books to read and what to do to be helpful.

One thing more at this point. The best reading teachers are those who help children to become independent readers *quickly*. But some children take longer than others, and some rely more and more on their helpers when they should be relying on themselves. In reading and writing you are working towards the moment you remember when your child said, 'No, let me do it' about his shoelaces, his coat buttons, crossing the road alone. You will be successful when you are no longer needed as the one who shows the way, but still accepted as equal partner in an enterprise that brings pleasure and profit to you both.

2

Beginning Early;
Before Five

Children are natural learners and well disposed to discover for themselves many of the things they need to know. Parents are natural teachers when they share with their children activities they themselves have mastered and enjoy. Good teachers never underestimate the ability of children to learn, nor overestimate the part they play in the process. This is specially true of learning to read.

There are good and bad reasons for teaching a child to read before he goes to school. In a situation involving books or reading, the first thing a child learns is the adult's attitude to it. Particularly if you are preoccupied with the problems of the educational rat-race and want your child to have a headstart at school, then you should certainly *not* disturb the happy toddler running round the garden, discovering how worms crawl or how his tricycle wheels go round. If there is the slightest hint of fear or anxiety or strain, the child will sense that this book business is different from other activities, so do not try to overstretch the child's natural instincts to learn. The best time to begin helping a child to learn to read, no matter what his age, is when he seems to want to listen to a story you can read to him from a book. He may look at books and recognize objects in pictures round about his second birthday. If he doesn't, don't insist. Do not begin to read with a child until you feel confident that when you show him a book he responds with some interest in it. If he wriggles off your knee and goes back to his toys, wait a little and try again. While it is true that children who have had some experience of reading and books come to school better prepared for school work, there is no point in putting a child off books for good with a forced early start.

The best reason for introducing books to children is that you enjoy books and want to share your pleasure in them. Do you like stories? Do you enjoy songs, poems, rhymes and jokes? If you do any of these things, then look for a book you think you might enjoy reading with your child. Trust your own judgment to choose it, or borrow one from a library after you have had a browse around in the children's picture book section. Sit, relaxed, with the child on your knee, and read the story with pleasure he can feel and share. If the experience is a good one, repeat it sometime later and see what happens.

The child takes his first steps towards becoming a reader by learning to behave like one. Let him help you to turn the pages. Look at the pictures together and encourage him to comment on what he sees. If he slaps the page in his enjoyment, be pleased by his response rather than anxious about the book. When he has had enough, let him go. If later he sees you reading your own book and asks to share it by climbing on to your knee again, pick him up and go back to the rituals connected with his reading. Remember, a new activity cannot always be restrained to fit your convenience. Give him time to look as closely as he wants at the pictures, and answer his questions as simply as you can. This sharing comes instinctively to most people and is all that is needed to make a start. It is neither methodical nor planned; it is always fun, and a special kind of discovery for both partners. You will know that it has been successful when together you meet in real life something that has hitherto been part of the child's experience only in a book and he recognizes it: 'Look, Mummy, a peacock'.

When we read to children in this simple way, turning the pages of a picture book and telling the story, the child associates reading with the pleasure that comes from close contact, unhurried enjoyment of a joint activity, and the feeling that this is a good thing to be doing. The story seems to weave itself around the reader, and this awareness is a lesson that lasts much longer than the time it takes to read the book twice or three times at a sitting. Your child has begun to be a reader because you have embarked on the enterprise in the same way as you have taught him other important things. You have let him join in and given him encouragement, scaling down the activity to fit his size. You did this when he first began to feed himself, to walk and to talk. In each of these things you expected his behaviour to match yours, and you put up with the repetitions of practice that brought him success. Why should reading be different? If we want a three-year-old to read, he will—in the way a three-year-old can.

As long as you are both pleased with this activity and you can find enough picture books, you need do no more than keep up this sharing. Do not be content with reading a story once; a book becomes a friend after a long acquaintance. You will find that reading offers periods of calm in the toddler's exhausting day, comfort after a bump or a fall, occupation for long waits in the clinic or the doctor's surgery or on boring journeys. You can assume that the child knows what you are doing as long as he is interested and you are not selfconscious about reading aloud to him. Gradually, he will begin to know what happens with a book, to tell you parts of the story, or to say aloud the words he knows or the phrases and rhymes that seem to come round regularly. This is the beginning of his taking over. Now be patient; do not try to go too fast.

A mild warning. You may find in bookshops, libraries or even in baby clinics, some ingenious schemes which promote a method or a device for teaching your baby to read. Most of them turn the enterprise into a great trial for the adult. You need not buy any special equipment, nor perform any complicated manoeuvre beyond reading with your baby, sharing the book and letting him help you to turn the pages until the time comes to show him how the print runs from left to right, and how the words are separated out. A library ticket, a copy of Dorothy Butler's *Babies Need Books* and some of the books on the list at the end of this book are all you need at this stage.

Why am I so sure? The experts have begun to examine in detail what happens when children learn to read on their own, and why they can be successful without a teacher. One of the best documented cases, not usually included in books for parents, concerns a boy from a poor home in a southern state of the USA who became an expert reader by learning the words of the TV advertising slogans by heart and reciting them as they appeared on the screen. Another study tells of a number of Glasgow children who arrived in school able to read and confident of tackling anything, as a result of their parents' help and an early understanding of what reading is all about. It is not the bookish home, nor necessarily the middle-class family (except in so far as they are usually aware of what is at stake), not high intelligence, good eye movements, acute ears, right-handedness, nor even extensive vocabulary that makes the successful beginner. The supporting adult, who shows him what a book is and how print works, who helps him to discover reading and expects him to be successful, makes all the difference. Together, adult and child learn about reading.

This is confirmed if we look at children learning to talk, which is the most complex, useful and exciting thing every child learns to do before he goes to school, unless he has some handicap or brain damage. As they learn to make themselves understood, children secure their place in the world and in the conversation of mankind. It all happens in two years, more or less, from the babbling in the early months, through the persistent questioning of the naming period ('what's that?') to the long monologues of the child playing at shopping or pretending to be a space pilot, and the later back-and-forth of family arguments. The more that language experts study children's speech, the more elaborate their descriptions become of what is happening. Yet this complicated activity is mastered by each child, in his own way, very quickly. The dialogue of adult and child is clearly at the heart of the matter. Before the child can speak, his mother supplies all of the conversation. When the child says a single word, the listening parent grasps a whole meaning.

'Out,' says the child, and his mother knows at once whether he wants to go out, to come down from the high chair, or to indicate that his father has gone out. The rate at which a child learns to talk is most closely related to the kind of talk he has with those around him, and the encouragement he is given to express himself in order to 'learn how to mean'.

Learning to talk is the clearest example we have of how children cope with a complex pattern of learned behaviour. Some children begin to notice that speech has different modes, tunes and tones. They know their father's emphatic order: 'Go to bed at once!' They distinguish levels of formality and friendliness and the forms of language that are appropriate for different occasions, in church, on television, with their friends or their grandparents. They know their local speech. Then, when they sit on the adult's knee to listen to a story from a book, they discover that books have their own language, the language of writing, the form that we call *standard* English. Children meet it as the special tone that accompanies reading and stories. For some time they may wonder where it comes from. Then they discover that whoever is reading to them makes the book talk. When, later on, they play at reading, they take up the tune of the story even before they can read the words.

Children's language develops with everyday talk; most of it is directed at getting things done. But there is another kind that emerges when the day's activities are over. You hear it in some children between the ages of two and three, especially if they sleep alone. The child is lying in bed, not expecting attention, talking to himself. If you listen carefully, you will hear that he is distinguishing sounds and practising them. Then he whispers, shouts, squeaks, sings and produces a whole range of the noises that make up words, like a violinist trying out a new instrument.

Sometimes the child laughs at what he hears himself saying: at other times he is correcting mistakes until he is sure he has got it right. There are rhythmic sequences and changes of emphasis: 'Don't *do* that', followed by 'Don't do *that*', for instance, or the rising tone of a question followed by

the stern mode of command. Imaginary characters are part
of the scene. The child talks to his toys about past events and
goes over what has happened in different ways of explaining
and telling:

'This is my house,
This my mummy house, my daddy house, my Billy house,
   my granny house
Houses, houses, houses, his houses,
And mummy goes to work, and Billy . . .'

For all that it seems inconsequential, this early talk is by
no means random. It performs many functions in children's
language learning, but its relevance here is that it is storytelling, the beginning of knowing how to *narrate*. When they
play with language, children separate it out for a special kind
of attention. They inspect the thing that it is, as distinct from
what it says. They play with speech forms in ways that
resemble the nonsense syllables of comic poetry, like Lewis
Carroll's *Jabberwocky*.

We encourage this language play when we make noises for
the duck or the boat in the bath, when we recite nursery
rhymes or sing old songs, family choruses or pop hits, that is,
whenever we make sound patterns apart from ordinary
speech. 'Ride a cock horse' is rhythm rather than sense. The
meaning of 'This little pig went to market' includes the fun of
pulling toes. When he hears the sweet sadness of 'Where are
you going? To Scarborough Fair' the baby need never have
seen 'parsley, sage, rosemary and thyme' nor wondered
about the exact geographical location of the place. The
spellbinding of the song matters most. The enchantment of
the language makes a kind of deliberate strangeness. Think
of 'Hey diddle diddle' and how we confidently say 'The dish
ran away with the spoon', which is a grammatical possibility, not a real one. Children discover early that they can
say things that turn the world upside down, where cows
jump over the moon and men go to sea in a sieve. Yet the
topsy-turvy world is firmly grounded in everyday crockery

and domestic animals. From here to the fairy story is a short step.

These early rhymes are important language rituals that link the child who is learning to speak with the old yet living language that English is. Because they are usually learned in close contact with someone who enjoys them, the texts become familiar with repetition. The rhymes increase the listener's security and confidence until he too joins in and remembers the words. All these old chants and verses that we seem to dredge up from early memories to pass on to our children are the rags and bones of a once flourishing oral tradition of folklore and song, one that our newer print-soaked society has driven underground or transformed into television jingles and other kinds of popular culture. No one knows where the old verses join the new; famous collectors like Iona and Peter Opie suggest that children are the guardians of the oral culture in a way that makes them the inheritors of a literary tradition that is older than books. The enchantment of this lore is what early readers know they can find in stories that they read for themselves.

If you want your child to read early, link your saying and singing of nursery rhymes to their presentation in books specially prepared for children. Find the best copy you can of *Mother Goose* and begin again with Simple Simon and Jack and Jill. Use the book to identify the characters until the child learns the verses by heart, then let him find the names on the page. This is the significant starting point for taking on the heritage of literature in the folklore of childhood.

The next best language gift from an adult to a child is a joke. It is a complete story, a verbal trick, another example of how we separate meaning from words. Part of the ritual of jokes is joining in the game of telling them, or asking riddles even before you know exactly why it is funny or how the trick works.

> 'Why is an elephant large, grey and wrinkled?'
> 'Because if it was small, round, and white, it would be an aspirin!'

As part of learning to read early, the young child discovers that all the varieties of language he hears and uses include the language that makes stories.

As they move about their world, children learning to talk seem to utter most of the words they know as a means of keeping in contact with those around them. At the same time, some of their speech seems to go inwards, to become what we call thought. Not all thinking needs words, but when we think about thinking, then words play some part in the process, especially if we are asking ourselves questions, or wonder what exactly we are doing. When he distinguishes one activity from another, for instance when he says, 'This is reading', a child is helping himself to think about what reading is. Even the idea of 'a word' is a puzzle at first. It is possible that very early readers have some idea that the kind of talking they do in their heads is like the kind of conversation that they engage in with a book. They may even see reading as another version of the game that they play when they recite things to themselves before they go to sleep. Certainly some children learn to read at about the same time as they stop saying things out loud all day long. Then, if they know that they are seeing the words they usually say, they are suddenly free to inspect both the writing and the meaning. A child who is told that the word he is looking at is *little*, may suddenly say, 'and small, and tiny'.

The clues about all of this come from children's play. We have known for a long time that play is not confined to childhood and that it is perhaps the most significant thing we do all our lives long. Important learning, for adults as well as children, begins as play, and it is from watching children play that we discover just how prodigious is the learning that goes on in early childhood. If reading looks like play to a child, it will be taken seriously. In play children imitate the actions that they see adults performing, not only when they make 'pretend' tea, but also when they learn to use a real hammer with a real nail. When they scold the dolls, they learn safely what it is like to master anger and frustration, and in so doing they discover how to separate the world outside themselves from the world of their inner feelings.

No one can make children play; it is their own natural activity. It flourishes best when they are free from the restraints of having to do what other people want them to do. They need only some space to move about in, a few simple materials, and a grown-up who cares about them more than about clearing up the mess. When they are free to invent a new game or to practise jumping off the bottom step of the staircase, they discover the satisfaction of mastering something, of being good at it. The adult's role is to promote play as adventure, while ensuring their safety.

Two kinds of play are worth a closer look in connection with learning to read. Quite often children stop in the middle of what they are doing to examine what they are handling, or to inspect the process they are executing. If a tower of bricks is not to fall down, the top one needs delicate adjustment. We see the three-year-old looking at a big brick and a smaller one, smoothing the corners with his fingers, or even putting the brick in his mouth before he reaches over to the tower. At this moment his attention has shifted from the tower to the nature and size of the brick, a thing made of plastic, like the duck in the bath, or something too big to stay up at the top of a tower. Shape, size and consistency become parts of his learning. One day he will pay attention to words and letters in just this way, but only after he knows what he does with them, to tell a story. Progress in play comes from making and doing, and *then* examining the nature of the material being handled.

At another time we may see a three-year-old building a house under the table. The walls are cushions which cut off the space inside and make it snug. There he lives as someone in another 'pretend' family, with its own rules about washing and mealtimes, although he makes up the rules with reference to the real family he belongs to. If we eavesdrop we discover that the menu for the day is jelly and Smarties. Sometimes he rides round the garden on a broom handle held as either a horse or a motor bike, or his own bike becomes a really fast car. The broom-horse is made to gallop; the tricycle breaks every known speed limit. He is not playing with the cushions, the broom or the tricycle. But because the cushions make walls, the broom is sufficiently like a horse, and the tricycle acts as a car does, the child is free to enter into these other worlds on his own terms. Without knowing that this is what he is doing, he separates the meaning he gives to an object he plays with from the object itself, and *acts according to the meaning*. The idea of the horse replaces the broom in his mind. This kind of play links the outside world with the world in the head, the place where we usually locate thinking and imagination. Here he can safely take risks to discover how the world works and how to make things happen.

What has this to do with reading? Language, both speech and writing, is a system of symbols, where one thing stands for another. By discovering early how to operate these symbol systems, both in talk and in playing with toys that 'stand for' real things, the child represents the world to himself. The pictures in his mind, his mental imagery, and pictures in a book can be dealt with in the same way, because he knows how to separate meaning from appearance, although he does not yet know that he does it, nor how he does it. A book or a story offers him an area like his play world. Tolkien called it 'an alternative world' and created one of the most famous examples for both children and adults to enter. As I said earlier, you can understand this if you ask yourself, 'When I read a story, where am I?' I am not in the novel, not in a space ship nor in the town where the author has set the story. But I am not in the real world either, for all that I am sitting in a chair. We agree to the illusion of being somewhere else. Successful early readers discover that the story happens like play. They enjoy a story and feel quite safe even with giants and witches, because they know that a story, like the house play under the table, is a game with rules.

Stories are the essential link between learning to talk and learning to read, because they are a special kind of play with language that separates it from speech. The simplest answer to the question 'How does a child come to know how print works?' is 'By being read a story'. So we are back to where we began. I have already said that it is never too early to read to children; we need not even wait until they have fully learned to talk; nursery rhymes and jokes depend on conventions of narrative which are forms of play. The child does not separate fiction and fact as we do, and he relates the illusory happenings of the story to what actually happens in the course of his day. The words of the book move into his speech. Early contact with stories and poems has the greatest single effect on a child's linguistic development. Stories are at the heart of learning to read because they make a pattern of the deep imaginative play in a special way.

There is a striking example of this in *Cushla and her Books*, by the New Zealand teacher and bookseller, Dorothy Butler. Her grand-daughter, Cushla, declared to be handicapped and retarded by the specialists who saw her after birth, was solaced from the age of six weeks by her parents reading to her. Because they could not abandon themselves to the despair of doing nothing for a screaming child, they soothed her, and themselves, with stories and poems. Later it became clear that Cushla found in stories a world to grow up in when the ordinary world was beyond her physical grasp. Her slower growth kept her from the society of children in her earlier years, but by the time she was six and a half she could read fluently and had derived a fund of experience from what had been read to her. Cushla was never actually taught to read, 'unless the provision of language and story, in books and out of books, can be called a method'.

Given encouragement, everyone is a storyteller. Any incident becomes a story in the telling of it, and the next simple step is to write it down. Children are often surprised when visitors say that they knew their mother when she was a little girl. They enjoy stories about adult naughtiness and ask to hear them over and over again. If we go one step further and write them down as our child watches us doing it, he discovers that the writing keeps the stories in the form in which he wants to hear them repeated. Here is a family story read many times.

> When I was a little girl I went to stay with my Gran—that's your great-grandmother—in the holidays. To get the milk we had to go to the farm with a pitcher—that's a kind of jar with a lid and a handle. I used to swing the pitcher because I liked to hear the handle creak. One day I was carrying the pitcher back full of milk. I thought I would give it a little joggle to see if I could swing it with the milk in, without spilling any. I swung it, but the milk bumped the lid and it all fell out on the road. I don't remember what my Gran said, but I remember I had to go back to the farm for more milk and I had to eat my porridge without any for two days.

If we read to the child the stories we have kept in this way, he will eventually come to read them for himself.

Stories are naturally associated with people. Many children like to say over the names of their friends and to recall visitors. Some families cut out cardboard figures of the people who cannot come often to see them and they become the characters in stories. At story time the children in the family take it in turn to choose some of the characters and to ask for a story about them. When the stories are written down they are made up into a book. The writing becomes familiar as the young reader discovers that what he hears and sees is made up of the words he knows, especially as he recognizes the names. Then he begins to tell the story in his own way, and to look at the writing in the way that a real reader does. His reproduction of what is actually written is only approximate; about half of the words that he says actually correspond to what is on the page. There is no question at this stage of his matching the writing word for word, but this is the beginning of behaving like a reader, by reading aloud and making the story work.

After this, or at about the same time, the child begins to draw figures for himself and tell stories about them. Or he

39

simply tries to produce his own kind of writing. What adults call scribbling is the beginning of composing, just as babbling is the beginning of talk. Once again, the adult's job is to interpret the child's meaning, this time from his scribbles. A little later, a version nearer to the accepted mode of producing letters can be put alongside or underneath what the child has written, and he can either just look at it or try to copy it. But from the start he can hold his pencil in the right way, between the thumb and third finger, to produce what will come gradually to look like writing, saying his own words aloud the while. Here again the child is making meaning in language. There is no need to insist at this stage that the letter shapes should be exact. It takes time to experiment with what a pencil can do, and see how it differs from a paint-brush. Gradually, the shapes begin to look like print or script, and practice is fun if no one makes a fuss.

The nursery rhyme with its picture in a book, the story written down, the scribbles that turn into meaning are all there to go back to. Writing and print stay on the page to be read again. Because they know what the words say, children expect to get them right, to be fluent when they read them. They will not let the adults change the text that they have heard many times, nor revise any story they helped to compose. When they know the story, and can follow it, children come to know how language works on a page. Stories have a beginning, an end, and a formula to go with each event.

There would be no point in insisting on all of these quite obvious things if we did not know from the sad cases of children who have not learned to read that these are the things they do not expect to understand. Teenagers who leave school unable to read are often very skilled in tackling letters to make sounds, but they have no idea of what a reader does or why he does it. The rest of us who learned how stories work by means of these early lessons have usually forgotten that they matter. It is important not to be so anxious to help children to hurry on that we miss the essential features of the starting point.

One of these obvious things is that the child's world is

full of print, and sooner or later he will notice it. Hundreds of children have learned to read from advertisements on hoardings. Many a non-reader has failed just because he did not link the way he looked at advertisements on his way to school with what he has to look at on the school noticeboard. Every London child who buys icecream knows the differences between the kinds offered by the two chief suppliers, and even those who are classed by the schools as hardened illiterates can distinguish the writing on the labels. Everything that children eat, wear, play with or pass in the streets has a sign or a symbol, usually in capital letters. The signs are embedded in the context, like the name of the motor car. In the supermarket the familiar cocoa tin and the cereal packet become traditional promoters of literacy, which is why the busy adult must tolerate the child's question, 'What does it say?'. Television advertisements are stories where certain words are isolated for repetition, and when the youngest in the family begins to notice them, he asks about them or makes sense of them. Most children promote their learning in this way. They guess the meaning of what they see; the surrounding context provides the feedback of whether they are right or wrong, and gradually, as they did in play, they look at individual words and letters.

It is so easy for us to take all public print for granted that we often forget our part in pointing it out as something to be looked at. One of the paradoxes of being literate is that we know so well what notices and signs are, and what they say, that we no longer look at them. The learner, on the other hand, can make good use of such things—particularly during those long waits at a bus stop.

If stories are at the centre of early reading, when does the real work begin? Where are children to learn their letters? Should we not be helping them with that as early as possible? Stories and scribbling are all very well, but in the end do they not have to decipher words and learn the rules of spelling? These questions are very natural, but it is my contention that children should not be taught letters as if this were the secret of learning to read. It is better to practise drawing letters for fun, to recognize them on signs for the train or the post office, or to see them as initials of a name. Some parents even bake them in dough or ice them on a cake. There are wooden letters for the child to handle, and magnetic ones to fix on a board. But at this stage, they are essentially toys, play material, and in the course of play they can be inspected and recognized.

Letters are normally associated with sounds. Songs, jokes and rhymes are the best way to explore sounds. It is difficult for a competent, logical adult to admit that it is a hopeless task to attempt teaching the spelling-to-sound correspondences of English as a system of rules. Yet very few readers ever learn that way. If your child seems to be asking about letters, point out examples either in a book, or when writing his name, or in the print you see as you walk around the neighbourhood. Try very hard to resist the temptation to insist that your early reader should 'sound out' the letters of a word to please you. If he does it by himself, that is a different matter.

The greatest conflict for even the most patient and helpful adult is to tolerate the child's mistakes in the reading or copying of print in a book. Here I must repeat that if the child under five can make a satisfactory meaning for himself out of what he tries to read, then he will come to get more words 'right' as he reads more. A two-year-old, turning the pages of a book he likes and knows, telling himself the story, or even a different story, is nearer the actual business of reading than a child who reads small units of texts without ever making a mistake, and without understanding a word. It *is* difficult to believe that children teach themselves to read, as they teach themselves other important things, because reading and writing are not as natural as speech. But we should not underestimate what children can do. What we have to rethink is the best kind of help to give them. The golden rule for helping a child is still: read *to* him, and *for* him, in a way that will let him discover what reading is all about. If you do this, he will never be bamboozled later on by what people say he has to do. Then, as he is gradually able to do more of the reading aloud, you can do less. It will seem like memorizing at first; this is quite normal, natural and right. Reading familiar books and stories brings fluency, which is a feeling of knowing oneself to be a reader, and not simply freedom from error. Even the most gifted reader makes mistakes when reading aloud.

In the four or five years before a child goes to school, he seems to have to learn so many things that learning to read as well may just be too much. You don't have to follow the programme I am now going to suggest, but I believe it can be pleasurable and profitable for both adults and children. There are stages in the shared process of learning to read; the age of the child is of much less importance than the experience he is being offered. Don't think that if you have missed a step there will be a problem. Children learn to read by discovering what to do and by making the most of the help they are given. The younger they are when they start the smaller the initial step they will take, the more help they will need. This is not a set of specific instructions to be followed exactly, but a number of suggested ways to help a pre-school child to become aware of books and a supporting adult to understand what is happening. There is only one rule: avoid frustration and enjoy the time that you spend together and the books that you share.

Stage One

In the very early days you will be too busy with other things to think much about learning to read. When you begin to be excited about your child starting to talk and you can linger over his contented periods after all the necessary rituals of play and walking and meals, be sure to sing songs, repeat rhymes and play games that have rhythm and word repetition. Do you know finger games, like 'Round and round the garden', and rhymes for swinging and jogging, like 'This is the way that ladies ride'? If you have forgotten all of these, look for a book like *This Little Puffin* to remind you of them. If you play guitar, the piano, or any other musical instrument, you will already have introduced the baby to its sounds. Records and cassettes of nursery rhymes will help if you run out of lullabies and rocking songs.

Read something to the baby before he can talk. Put him on your knee with the book in front of you both. You can choose a book with stiff pages, like the Bodley Head board books, or *My Big Picture Word Book* where the game is to name the objects on the page and to talk about them. You will soon begin to notice how many early books for children are about animals and creatures smaller than they are. Don't be in a hurry to find an alphabet book, even a simple one. Look for a well illustrated book of nursery rhymes (I have listed some collections on p. 229). *Cakes and Custard*, edited by Brian Alderson, illustrated by Helen Oxenbury, is a beautifully produced one to borrow from the library or to ask for when someone wants to give a birthday present. You will soon discover which books please you both, are easiest to handle, have the pictures your child recognizes with most pleasure and the words that make a pattern and so become memorable.

The first stage of reading with a very young child, or even with one approaching school age, establishes how a book works. Turn the pages together and show where you are looking for the words, on the left-hand side after the first page. Read stories that have a distinct shape, then look at a picture book with no text. When you look at the book a second time, let the child help to turn the pages. When he can talk, let him guess-remember what is to come when he turns over. Gradually you will discover if he has grasped the idea that the reader makes the meaning from what he sees. A good book to begin with is Pat Hutchins' *Changes, Changes*. Artists know how children link ideas with images before they can explain themselves. In this story a wooden toy man and woman use a set of bricks to build for themselves the kind of things they need—a house, a boat, a lorry—as the story develops. The text is what the reader says he sees. The reading lesson is that books are handled in a particular way and inside books are stories in pictures. Gradually the readers of these wordless books settle for a version of the story which they can repeat until they are satisfied with it.

Some books are toys in disguise, like those with pop-up pictures. Some are no more than a tribute to the maker's ingenuity with movable parts; others have enchantments that add to the illusion of the story, like Eric Carle's *The Very Hungry Caterpillar* who eats his way through the pages. Early word play reappears in the splendid rhymes of *Drummer Hoff*. When you read it for the third time, even the youngest reader anticipates the rhyme of the couplets. Among the old and the new there are many story books of undoubted imaginative worth which you will discover by looking and reading. You will find some old favourites in a new guise and a host of new illustrations of traditional tales.

If you do not like children's stories and are happier with books that reflect your practical interests, there is no need to force yourself into the world of children's fiction. We only read well what we think well of. If, as a result of your enthusiasm, your child wants to see pictures of motor bikes or aeroplanes, begin there, even with quite young children, for you will be able to fill out the text with your own expertise. But be careful not to let the book take the place of looking at familiar or special things in the world outside that you encounter from day to day. If you want to look at pictures of mountains when you have no chance of climbing them, that is like imaginative play; the child will turn it into a story. But avoid at all costs a book that assumes that your child has no everyday experience of ordinary things. There is no need for a children's book to begin 'This is the front of a motor bike'!

By now the child will have learnt in all of these ways that books, pictures and print are meaningful, and to read is to attend to meaning, in the way that we said the broom becomes the horse. When he begins to look at the words in order to say aloud what he thinks is written for him to read, the beginner *approximates* to what he sees written down by using the pictures to help him to guess what the words say. Gradually he discovers that the words do not change; every time the adult reads, the same words come out. So the beginner teaches himself to be more and more exact. In the case of a nursery rhyme, he may already know the unchanging sequence of the words so he is free to examine what they look like in their written form, and he practises his matching that way.

Stage Two

Now let him turn this reading-like behaviour on to print. The classic is Pat Hutchins' *Rosie's Walk*, a text of thirty-two words which can be read over and over for the fun of the story. It also teaches some fundamental reading lessons directly related to the process of becoming a reader. If you open the book face downwards, you and the child can see the story at a glance on the cover. Rosie the hen walks round the farmyard followed by the fox. Both are instantly recognizable in the fine stylized drawings as the archetypal figures of the fable that goes back to Aesop and beyond.

As you turn the pages together, the words *Rosie's Walk* appear three times more, as is the way of covers and title pages. The shape of the letters changes but the words are recognizable as being the same. The young reader is now learning what to look at, and to notice the sameness or the difference. (Incidentally, as long as the letters in early books are well spaced and not too small, the typeface is not a serious matter.) Then comes a page which says: *For Wendy and Stephen.* If your reader is at the conversational stage, it is worth pausing to explain that the artist who made the book had two special children in mind who might read it, but the story is for all to share. This may not be clearly understood, but the idea of the dedication will be picked up again later. The surprise that greets information of this kind when it is offered to inexperienced readers in their teens suggests that here is another thing about reading that initiates take for granted.

Now you read the story: *Rosie the hen went for a walk/across the yard/around the pond/over the haycock/past the mill/through the fence/under the beehives/and got back in time for dinner.* On the pages that have only pictures, the fox is in trouble. Does Rosie know he is there? Is she wisely not looking? Most children of four or under can learn to read the words by themselves. Look at *haycock,* a bookish word if ever there was one, but familiar if you know 'Little Boy Blue'. See how the sequence works. The fox is never mentioned. That he is following Rosie is implied in the pictures, and his troubles are seen as just retribution for not looking where he is going, but the author leaves him out of the text. The reader is in league with the author; this is one of the rules of the reading game, and best learned early. Some children never learn it, not because they cannot read, but because the books they are given do not include this need to attend to what the author is *not* saying—the beginning of an experience that leads to Jane Austen. The organization of this book also offers the readers the chance to anticipate and guess what is coming in the story, even when there is a comic chance of their being wrong.

All good readers learn to predict both words and events. Knowing how sentences, words and episodes are strung together makes us confident that we shall understand them. This beautiful little tale has most of the conventions that a child needs to learn at this stage, in addition to the vital one about his collaboration with the writer.

This may seem a long roundabout way to explain what a child learns from his early reading experiences. But too often the adult's anxiety is focused on the text, on saying the words, on getting it right. There is a time for all that. At this stage, only getting the words right would be no reading experience. In the case of *Rosie's Walk* it would be a denial of how the book is to be read. It is natural to want the reader to know the words and to recognize them, because it would seem that, in so doing, he would progress logically to other kinds of word and letter recognition. But everything we know for certain about the way children learn suggests that they do not follow an adult's logical analysis of the process. A child who has read *Rosie's Walk* in the way that makes the story meaningful to him arrives at school with an expectation of what reading is, that will carry him into the rest of his learning with confidence.

This is the time to begin writing stories together. It may seem strange at first, but you can begin by drawing a picture and encouraging the child to do the same. If you recreate an incident, the shopping expedition, a bus ride, a visit, you will talk about it and the story will tell itself. Or you can draw pictures of other members of the family and read something about each one.

'Aunt Mary comes to see us on Tuesdays. She comes in a train.'

It is not too soon at three and a bit to let the child have pencils and crayons and sheets of writing paper or of wallpaper lining or of the kind that butchers use. Again, you have to be patient at the start because not every child instinctively knows what to do with drawing materials. If you are a competent artist you will know how to help, but at least anyone can write the child's name and encourage him to copy it in his own way. Don't guide his hand unless he wants you to. He should make his own attempt first. It will be only one letter at a time at the start.

All of this is still an extension of the child's play. For the adult other satisfactions emerge. Some parents discover the joy of reading for the first time, simply because of the abundance of reading matter, picture books and stories. Others rediscover the pleasure they thought belonged only to childhood. Those who have given up what little time they thought they had to reading with their children have found that they no longer say they have no time to read, and become readers again. You will also discover, when you have been looking at children's books for nearly a year, that you develop some genuine expertise in selecting. By this time you will have views about the stylised drawings of Dick Bruna, for example, and know how artists can either support the text or extend it with their imaginative response to the story. You will know which illustrators draw children into the picture so that they, in a sense, walk around inside it. This is very important for understanding a story, and *getting the feel* of the book. Colours, shapes, shadows and lights are learned as reading skills, just as words and letters are. You will remember the day when your child first laughs at a picture even if you do not understand the reason for his glee. My conviction about the imaginative power of Maurice Sendak goes back to the day when my three-year-old found a copy of *Where The Wild Things Are*, and with prodigious mirth pointed to a monster on the middle page and said, 'Look Mummy, Granny'.

By the end of this stage, the young reader knows how to turn a book the right way up; he looks at the left-hand page first; he knows the story is in the print as well as in the pictures. He can recognize most things in their pictured form and he can remember the sequence of a tale and predict possible actions that the chief characters may become involved in. In some cases, he has begun to talk about the characters as if they were real people, often asking questions about what they are like and what they are doing. There is also the beginning of a sense of suspense, the idea that in the course of a tale things may go wrong, but by the end there is a resolution of the difficulty. These are all reading lessons, and important ones.

Stage Three

By now your child should have some books of his own that he knows to be among his possessions and his toys. He will have been to the library. He will have heard nearly thirty nursery rhymes. (You don't need to count them; that's an average repertoire for a parent who has recalled his or her childhood collection and added some new ones.) Grown-ups will have begun to tell him stories, especially funny tales. He may have begun to count the stairs as he climbs them and have pushed letters into a letter-box. As you go about with him you have begun to point out pictures and public print. He may even know which notice says his dog cannot go without a lead, and when he presses the button at a traffic crossing, he will recognize the word that says, WAIT. Above all, he is now talking with greater fluency and asking all kinds of questions.

Play is still all-important as a means of trying out new things, so this is a specially good time for longer stories and for distinguishing the kind of activities that belong to reading and writing. Read together regularly now, not only at bedtime when you are both tired, but after breakfast or lunch. If that is too idealistic for working mothers who are bound to entrust their children to others during the day, then encourage the baby-minder to read a book the child may bring with him from home. Then sit with him—ten minutes will do—when you are both together again at the end of the day. Reading is such a good way to unwind, better even than the flickering distraction of the television, if only because it's quieter. The supper will still be on time; the clearing up will wait. You will never have this vital playing time again.

When you read together, try to go right to the end of the book at one sitting. Talk about the pictures and the text and encourage questions about both. Don't be too anxious to discover if your child understands everything, and don't be afraid of the new words that authors introduce, or the new ideas that seem to be puzzling at first. Above all, keep going back to favourite stories as well as forging ahead with longer stretches of print. Look at Beatrix Potter's *The Tale of Peter Rabbit*. This is the classic tale to be read at any time. If you think it is a little old-fashioned, try to find the small books by John Burningham: *The Dog*, *The Blanket*, *The Baby*, and *The Rabbit*. Each is a perfect example of how short a story incident can be. See how John Burningham conveys in a sentence ('I wish the dog could stay with me') the feeling that accompanies each stage of the action, and how the pictures extend the reader's feelings beyond the text. If you are in any doubt about reading to your child, compare these books with the ones prepared for reading schemes and you will then see the difference. I could easily be emphatic and say that the best books for children, at this or any age, are those that reflect the author's and illustrator's pleasure in making them as well as they can. I believe that. But I know that some little books of indifferent value can also help at this stage. Enjoyment is what matters.

Stage Four

As school approaches, it is difficult not to worry about all kinds of things, and anxiety about reading always gets worse. For one thing, there is now no lack of advice from many sources, and this in itself increases the parents' fear of the child's possible failure. There are so many reading experts that the efforts of interested adults seem amateurish. As we watch children looking at books, turning the pages quickly and guessing the story, we are tempted to believe that this is 'just play' and that real reading begins when the school takes over and the reading becomes accurate, the exact reproduction of the words on the page.

At the risk of being repetitive, I must say again that the most important thing is the learner's belief that he can turn print into sense. The stages of learning are the developing ways of making the print mean. Sometimes direct instruction about what to do stands in the way of a child's learning. We have to believe that if the young reader expects to take in hand the task of turning the print into meaning, getting the words exactly right will follow. But that's the order. Many a child can reproduce aloud the author's words without any understanding of the story. Knowing what reading is all about is the most important reading lesson of all.

In all that I have said so far, I have insisted that the child should behave like a reader. This includes asking questions about the pictures or the story in the book that is read to him and gradually increasing his experience, with adult help, of the kinds of books that are available. By the time they go to school, most children who have had experience of books have begun to see that some things happen in stories that have not happened to them. When you read *The Tiger who came to Tea* with a four-year-old he knows that the chances of this happening are not high. But he doesn't reject the idea.

51

Instead he considers the possibilities. Reading, even for four-year-olds, has its speculative modes.

By the time they are four, children really enjoy being told stories. Television and radio programmes enhance this; they are greatly to be applauded for the support they give to children's reading, especially as they bring new books to the notice of parents, teachers and librarians. If your child listens to a radio story or watches *Jackanory*, you are bound to be making good use of the time when he is thus occupied. Try, however, to let him talk about what he has seen or heard. You will soon discover which stories he would like to hear again.

As the span of his attention increases, let him look at a book with you and, as far as you can, let him take the initiative in talking about it. See how long he can give to what he is doing. If he is being hasty or casual, try to encourage him to look a little longer, without coercion. By now you will have begun to vary the kind of books you read. There is no reason why he shouldn't look at pictures in a newspaper or in an adult book, if he is interested.

As you read together let him say aloud with you the words he knows, so that he gets the feel of the rhythm of the written language in utterance. You will probably enjoy looking at picture books of cumulative rhymes ('This is the house that Jack built') or traditional tales (*The Old Woman and her Pig*). You are bound to go back to earlier favourites. Let the child take over more and more of the saying. If you point to the words, let him point too. Show him how the print runs from left to right across the page, then show him where to put his eyes as he turns the corner into the next line. Don't be more emphatic than he can stand, and rather than insist that he should do it, say, 'I'll show you where my eyes go when I read and how I know what to say.' This should give him the idea of looking ahead. If he can do this and expect a meaningful story, he is in good shape for beginning to read at school, provided that the idea of reading still appeals to him and he looks forward to school with enjoyable anticipation.

Try to vary the kinds of books you read together rather

than to step up the intensity of word recognition. If you are really keen to make him recognize words and letters, then use the public print of outdoor signs, where the environment gives the context clues, rather than spoil a story by making it a word-recognition exercise. Encourage him to talk about what he sees and the words he recognizes.

Don't forget that the rhythm of language is one of the greatest helps to extending understanding, and the sounds of language are intimately bound up with meaning. I have a passionate conviction that this is the stage when poetry becomes a special way of saying things, a kind of enchantment for which there is no substitute. *A Child's Garden of Verses* and *Come Hither* are so surely part of my childhood that I want every child to know what words *make*, as well as to understand what they say. When school reading takes over from the pleasures of early discovery of books and stories, reading aloud will be all the easier if the child's fluency in spoken language is also grounded in a poetic tradition older than writing.

By this time you will have written stories together and your child may read them fluently and be able to dictate some for you to write. Concentrate on these familiar things when school comes near. Don't push him to read longer sentences or to decipher new words. None of the security and confidence that you have built up should desert him now. Don't worry if you are more often reading old favourite stories. Even if he seems to be 'only memorizing', that is perfectly all right. Do not become impatient with him if he guesses a word wrongly or doesn't always want to read. Above all, don't threaten him with school, or emphasize unduly the part that reading will play in his progress there. Remember, many of his future classmates will be just beginning.

It is tempting to want to teach him the alphabet, and I cannot say you should not. If you want to, be sure to treat it as the same kind of play as the other early steps. The Victorians were as good as any in devising alphabet books (some of which are really very old indeed) and their rhyming ones have much to commend them:

A was an archer and shot at a frog.
B was a butcher and kept a great dog.

On p. 231 there is a list of modern ones from which the child can select those he likes. Remember, he is unlikely to repeat the alphabetic sequence straight off. If you insist that he should, it might be at the expense of something else he ought to be learning.

When children begin to make progress we are tempted to believe that they will keep up an even rate, or even go faster as their reading ability increases. They won't. They may even slow down at the very moment when they are beginning to understand something better. If you have doubts about any stage, go back to the last book, to the most recent experience that was a success and remember the pleasure of it. Many four-year-olds are nearly able to take off on their own because they have experienced *real* reading. But sometimes their independence is delayed because they have had their natural inclination to play and to practise cut off by the adults' over-insistence on only one aspect of the process. We have to understand that, just before he becomes independent, the young reader has worked out for himself what he has to do. All children do this differently. Our job is not to get in the way, but to be patient and not take the operation away from the child. Some discouraged readers I know have had so much help that they have lost confidence in their ability to read for themselves.

Throughout this section you may have thought that the ideas and the activities associated with them assume that most children spend their pre-school days at home, or in the company of caretaking adults who give them constant attention. Not so. A great many children go to nursery schools, to playgroups, or are looked after outside the base that is their home. Would they get the attention that this reading activity seems to require? Parents who come home late are not in the most relaxed state to begin a quiet read, and sometimes the bedtime story happens in a hurry in even the best-regulated households.

Nursery schools do not usually undertake to teach children to read, and those that do so are similar to infant schools with younger children. Nevertheless, in many nursery schools a teacher will read to children with great success. In the social situation of the group, children discover that being read to can be a different kind of spellbinding experience, the group in thrall to the storyteller—the nearest we ever come to what our forefathers knew when the ballad 'drew children from play and old men from the chimney corner'. It is worth going to school for.

If, at any time, reading becomes a source of worry to a child or to his parents, it seems worth taking stock of all that it is possible to do in the time that remains before school, even for very busy people, to foster a good feeling and some confidence about it in both the adult and the child. As long as he is at home, the child has a certain amount of authorized favouritism that becomes less as soon as he spends most of his day in school. Studies of early readers make it clear that adults are necessary to ensure that the child has the time and patience that practice needs.

The child who is a successful early reader will remember practically nothing of the way by which he learns to read. But all young readers recall, with a powerful nostalgia, their earliest books: the thrill of Peter Rabbit in Mr Macgregor's garden, the little red engine, the giant turnip, the magic, the mystery and the strange spells that reading wove. They have only to pick up a book, from adolescence to senility, to remember how 'Once upon a time . . . ' brought both delight and power. Asked once by his mother what was the nicest thing that ever happened at Christmas, a child replied, 'When it was raining, and you read our new books to us *for a whole day*'.

3

The New Partnership;
Five Plus

School is the society where children are more important than
the adults, but the adults are in charge. It is not like a family,
where the child expects to make claims on the attention of his
parents. When he goes to school, he has to share his teacher's
attention with all the others in his class. Parents see schools as
institutions which take over the care of their child and they
vary in their reaction about this. No parent sees the approach
of the first day at school without anxiety because each knows
that the organization of the child's life with adults will change.

The child's worries about school are vague apprehensions. Even if he has been to nursery school or playgroup he
knows that the move to the official school building is a
significant one. People say 'So you're off to school next week
then!' and leave a trace of both excitement and uncertainty
in the words. Even if the school is a familiar local landmark
where other children in the family have already gone, and
the teachers can be seen with shopping baskets on Saturday,
it is difficult for a child to imagine this new and widening
world. Television presents schools in many forms, both
documentary and fictional, and the lore of the playground
spills out into other playing groups. But it is still puzzling to
know why children, when they anticipate what might happen by playing at school, often put their toys in a line,
assume a commanding air, and with a ferocity long since
banned by law, give lessons in stern voices to the immobile
playthings who are then instructed in reading and kerb drill.
We are bound to wonder where this picture of school comes
from.

Some people have never been in hospital or in an aeroplane, and there are those who have never seen the sea. But, with very few exceptions, we have all been to school. Our reactions to it cannot be neutral because our personal lives were in some measure shaped by what happened to us there. When our children are about to go to school, we remind ourselves of what it was like for us, and we are often determined that our children should enjoy it more than we did. Anxiety is natural, but it is better not to share with a five-year-old whatever reservations we may have about the local school before he goes there. Most parents nowadays have been at school for longer than any others in history; they really know about what happens there in more detail, for all that school ways and customs have changed in the last twenty years. So when we scurry round looking for a pencil-case and clean socks, we are acknowledging that education is a shaping force in the lives of our children, and preparing for the first stage of their partial separation from us. For years we have accepted full responsibility for what our children do and our caring has deep roots. As we see our children off to school, we feel we are making them ready for activities they will share with others before they share them with us.

Most infant schools take pains to introduce new pupils gradually. A visit to the headmistress, a tour of the hall, the cloakrooms and sometimes the library, a view of the class-rooms and an introduction to the teacher are all meant to make the transition easier. Even the friendliest of chats, however, tends to convey the message that there are school ways of doing things. On the first day itself, the initiation rites are as memorable as anything ever will be again, until the first job, perhaps, or leaving home as an adult.

The first day itself, exacting for the child, a strain for the parent, often passes without comment beyond, 'we had green peas for dinner'. The anxious parent is left to wonder what happened to the dinner money, was the child suitably polite, did the teacher like him? The first hurdle for the parents is, does the school want parents to come near enough to see what is going on? It is a good idea to find out during early visits what you are allowed to be part of. The more you can discover about the kind of relations that exist between the school and the families it serves, the easier it will be to know how much you are expected to be involved. It is natural to want to know what goes on, so take advantage of any invitation, formal or informal, to visit. During the first year, some schools even let one or two parents stay for assembly, or invite them to spend the last hour of the day with a class.

Children begin school with a great sense of anticipation of the possibilities that stretch ahead. A few complain that they have not been given a reading book straight away, and others, less certain, think that one day a week is enough to be away from home. Many children are not easily sociable; they need time to adapt to a new situation. They discover that they have to take turns, to wait for the adult to notice what they are doing. Above all, they are sometimes puzzled when a parent asks questions like 'Did you tell Mrs Evans about your holiday? Have you got a reading book yet? Who do you sit next to?'

Anxious adults learn the hard way that children's concerns may no longer be theirs. A new kind of patience is needed. If we persistently ask, 'What did you do today?' hoping for the answer 'Reading', and hearing in fact 'Just played about', then our anxiety sets up the first tremor of tension. All the public debates about education, visions of teenage illiteracy and examination failure are never far from our minds. We wonder if our child is 'different' in some way in the school setting, or if other people see him differently. If our family has standards, values, religious attachments or dietary habits that belong to a minority group, we are specially sensitive about our child joining in school activities that highlight these as extraordinary or strange. A sudden crisis about the lavatories, or the drinking water, brings back our worry in case the child should attract too much attention in one area, and then be deprived of the kind of favour he needs from his teacher in areas of learning. We worry about being 'pushy' parents in case our child is made to bear the brunt of our interference. What is so easy at home can become very strange in the setting of school, and the strangest thing of all for parents is not to know what really goes on.

Despite these natural apprehensions, we usually find that the quality of life shared by pupils and teachers in primary schools is better than at any other time in our children's education. Most schools provide an environment where real learning can flourish; no teacher, headmaster or headmistress would have any other desire, although their interpretation of 'real learning' may differ. They work within the same constraints that affect life outside school, and like other human beings, they have their creative and their fallow times. If there is a breakdown of confidence, it may be that the school has alienated parents, or the local authority, by failing to explain adequately its intentions on behalf of the children. When the teachers and their pupils meet naturally outside school, their lives have more in common than those who meet only in the classroom. Where falling numbers of children and transient populations create difficulties, especially in the inner cities, it takes more patience on the part of all concerned, from the chief inspector to the caretakers, to integrate the school with the community.

The primary school is saved by its size, by the feeling of domesticity that pervades it. The dinner ladies and other helpers humanize it. You cannot tell what a school is like from the outside. Sometimes new prize-winning buildings are full of bored children, and Victorian temples of learning, with high ceilings and stairs of everlasting stone, are full of bright paint and creative energy. When you visit, you will get the feeling of the place at once. Look for evidence of what the children do, and the care taken to display it. Are the books worn with use or neglect? Most important, what kind of welcome is given to parents?

In their new social setting, children learn significant lessons all day long: new rules of behaviour, such as how to ask for things, and how to do things together. People talk to each other in different ways. The headmistress addresses the school as a whole assembly; the nurse says 'dear' when she looks at children's feet. In group activities, each child hears more voices saying things he never thought of, asking questions about things he took for granted: how the rabbits' eyes move, why water turns brown when you mix all the paints in it. Playground games have rhymes, friends have nicknames; there are jokes and secret swearing. The child's actions and sayings now have a different value as his focus shifts to school. Even drawing and painting, talking and making things are all part of a new learning pattern. No wonder parents suddenly find that their role has diminished.

Parents should feel confident of their right to know about what happens in the first weeks of school. Ask questions early, when it is accepted that you are unfamiliar with what goes on. You should know what the child is doing, or ought to be doing. A school recognizes its obligation to explain its organization, usually by sending home a booklet or a prospectus. Teachers are rarely as hostile, and parents seldom as 'stuck-up', as each may believe of the other.

But you may find, even in a very friendly school where you are often invited to come in, that the professional blinds come down if you ask questions about reading. Persist, gently, until you are satisfied that you know something about how it is taught. Remember always that your aim is to establish a working partnership with the teachers on behalf of your child. Assume, in the first place, that the school wants to respect your child and to offer him a satisfying social and intellectual experience. When tempted to criticize a particular school, or schools in general, we also have to remind ourselves that, for a significant number of children, school is a haven, a means of escape from darker lives outside, and sometimes the only hope of self-fulfilment.

When you see your child off to school, you become involved in school as part of his life. Many people enjoy this. They join parent-teacher associations; they become school governors or managers. They concern themselves with education in local government where they can influence the way money is spent on schools. Others build equipment or raise funds for special projects. There is some interesting

evidence that the children of young parents who are committed to social enterprises take more easily than others to the
social world of school. The parents of new pupils have most
to gain by joining in such activities. As children move up the
school, the enthusiastic volunteers need others to replace
them. To help raise funds for a minibus is one kind of
partnership in a school's activities. Enquiring about the
curriculum, including the school's approach to reading, is
another. The difficult question to ask in a school is, 'How can
I help my child to do what he should be doing?' without
implying that the school is falling short in its obligations. But
it still must be asked. Some parents seem confident in their
approach and they are able to tell teachers what they want.
But for the most part, adults are timid inside schools, until
they are sure they are welcome as the teacher's ally on behalf
of the child.

Soon you will begin to watch to see if your child is learning
to read. The first steps may surprise you, even if you already
have a child who has passed through the school, as teachers
are always looking for new initiation methods. One day your
child may bring home, in a small tin or an envelope, some
slips of card on each of which the teacher has written a word.
This may be his 'sight vocabulary', the words he is to
recognize later when he meets them in a book. In some
schools, being able to recognize these words at sight is the
passport to a reading book. The child's explanation about
the words in the tin may not be clear. (If he can already read,
you may never see them.) What are you to do?

If your child brings words home in this way, he will expect
something to happen. Clearly, you help him to understand
what he has been told by talking about what goes on in
school. You explain that people who can read recognize
words when they see them, just as he recognizes and knows
other words when he sees them. You may play a game with
the cards, take turns at guessing what is on the other side. If
you think this is a curious way to begin reading instruction, it
is better not to say so, for at this point confidence and success
are important. If you wonder what words on slips of card in a

tin have to do with reading, ask the teacher, not the child.

If this happens, or something like it, you will realize that the child, the teacher and the parent all have a view of reading, what it is and how it is learned. The fortunate child is the one who can profit from the partnership of his parents and his teachers, because, for the child, learning to read includes pleasing people, and he wants, above all, to please the people he likes by doing what they ask of him. If your child can already read and has no need to perform this word-recognition exercise, let him do it as a confirmation of his skill and to please his teacher, but continue to do what you have hitherto enjoyed about reading. If you have left the teaching entirely to the school, and you think this is a slow start, begin to interest your child in books and public print. Do not let the child think you have a poor view of his teacher or her view of reading. That way lies confusion, the only real threat to a child's progress.

To establish a good partnership there must be a basic trust among those involved. If the child is in any doubt about what the adults want him to do, his view of the task of learning to read will become shaky and unstable. If he does not understand the teacher's instructions, or if he sees a look of disappointment on his mother's face, he will begin to be threatened by reading and to doubt his ability as a learner. To overcome this he needs to feel that adults at home and at school want him to succeed in learning to read, and that, in the end, he will. If the teacher thinks the parent will help but not interfere, she will be relieved. The most difficult thing for the parents at this stage is to be patient, to accept their changing role on behalf of a child who is often only too anxious to tell his mother how much less she knows than all the significant adults he now meets. If your child has just gone to school, find time to ask questions of his teacher, and see what you can do to promote the partnership of home and school.

If a child is already familiar with books, if he has some idea of what reading is, he begins school with an undoubted advantage. He will take up books in the reading corner confidently, look at the pages from left to right, tell himself a story from the pictures, recognize some words and remember a sequence of events from a story read to him. The teacher's task is to notice his ability and extend it. There is every chance that she will do this, for in a class of twenty-five to thirty children, the teacher is always on the lookout for those who are not absolute beginners. They make her life easier, and their example is a help to her when she is introducing less experienced children to reading activities.

The children who make a confident start in reading usually fall into three groups: those who look at pictures and link them together into a story; those who are fairly sure of a known or familiar text—a book they have read many times—and can read for themselves; and those who are fluent enough to tackle the words they don't know. They all still need help, but by and large the teacher assumes that they are secure enough in their attitude to reading to be given books, as wide a supply as the stock allows, and encouragement. She will judge their progress by the extent to which they become fluent, faster and silent. If your child can read before he goes to school, the teacher will look to see what he does most naturally, encourage him to continue, and, for a week or two, even seem to neglect him.

If you think your child is not receiving as much praise or attention for his reading ability as you would like, remember that the teacher has an obligation to less advanced children, the real beginners, and it is natural that she should be careful about their initiation. Do not feel you must step up your instruction or accuse the teacher of dereliction of duty. Continue to do with your child all the things that you have enjoyed in the ways that you know. The only possible source of worry is that the teacher may not know how competent your child already is and begin to teach him according to the school's 'reading' method. The child may then adopt the teacher's view of reading as something different from what happens at home.

Even if this is the case, your main task is to *confirm* and *extend* your child's experience of books and text, and his awareness of print in the outside world. You do this by remembering and enjoying again all that has been fun in the early stages and the first books, and then by sharing new ones that he can almost manage on his own. That is, you extend his repertoire by reading stories that are good enough to be read more than once. There are always new ones available, and the chances are that you have even more time (it may not be much, but it is more) to select the latest books from the library or the bookshop, or to find a fresh supply at the jumble sale or the Oxfam shop than the teacher who has the reading of twenty absolute beginners to take care of. She will be only too pleased that your child is managing on his own and having help and support. She will not withdraw her attention. After all, he will remind her, on the day when the others seem to be moving very slowly, that five-year-olds really can learn to read well.

Parents of early confident beginners should not feel embarrassed by their child's achievement. It represents an earlier successful partnership and that is no threat to a competent teacher. But it is perhaps not a good idea to boast about it. Then it is the child's turn to feel embarrassed, and you may find that other parents with whom you enjoyed a chat as you waited at the school gates now hurry off when they see you coming.

All good reading teachers like reading, at their own level as well as on behalf of their pupils. They read enough to know what is available, and to discriminate among the many picture books so that each child has a chance to make a *readerly* response to what he sees when he turns the pages. We are apt to worry about what teachers *do* when they begin to teach reading. I always want to ask: does the teacher want to read with the children, and does she enjoy reading at her own level? The child's first teacher is an important model in his life. The first thing a teacher teaches is herself, and her attitude to reading, her pleasure in it, will come across to the child even before his first reading lesson.

In the child's first few days at school the teacher will both read stories and tell them. The class comes together to listen, and there is a kind of communal spellbinding that holds them for as long as the story lasts, a shared experience that the children remember long after everyone has learned to read for himself. Some children have their first encounter with well-known tales in this way: *The Wolf and the Seven Little Kids, Goldilocks, The Three Billy Goats Gruff* and others. Part of the enchantment comes from joining in when it is time to say, 'I'll huff and I'll puff and I'll *blow* your house in.' Reading is a social as well as an individual activity in the early days, and right from the start a good teacher will encourage every child to see himself as a reader among readers.

You will quickly tell how a teacher values reading and her pupils as potential readers. Here is Jill Bennett, a teacher with special responsibility for reading in an infant school, who has written a pamphlet, *Learning to Read with Picture Books*, which demonstrates how reading is learned by reading.

Fundamental to my approach are a number of expectations, both on the children's behalf and on my own. I expect them to read books and enjoy doing so. I am a bibliomaniac myself and this enthusiasm seems to be highly infectious. I do not expect one hundred per cent accuracy, but meaning is vital. The children expect to be able to read the books offered. I show them the appropriate books. At the same time all the books are available to all the children all the time. A five-year-old may select, say, *Burglar Bill*, which he cannot read for himself, and ask a more experienced friend to read it to him or merely enjoy browsing though it himself. On the other hand, an older child may return to the simpler *Meg and Mog* and read it on his own, or to two or three younger children. In this way a substantial proportion of the learning-to-read process takes place independently of me. When finding a book to read aloud to me, however, it is essential that the child chooses one that is within his capabilities, otherwise he will not get the meaning, reading becomes a senseless task, and the enjoyment is lost.

Jill Bennett approaches the teaching of reading for those who start at school in the same way as I have suggested for early readers at home. It looks easy, relaxed and not at all threatening, but it is firmly based on an understanding of what the new reader has to learn—that a book is a special way of telling a story that lets the reader go back to it as often as he likes, that the words stay the same, that the pictures help the reader to understand the story, that the story has a shape and the author a voice. I call this kind of awareness in children *literary competence*, because in learning to read the beginner comes to know far more than how to get the words off the page. He discovers how to become independent in recreating the story for himself. In so doing, he learns to expect the text to be meaningful, but the meaning is something he helps to make, from the pictures and from his experience of what happens both in life and from other stories, told or read. It is natural to want children to 'get the words' right, but the first thing is to get the *story* right, to expect to make the text mean. All beginners should be given the chance to develop literary competences as part of their earliest experiences of reading in school.

We know that not all reading teachers have these insights, this experience, this conviction about the importance of real books and this view of the child as a learner. But their number is growing. Do not be worried that your child's teacher is not 'modern' in her approach if most of the children emerge from her class able to read and with pleasure in reading. The truth is, a good teacher makes more difference than any method. The best method in the world will not compensate for an indifferent teacher. Some reading specialists have tried to offset the inefficiency of instructors by designing 'teacher-proof' materials for children's learning, but this is a hopeless endeavour. The best teachers are convinced that reading is a pleasurable and profitable thing to do, and *they do it* to please themselves. I cannot say often enough that the concern of an interested adult or adults, books and significant print are the crucial factors in learning to read.

It is difficult, however, to shake most teachers free of the conviction that to teach reading they need a structured method and the special materials that go with it called 'the reading scheme'. If your child is not in a class like Jill Bennett's, you will, in due course, encounter the cards, pictures and numbered books that embody the view of reading held by the producer and the publisher and sold as a package to the school. Teachers use these materials not because they believe they teach reading, but from a need to be able to demonstrate a child's progress in some way that reassures everyone—the teachers, the parents and, in turn, the child. If success seems to come from moving up the ladder of the reading scheme, the child will judge his performance by the number on the cover of the book. When he announces proudly, 'I'm *on* book three', he really means, 'I am learning, I haven't stuck on book one'. His parents are pleased and commend him. In fact, there is little virtue in most reading scheme books, as books. No child would dream of reading book three more than once, and no one would keep it as a book to possess and return to. At best, the reading scheme is to be passed through and forgotten.

How quickly we all play the numbers game. The head of the primary school may say that young teachers need the reassurance of this graded material. Even skilled teachers take refuge in the so-called 'standards' of these initiation books and judge children's progress in terms of what the books offer. So everyone—children, teachers, parents—is mesmerized into believing that the magic formula for learning to read is the number of words on a page, the number of pages in a book, or the number of books in a scheme. Worst of all is the situation where a beginner has to accomplish an oral reading of all the numbered reading books before he becomes a 'free' reader and is entitled to borrow books from the library.

If you have already experienced the effects of a reading scheme on your child's view of what reading is, you are bound to take steps to counter its influence, not by suggesting

67

to your child that his teacher is incompetent, but by making the most of every chance you have to read real books and to enjoy stories. Authors who genuinely want to write for children do not count the words in sentences. They know instinctively where phrases start and stop because they shape narratives and incidents. Literature makes readers in a way that reading schemes never can. But teachers are still reluctant to trust their instincts in this because the weight of school pressures actually forces them to believe that beginners are to be given texts that no self-respecting author would ever compose.

As fully as you can, acquaint yourself with any mass-produced reading material which your child uses in school. Do not buy it, or have it at home. Above all, do not spend time coaching your child to read the next book in the series. That will double the boredom. Borrow a copy of the teacher's book from the library to see what the originator of the scheme says it is designed to do. Every good teacher who uses the material is more enterprising with it in her classroom than the instructions suggest, and the designer's orders are rarely carried out to the letter. You will soon see how necessary it is for you to supplement the child's view of reading that these class books present. If your child has moved from one book to the next very quickly, be glad that he need not spend too long with them, but let him know that reading is more than that. If he goes slowly, or seems to take too long to read a thirty-two page book with more pictures than text, assure him that there is more to reading than getting the words on the page right. Give him other books that open up the idea of what reading is all about. But the fact remains: the book your child brings home from school, and what he says about it, reflect the school's view of reading. If you are to help in a positive way, it is useful to know as much as you can about what he is being told about reading, and that includes the message that the reading scheme conveys.

Very few teachers use one pattern of instruction exclusively. Most refer to their 'approach' rather than to a 'method'. You will soon see what they believe the reading process involves when your child tackles an unfamiliar text. No matter how strongly teachers hold to the belief that they use a variety of methods and approaches, they instruct the child in a basic strategy which he uses as his first 'attack' on an unknown word. See, for instance, if your child is encouraged to guess, or if he has a systematic way of 'sounding out' and believes guessing is bad. Remember, whatever is offered as a general rule usually needs interpretation by each individual child, and that is where the teacher needs you to tell her if her instruction has been understood. Some early reading difficulties are caused by the child's misunderstanding of what he is expected to do. If his teacher says 'sound the letters together' he may be puzzled for a long time, especially if other children seem to do this without difficulty. If she holds up a card, asking, 'What does this say?' the child does not always realize that it is he who *says*.

Here are some of the ways in which teachers talk about teaching reading. They are a kind of professional shorthand that has grown up over the years. You don't have to know everything the teacher knows, nor yet to use her ways of referring to her teaching. But sometimes when parents come to see them teachers in a hurry assume that parents understand more of these matters than they actually do. So for that reason it seems sensible to explain some of them here.

The language experience approach may be the least familiar to you, but it plays some part in all reading sessions nowadays. Language experience is a child's ability to talk about what happens to him, to express himself, to make himself understood in speech and to respond to talk with others from his understanding of what they say. That capability is to be put to use in teaching him to read, by turning what he says into language he can see, into writing. The child tells the teacher about a picture he has painted, or an event that has happened to him, or something he hears about. The teacher writes down what he wants to tell the others. Because these are his own words the child knows what they say: 'My mum goes to work in the morning and fetches me on her way home' appears under a picture of school, for instance. Then the children share what they have written by reading to each other. Gradually they copy the teacher's writing and produce their own. They may even make a book of stories. The approach is linguistically sound. The learner gains insight into the relationship of reading and writing in ways he can control.

The best feature of this approach is that it enhances the child's view of himself as the person who makes reading happen. He experiences the power that comes from producing written words, which is a literate thing to do. He declares himself in what he says, and good teachers do much more than write captions under pictures ('This is my house'). Some of the children's early stories are powerful and not as bland as we expect. ('On my way home from school I saw a dead cat. It had been squashed by a bus.') With genuine encouragement (mostly discussion of the content) children gradually extend the length of their stories into sustained pieces of composition which they read fluently and well.

The chief drawback is that dictating and reading a story, however short, needs a fair amount of time in the early months of school and the teacher is not always on hand to take dictation. She must keep a lookout for those who are not keen to enter into this activity and still encourage the others. Some children want to carry on at home with writing they begin in school, so where that is the case, parents should act as scribes and understand as much as they can about this approach to literacy. (The book to consult is *Reading*: *The Language Experience Approach* by Norah Goddard, Macmillan.)

Teachers who concentrate on linking reading with writing know that children need to read more pages than they ever write. Your contribution is the practice that comes from taking time to read a story that is longer than one the child can write for himself. When you read together, you will find that you are still doing most of the reading for a five-year-old, and a little less for a six-year-old. Do not expect children of this age to begin to read on their own until they are familiar with both the words and the subject matter. When your child is trying to go ahead on his own, do not correct him as long as what he says makes sense. Glance indirectly at what he does when he comes to words he doesn't know. If he can't guess, tell him the word and let him go on. If he seems to stick often, go back to an earlier book that he knows, one with familiar pictures or rhymes, for instance. If he remembers an earlier success he will feel confident again.

Sometimes school beginners expect to learn very quickly and some certainly do. But if your child has chosen a more difficult book than usual and he is stumbling at unfamiliar words, ask him to supply a word he thinks will make sense. See if the word he supplies indicates that he is making his experience of spoken language help him. If the words he offers seem to be entirely random, indicating that he is not concentrating on the meaning, you may be pushing ahead too fast. On the other hand, do not choose only the books that have words he knows or else his reading experience will be as confined as in the early stages of a class reading scheme.

The best-known language experience approach used in schools is *Breakthrough to Literacy* which appeared on the scene in 1970 as the result of a partnership of linguists and practising teachers. The researches that produced this material confirmed that the child's most valuable first reading book is the personal one he writes with his teacher or his parent. *Breakthrough* has a number of devices, such as a Sentence Maker, a plastic stand on which the child assembles the sentence he wants to write by means of word cards. The advantage of the Sentence Maker is that it lets the child think about what he wants to say and then find the words to compose his thoughts or speech into written language before his handwriting and spelling are fully developed. The *Breakthrough* scheme also has a series of books based on similar ones written by children. The books are easily read and I recommend them to parents who are both anxious about their child's reading and as yet unsure about children's books.

If your child is taught by means of *Breakthrough* materials, you will be given a chance to look at them when you visit the school. You can get a good idea of how the teacher uses the Sentence Maker from the illustrated edition of the teacher's manual (Longman, 1979). If you would rather inspect the books, look especially for the poetry book called *Lollipops* by Brian Thompson.

Those who devised *Breakthrough to Literacy* know that as soon as children begin to write they encounter the complication of English spelling and all the problems that follow. Our alphabet, an inheritance from the imaginatively inventive Greeks, is too small to represent all the sounds of spoken English. We need about 40–50 letters to do that, and we have a writing system with only 26. So when people think about making learning to read easier, they invent new ways of modifying the alphabet, only to discover that each change brings its own problems. For all that we complain about it, English spelling is neither senseless nor haphazard. We could adopt some American simplifications, such as *odor*, *labor*, *humor* and *program*, but beyond that we tinker with it at our peril. We could not devise a new system for representing sounds by letters and then expect people in Newcastle and Bristol to spell *gate* in the same way, for the simple reason that they don't say it in the same way.

When we see our children struggling with the complexity of 'c' in *city*, *necklace* or *coach* we wish we could make writing easier. But while we all agree that our spelling is puzzling, no one knows what an improvement would be like. We learn to spell by teaching ourselves what to look out for. We make up rules for ourselves where we can. 'I' before 'e' except after 'c' is a fairly good rule, but even there the exceptions number about fifty. (What do you do about Leicester?)

Reading and movements for spelling reform are closely linked because of the belief that the latter would make the former easier. In the 1960s Sir James Pitman invented the *initial teaching alphabet* (ita) which consists of 44 letters (no capitals) to correspond to the sounds of modern English so that children learning to read could 'sound out' the words

and not be confused. *Daughter* would be written **dautu** .
To use this new writing system (for that is what it is)
interested teachers in the sixties studied the teaching of
reading with renewed enthusiasm and there were reports
of early success for the new alphabet. But public print is
not written in ita, and the number of books published in it
was small. The moment of transition from ita to the
traditional spelling was fraught with as many difficulties
as learning to read in the old style. So the experiment,
despite much early support and research, has faded out.
The attempt to introduce ita on a national scale failed, but
one important result remained. In the schools which had
tried the ita experiment, the parents and teachers discovered that they had to work together to understand reading
and writing. Their joint interest had significant effects on
the children's progress. The children learned to read, not
so much as the result of the new alphabet but as a
consequence of adult co-operation.

If your child is in a primary school where the teachers still
use ita, you will be given full instructions about the part you
can play in helping your child. He will begin with books
printed in this alphabet, and if ita makes him a confident
reader, you can count on his resilience to respond later to
traditional print and spelling. It would be very wise to read
to him from books in the more usual style so that he knows
that both writing systems exist. Concentrate on pointing out
conventional writing in public places, such as on notice-
boards and advertisement hoardings.

Public print is the most obvious drawback to any attempt
to modify an alphabet. We could not change our writing
system as easily as we changed our coinage or moved to the
twenty-four-hour clock. There is no conclusive evidence that
ita does any of the things claimed for it; yet for a time it
caused teachers to think about reading and writing as
language *processes* and those who studied ita carefully
became more aware of how understanding language relates
to the business of teaching reading. However, if you are
asked to support a move to teach children by ita, my

suggestion is that unless the school and the parents are in accord, it is better not to begin in this way.

Each of these three approaches, language experience, *Breakthrough* and ita is related to learning to write. Literacy is presented as reading-and-writing and linked to the child's need to become a writer as well as a reader. All three modes demand a strong commitment on the part of the teacher and support from parents. They are not taken in hand by indifferent practitioners. But whereas all reading teaching needs time, these make even greater demands on the teacher to work with the child, either individually or in small groups. You will see these approaches to reading in classes with smaller numbers. As there is a strong emphasis in the class on writing as a tandem operation with reading (and of this I approve), the child may become impatient and want to read much more. This is your cue to provide the time and the books at home so that he can see the scope and range of reading in a way that may not be always available to him in school.

The more traditional reading methods which are still in use with beginners are: *phonics* and *Look and Say*.

All teachers of infants have to teach reading whether they feel able to or not. This is specially hard on young teachers who find the complexity of a class of beginners very daunting and the responsibility very great. It is estimated that more than eighty per cent of all children in school have some experience of the teaching procedure usually called *phonics*, because insecure or inexperienced teachers find it one they can both understand and administer.

This is the systematic instruction given to children about the correspondence of letters and sounds. It usually begins with three-letter words: c.a.t., and b.a.t., and the child is encouraged to see how the sounds attributed to the letters are blended into the word. At this point the child is also discovering what letters and words are; many children don't know at this stage. The material to be read lets the child apply the rule with success. 'The pin is in the tin in the bin.' The vocabulary of the reading matter is chosen so that the rule is reinforced by repetition. The teacher's understanding is that when the child 'acquires' enough 'sight vocabulary', that is, words he can recognize as familiar, and a number of phonic rules (e.g. to explain 'th' and the sound of two vowels together, as in *head*) he can tackle new text with confidence. Many teachers want to persevere with phonic sounding and blending because in our imperfect world it seems to be the most efficient system we have yet devised for beginners.

In fact, it is highly inefficient and full of traps. Words in everyday use—*daughter*, *neighbour*, *cream*, *friend*, *sea*, *where*, *were*, *wear*, *road*—will not yield to phonic decoding which produces as many confusions as rules. In fact, we need 166 rules for the relation of English sound to letters, and there are still 661 exceptions. My objection to the dominance of phonics as a teaching strategy comes from my acquaintance with adolescent and adult illiterates. In almost every case, failed readers have learned the phonic rules so well they cannot do anything else to help themselves. They sound out the letters and try to blend the sounds together with patience and perseverance and ever-growing despair. What use is the famous rule about 'magic e' at the end of the word changing the vowel in the middle (e.g. *hat–hate*) when you want to read *axe* and *have*?

When a child can read, even a little, he should be encouraged to be curious about the sound and letter combinations of words he *knows*, rather than to use a hopeless rule to decode a new word. He can inspect a name: George, Charlotte, Sophie, Raymond, Thomas, Michael, Elaine, Josephine, John, Anthony, Hannah, to see where there are letters without sounds. Far better than learning any rule is the encouragement of a general curiosity about language, in all its forms and varieties, so that the learner can make up the rules later from his experience of successful reading. The quickest way to discover an unknown or new word is to ask someone, to read on, or to look for a picture clue.

As a method for teaching reading, *Look and Say* relies on the child's visual memory. He recognizes words he has seen before, especially if they recur in the same place. A parent riding on the top of a bus and pointing out the signs, or a driver encouraging a young passenger to keep a lookout for a certain petrol station is promoting this kind of behaviour. We do it all the time when we look for stations, restaurants, toilets, and so it is easy to think that the word 'stands for' the thing because the word or the sign is embedded in the context of its occurrence. We would be surprised if we saw 'Midland Bank' at the entrance to a garage.

Beginning readers are encouraged to recognize words at sight and to associate things or meanings with words they remember. Some teachers put labels on objects in the classroom: the door, the piano, the rabbit hutch, not to tell them what these things are, but so that children associate the word with the context. Then the words are removed and the children are given the labels to distribute again. These words, like those sent home in the envelope or the tin, are the child's 'sight vocabulary'. He is expected to recognize them wherever they occur, but most especially in his first reading book or for early writing.

We know now that children remember a written word by the features that strike them, that is, by the way they tell themselves to remember it (e.g. by the up-and-down letters in a word like *little*). Each child has his own way of looking, his own way of remembering. But teachers give *general* instructions. Where the child can fit what the teacher says into what he does, he will make the way he remembers accommodate what the teacher says. But if he is told that *bed* looks like a bed and he doesn't see that, the process can become very complicated. Reading then becomes a different kind of puzzle where he matches what the teacher says with something he is supposed to see.

The chief problem about *Look and Say* arises when the teacher uses flash cards. These are cards with words in large letters for use in a group. The teacher holds up the card and the children say the word. There is always a quick child whose responses are heard by the others who repeat what they hear. Some children grasp the relation of saying to seeing, others are thoroughly confused by the whole exercise because the words are introduced outside any context of use.

The children are learning words in the same way as the Chinese learn their characters. But this is the very difficulty our alphabet is designed to overcome. No one can learn enough words by heart to read all he wants to, and in English this memory feat is not necessary.

Children quickly learn words with distinctive features; they seem to have no difficulty with *elephant* and *aeroplane* and they recognize words that are important to them: the names of shops, and the kinds of motor cars (no problem with Porsche, Renault, Triumph). When they begin to tackle continuous prose their parents are often surprised that they can manage *soldier* but stick at *they* and *her* which they try to isolate in the same way as the content words with which they are familiar. But *at*, *over*, *to* and *too* do not represent things. In speech they are rarely heard separately, so the first necessary modification of *Look and Say* is to put the known words into a sentence with the 'little' words so that the structure of phrases becomes part of looking and saying ('in the net', 'over the road', 'to the park'). As in the case of phonic instruction, natural text—what people naturally say or write —has to be changed into a strange no-man's language to make materials for children to read in this way.

As our knowledge of children's language development increases, and the study of linguistics is applied to learning to read and write, so we become aware of the intricacies of these processes. At the same time it is clear that children learn to do these things with no conscious grasp of the complexities. They are in pursuit of *meaning*, and their greatest asset is that they speak English, the language of the text, and every day they hear many varieties of that language, some of them more complicated than they will read or write for years to come. But they know the language as theirs. When people speak to them they expect to understand. Crucially, they have to see reading as something they *can* understand because what they see will resemble what they can say. When they learned to speak they made meanings. In learning to read and write they learn how to understand what others say, and to offer their sayings in

77

return. Extreme devotees of phonic and *Look and Say* strategies, and even some linguists, promote learning to read and write as if the child were tackling a foreign language.

Most teachers know that they cannot teach reading by following a programme that someone else has devised. They must respond to the child's efforts and promote these in ways that bring success. A method is good if the child learns. It is possible to blame the method of teaching if something goes wrong, but it is much better to look more closely at the child's view of what he thinks he is expected to do. If he is simply sitting and waiting for reading to happen to him, then you have to take a hand at once in what is going on. The most serious problem is the discrepancy between what the teacher says and what the child understands. When this happens, the learning becomes entangled with the child's fears and the teacher's exasperation. A six-year-old I knew was always sick on Fridays until it was discovered it was 'flash test day'. His difficulties lay in understanding the language of the instructions.

When you know what is going on in your child's reading lessons, it is better not to try to interfere at school. I remember very clearly how hard I found this because I knew that my five-year-old divided his reading into two distinct activities, the reading we shared together at home and the exercises he performed at school. His problem, and mine, was to relate the set method he tried to understand to the storytelling he could do when he read familiar books with pictures. Reading at school was work; reading at home was fun. Unfortunately work begins to assume more importance than play, so the parent needs to help the child to become fluent and independent before the idea that reading is fun gives way to the absolute necessity of doing what is required. The parent's role is not to supplant the teacher nor to prove the reading method unsuitable, for that would only undermine the child's confidence. It is to make sure that he has access to real reading experiences, especially in books and stories about what interests him, so that what he is reading is firmly linked to what he enjoys.

If your child was almost a fluent reader before he went to school and then he brings home his reading book so that you can help him, accept it and then listen carefully to what the child says he has to do. If the teacher wants him to practise or prepare a special piece, the chances are that she will expect him to be word-perfect when she hears him read it. Let the child read to you. If he sticks at a word or stumbles over a phrase, don't rush in with the correct version too quickly. Ask, 'What does the teacher say you do now?' Let him guess what should make sense. School reading books are organized to fit the so-called rules, so you are looking to see what your child has made of the instruction he has received.

It is a complicated time, not least because reading, even in the early stages, makes children pause to puzzle out the nature of the task and the kind of things they are dealing with. They hear adults talking about 'words', 'letters', 'sentences', 'meaning' and 'sense' and they have to re-organize what they know to fit the adults' reference pattern. Keep everything calm and simple; avoid complex explanations, but answer all questions as best you can. Never, never say: 'Don't do it that way' if the child is tackling a new word as he has been instructed. Say rather, 'The word is . . . Can you see how it works?' But don't delay the story unless the puzzling out of a word is absorbing the child's interest.

When he reads to you from his school book, his intonation may become strange, or seem to be so, if he has been reading 'naturally' up to this stage. There is a kind of school reading voice, a one-toned word-by-word effect that often makes parents weary because its jerkiness seems unfluent and not like real reading. Tolerate it a little, as this is what he hears at school, but when it is your turn to read, slow down so that he can now try to match what you say with what he sees, if you are sharing the book. He may be surprised that you can make the reading-book reading sound like a real story. (It is difficult: not many school reading books have real stories.) Finish with the exercise as soon as you can when he has done enough to count as homework, and then go back to the books you both enjoy.

You may have to find an old favourite to remind your-selves what reading can be like. All you have to do is to read for the pleasure of the story. Encourage the child to guess and to read on. Concentrate on the sense and do not drill him in word recognition or ask about the meaning of single words. Sometimes he will recognize a word from his school book, or stop to inspect something: 'That's the same in my school book'. Then you know the transfer from home to school and from school to home is safely accomplished. Print is mean-ingful in both places.

These things are true of both the absolute beginner and the child who has had some reading experience before school, and they are worth taking care about. First, find out, with a subtle mixture of boldness and discretion, what happens in school reading lessons. The Head should be prepared to explain the school's teaching policy. If you hesitate to ask, invite another parent to join in approaching the school. Then, let your child know and feel that you expect him to learn and to be successful. The best way to do this is to treat him as a fellow-reader. When you read together, let it be at other times besides the ritual bedtime. Discuss the story, to wonder what will happen next, to talk about the characters and to let the reader say what he finds interesting. Spend time on poems and traditional stories and tell stories about your childhood.

Next, when you can appear almost casual about it, that is, not as soon as you meet at the school gate, let him discuss school reading lessons. The fact that you don't hear anything may mean all is going well. On the other hand, it may not. See if you can determine whether or not he understands the instructions, what ritual phrases the teacher uses, and if he is encouraged to write. If he wants to practise, let him, and see if you can turn what he does into a game that will prolong the activity for a little just as he is beginning to tire. Do not insist he continues until he has mastered what he is doing to your satisfaction, but only to his own.

It is difficult for the supporting adult not to become entangled in school practices, and for the child to understand that knowing how to read does not come at the end of a set of books or exercises but can be real right from the start. Many children believe that they learn to read in the last term in their infant school because they have performed successfully all the introductory exercises. In fact, this is the moment they are expected to become independent readers. The simplest practice at home is to find a number of stories that the child can become really familiar with and read them as often as he wants to. Memorable writing can survive endless repetition: boring and insignificant language cannot. By reading a story he likes so that he gradually takes over the telling, a child can become fluent on a known text and thus experience what reading success is like, and what real readers actually do.

Two things to avoid at this stage. Try not to point to single words on a page and ask, 'What does that word say?' He will like the story less next time. In the same way, try not to test his awareness of letters at every street sign or hoarding. Good as it is to point out public print, you do not want him to avoid his favourite walks because the airways notices are no longer comic pictures but reading exercises instead. Don't miss the chance offered by legible graffiti. 'Spurs rule ok' is no bad thing to be able to read.

School instruction includes rules about other reading practices that sometimes assume the proportion of great debates. Pointing, for instance. Parents are sometimes ordered to stop children pointing. But if it is a help, a steadying device, the child will benefit. Most children point at some time. Pointing helps the eyes to move in the right direction and certainly saves the 'Where am I, where am I?' that sometimes panics a young reader as he goes to the beginning of the next line. The objections usually come from teachers who know that older children who are poor readers still point and read at the rate of their fingers instead of at the speed of their eyes. If your child is not yet seven, let him point if it helps. If he is just five, you may need to point for a little. But, in the end, the finger has to disappear when the eyes can take over. In the early stages children point to the first word and recite the sentence, then point to the last word. They even say the sentence forwards and point backwards. The essential feature of this learning is not to say the words aloud in order, but to discover the direction in which print runs. You will know that the finger is no longer necessary if the child co-ordinates his pointing and his saying, that is, if he moves his finger on to the next word as he reads it.

Another question that crops up in the early days at school is: should a child learn to recite the alphabet? If so, when? Obviously, in the end, he will; he must. In school there are alphabet friezes, letters and pictures, but the sequencing of the alphabet is mumbo-jumbo to a child who cannot write his name. It is better to play with wooden or plastic letters, arranging them into words he knows, or tracing over someone's writing of his name, or making his own attempts to write, all before the alphabet becomes an end in itself. Ask the parents of older children how they learned the alphabet, then ask the children. You will find there are as many ways of learning it as there are children. Do not insist before the child is seven. Then, if the teacher is making a fuss, turn it into a game.

Books will help, not because they teach the sequence but from their inventive cheerfulness the child begins to see what the adult's concern is all about.

Look at *The Most Amazing Hide-and-Seek Alphabet Book* by Robert Crowther; find others in the library or, best of all, make your own. I have included some in the book list on p. 231, but there are many more.

It is not difficult to see when a child's reading is improving. He stops reading word by word, he 'chunks' the meaning in phrases, his eyes turn confidently at the end of the line, and his intonation declares his grasp of the meaning. If he stumbles, he retraces his steps confidently. His mistakes are those made by skilled readers. (*Everyone* who reads aloud makes some mistakes.) Before he reaches this stage of fluency, he has probably begun to read silently.

Do not expect this to happen suddenly. Some children go through a stage of pointing and uttering under their breath.

Many imitate, in a slightly exaggerated form, the story intonation of the adult on whom they model their reading, emphasizing the words or intoning the conversation ('Who's been sitting in *my* chair!'). If you think your six-and-a-half-year-old should try to read silently, you can encourage him by saying, 'We'll both read to the bottom of this page without saying anything. Run your finger along with your eyes if you like.' A little later you may find, especially with a book he knows, you will be told, 'I can do it by myself by looking'. If it takes as long as two years from the start to this point, there is nothing to worry about.

Ideally, your child will now be able to do a great many things which relate to the business of being a reader. As a result of reading with you he will know about all kinds of books and many kinds of stories and storytelling. He will tell a story from one picture or a series of illustrations, even when there is no text. When he reads a text he knows, he will see where the words begin and end and be able to match most of his seeing to his saying, even if he doesn't point accurately. He will follow the direction of the print, even when it is on the illustration as well as below or alongside it. From what he says as well as what he sees he will look for meaning in a sentence or a caption, because he knows that what he says when he tells a story can be written down and said aloud. He can look for the beginnings of sentences and paragraphs and recognize names by their initial letters. All of these are specific and exact ways of knowing.

In his reading practice he will be operating various kinds of matching: speech and text, word for word, finger, voice and word. He will match meanings, and for 'truck' he may say 'lorry', which is good matching. When he recites a caption back from memory, he is matching what he remembers with what he sees. When he writes his name and says it as he does so, or copies a line under his drawing, he is also matching meaning with appearance.

As these things proceed, so his expectations of the nature and product of reading enlarge. He expects print to be meaningful: to explain pictures, to tell stories, to name objects and places. He learns to do some reading on his own, to guess the sense of what he looks at. He wants help from adults, and above all he expects reading to be pleasurable. On this his confidence rests.

As he practises reading, first as play, and then as a thing on its own, he adopts the behaviour of a reader. He sees the story as a whole and shares his pleasure in it with others. Later he discusses what is happening and becomes a story-teller on his own account. He chooses library books and enjoys being read to. Gradually he attends to the material he is handling: books, print, letters, words. He laughs at verbal jokes and enjoys the topsy-turvyness of being able to say what is not the case, to invent and to fantasize. Believing that he can read enough, he knows he can read more.

These are some of the things a beginning reader can do with success and skill. They are the foundations of literacy and the assurance of coping with a book successfully. It all seems so pleasant and not too difficult. Why does it not always work? Why are there children who do not want to read?

One of the wisest reading experts, Marie Clay, says, 'Good reading depends on rich sources of information. If we think that there is only one way to teach a child to read, we produce an imbalance in his language systems, the very root of his strength. If, for instance, we insist that he has to get every word right, sounded out letter by letter or remembered exactly, then reading becomes for him the performance of these rituals, the carrying out of these instructions. His focus on the task narrows until it becomes meaningless.'

Be assured that, unless he has brain damage, no child below the age of seven needs *remedial* lessons in reading. Above all, he should not have special instruction in decipher-ing letters, sounds or words, as if he had failed to gather items of information about these things on his way along the road to reading and now needed his collection replenished. Narrow, specialized teaching buries natural response to print. If you think your child has specific problems with speech, hearing or seeing, these should be obvious before he begins to learn to read, and they will manifest themselves in other areas too. These are problems that are very rarely confined to reading, but early days in school may show them up more clearly.

You may hear people talking about the difficulties experienced by left-handed children. There is no need to worry about this if you know that your child is having instruction and practice in the direction in which print runs. (There is nothing *natural* about writing from left to right. Other countries have writing systems which go in the reverse direction, and right-handed people learn to read them.) When he begins to write, a left-handed child should put his book over to his left side and work towards the middle of his body with neither too much fuss nor too little attention. Do not look for defects in your child that you think might interfere with his reading. The saddest case is that of the failing child who is completely equipped by his parents with excuses for his failure. Expect him to learn and to become independent, and he will.

The worst thing that can happen is that a child can be 'turned off' by believing that reading is not for him because he has found the process puzzling or boring. If he can make no sense of the instruction he is given, he may believe that it does not refer to him, so he goes off to do something else. He needs encouragement to explore how books work and to discover the kinds of detail in print and pictures that reveal what happens when he tries to read.

The partnership of home and infant school is most important in the case of the bilingual child. Language experience approaches will certainly be the basis of his reading programme if he is learning English during his time in the infant school. But before any formal teaching of reading can begin, there must be an informal dialogue between the parents and the school. The parents must understand what is happening, and be assured that their own language, and the child's, has the respect of the school and is assumed to be an important part of the child's development in learning. Information must flow as freely as possible from home to school and back again. In many areas, the home-school partnership is already well established. In others, experimental schemes are under way. The parents of bilingual children should take care to see that the school day produces genuine involvement for their child in the life around them. Instructions such as 'Just draw a picture' will clearly not do. The bilingual child can begin to read in English in the same way as other children if he is not yet seven. He can certainly enjoy the same wordless picture books. He should be kept in the same class as other children of this age, even if he has extra lessons.

The particular difficulties experienced by the bilingual child, especially the parents' need to understand the school's expectations, point to the necessity for support from confident parents on behalf of all children. When parents visit the school, they will discover quickly the extent to which their interest in reading is encouraged and if they can ask about methods, materials and suitable books. If the teacher gives the impression that they should not be involved in these specialist matters, the parents are right to feel uneasy. The teacher should show you the books for the beginners, explain what happens, and go into as much detail as you want to know about the procedures for helping children to learn. Above all, she should give special attention to what you tell her about the reading the child does at home and invite you to help in quite specific ways. The best co-operation I have seen is in a school in a multicultural area where library books are taken home by the children with 'guidance' cards for the parents. The cards are written in the principal languages of the locality—English, Turkish, Spanish and Portuguese —and say: 'This book your child can read'; 'This book you'll need to help with' and 'This book you'll need to read to your child'. The expectations of both teacher and parent are thus directed towards the help the child actually needs to enjoy the book so that the task is not homework in the strict sense, but a genuine sharing.

Imaginative arrangements such as this give parents a distinctive part in the development of a child's reading. In other schools, this happens in 'library time'. Once a week, at the beginning or end of a school day, parents and children come together in the school library, or wherever the books are stored and displayed, to talk with the teacher about books other than those used in reading lessons. Parents can sit there and read to the children. They can take books home. Other parents and children talk about books they have enjoyed and look at new ones. Because the borrowed book comes from the school, some parents feel it has a special sanction, yet it is not a teacher's reading book.

Library time also includes storytelling, by parents or children. If a child has a story to tell and needs a scribe, the adults are pressed into service. When the story is finished it may be written out again, if the other children like it, so that it can be put into the library for others to read and borrow. Not all parents can come to library time, but the presence of one or two regular visitors gives a significant lift to the reading being done. The teacher's voice mingles with other voices; reading is shared, writing is important. If your child's school has, or is contemplating, a venture of this kind, join in if you can.

To be effective, library time has to be regular and smooth-running. Any library, however small, needs help until all schools, especially primary schools, can afford to have trained librarians. Parents can mend books, arrange them, display them, organize the borrowing procedures and keep records. They can also help other parents not to be nervous of borrowing books, even at the risk of accidents. Above all, they can give time if they are not at work outside the home, and this is the most expensive commodity of all in a school. A teacher who is attending to the needs of thirty children at a time appreciates most being freed from clerical duties and other routine chores in the library. A teacher will come more often to library time if she knows someone else is in charge of chasing up the missing books. Teachers who make good relationships with parents on the basis of a shared enterprise are always appreciative of parental inventiveness, especially about reading and how to interest children in books. See if your child's school has a special programme for Children's Book Week or if there is a local writer who would talk to parents and teachers together.

The growth of the school bookshop and the success of the School Bookshop Association in the UK has done more than any other single movement to bring books and children together. Except in large cities, specialist bookshops for children's literature are few. It is difficult to see a large display of children's books except in libraries or at special exhibitions or when one of the National Book League's travelling collections is on show. Parents whose choice of books for children is restricted by the policy of the local stationer have too few chances to handle books that are reviewed in Sunday papers or shown on television programmes. Owning books is a special kind of possessing, a hoarding that all readers share. To browse, look, feel, let oneself be taken over by a new book, all of these things are the indefinable pleasures that a bookshop supplies. Children have to experience this, but some booksellers are wary of browsing children. Inexperienced adults are not sure how far you can go in reading something before you buy it. The school bookshop is the place to learn bookshop behaviour and to become an owner of books in a way that cannot be learned in class or in libraries.

Help to run the school bookshop is essential. Only in very few favourable circumstances can teachers undertake the enterprise single-handed, despite the excellent advice in *How to Set Up and Run a School Bookshop*, the handbook published by the School Bookshop Association. If you want your child's school to have a bookshop, you may have to assume responsibility for organizing the help. If you decide that this is how you can best help your child's school, you will do a great deal to raise the general reading standard. Be sure, however, to look for your successor while you are still enjoying the children's eagerness to read and to be involved in what you have to sell. Also, some of the activities appropriate to library time can take place in a school bookshop if no library is available.

Library time and bookshops make heavy demands on those who organize them, but they are worth the effort if for only one thing: they bring the book to the child to promote reading as reading *books*, the reader as someone who owns books. These activities offer parents and other adults a genuine role in teaching children to read. The more we know about children's literature, the more we shall understand reading in the modern world. Children whose parents never go to bookshops are entitled to know how they work and what they are like. It's part of the function of literacy; it cannot begin too early.

As the reading partnership gives parents a role in school, it also assumes that teachers have some interest in what goes on at home. To send a child home with his reading book is one thing; to know what happens when it gets there is another. How does your child's school reading fit into his life at home? What is the teacher taking for granted in addition to your support with homework? What are the undiscussed parts of the partnership? What happens when the book bought in the school bookshop or the book club or borrowed from the library comes home?

It is perfectly permissible to let it remain unread for a day or two. If a new book is instantly turned into homework, the attraction of the bookshop will wane. Offer to read it. If the offer is refused because he wants to go it alone, don't insist. You can suggest that a library book should be read fairly soon as others may want to borrow it. Otherwise, bide your time. If your child is reading his own book as well as the school book, keep the enjoyment of his own book uppermost. Help him with words he doesn't know; encourage him to give up his 'reading' voice. Make him familiar with the text, keep him from frustration and concentrate on the story. If, when he knows the story fairly well he is making gross mistakes in the sense (not necessarily in the words) more than once in every six words or so, then the text may be too difficult but don't jump to this conclusion. Be patient and let him guess, let him approximate, if the meaning comes through clearly. If he seems to stick, say, 'Can you read the next word?' You may then discover that he will go back and correct himself. With new, real books for school beginners the rule is: turn a new book into a familiar one as soon as possible, usually by reading it to the child first. Keep the story as a whole: encourage looking at the pictures and show him how they help him to guess what the words on the page are about. Help him to follow the way the words go. Discuss everything he wants to ask about. Be sure that he looks at the left-hand page first when he turns over and check that his eye moves from left to right as he prepares to read. This is learning to read by reading. If it is not happening in school, it has to happen at home.

The advantage that the early beginner has over the school starter is a longer time with a parent and real books. Everything the early reader enjoyed should be part of the life of a five-year-old in reading at home. Without dismay, go back over the previous chapter of this book and see if it suggests anything that you wish could have happened to your child before he went to school. It is by no means too late to do it now.

If you think the school is being slow in helping your child to read, if you cannot really believe that you can teach a child to read by reading with him from a real book and not a school book, then put your energies and anxieties into helping your child to write.

Encourage him to draw, to imitate writing with different kinds of pens. Hold his hand while he writes his name. Encourage repetition; tolerate the scribble appearance of the first attempts. Capital letters are fine because they are easier to draw. Some will come out backwards. Some letters will be missed out. Children at the first stage of writing have almost no idea of the possibility of letters occurring in fixed sequences, so they have to look at what they are copying very carefully, and this makes them slow. Begin by letting him trace letters (greaseproof paper over newspaper) if he doesn't want to copy, and talk about what he is doing.

Let him invent words of his own, as well as encouraging him to write more than one word at a time, so that he discovers the space between words as greater than the space between letters. The very act of writing increases the child's awareness of which letters can be expected to occur together. Do not be too fussy about letter shapes, but give him time to try out the same words many times until he is satisfied that it nearly resembles what he is copying and tracing.

After he has painted a picture or drawn one, ask him what he wants to say about it for the people who will look at it. Then he can trace the caption over your writing. Be sure to let his words, not yours, remain, even if he wants to say 'I think the baby is very naughty. This is a dog biting her.' Several pieces of occasional writing, together with cut-out pictures, make a good scrapbook. Here you can encourage more copying. To learn to use a pencil to record one's thinking—such an automatic thing for an adult—takes most of his primary school days. If he finds a poem or some verses he likes or a joke, or a football score, or the names of his team or a list of his friends, let him copy them out. The words of a pop song, copied out, then stuck to the wall above his bed or on the door of the fridge, is as good a way to learn to read as any, and does not interfere with school instruction. It may not look like partnership with the teacher, but it is the kind of thing that most teachers, themselves the product of encouraging literate homes, take for granted as going on in others. They are wrong, because parents more and more *seem* to be leaving reading teaching to the experts, but that does not stop the teachers from assuming that the children's life at home includes some reading and writing done for the fun of it.

Here is a recap of these suggestions in a tentative order. There is no need to do all these things, but the later stages are more complicated than the earlier ones.

* Make it possible for him to trace an outline—a big letter or a simple design. This is better than colouring in a colouring book, although there is nothing wrong with beginning by using a pencil to fill in a given outline.

* Help him to trace a word or a name. Hold his hand and show him the most economical or smooth way to form the letters.
* Let him draw a picture of a person; help him to write the name, first by having his hand held, then on his own.
* Make a scrapbook story by using photographs that are not good enough for the family album or with some drawings and some pictures cut out from newspapers. Write funny things under them for copying and tracing.
* Let him show and read his writing to someone else.
* Encourage him to write something on his own, however indecipherable. Let him tell you what it says. Then you read it.

The enjoyment of growing skill, the power that comes from saying what makes a difference, is genuine 'language experience approach' to reading and can be undertaken at home as well as in school, although the feeling about it will be different. It will be fun, not a test. Then comes the moment when the child writes 'Two pints please' or 'Please feed the goldfish if I'm late', or he helps to write in Christmas cards 'Love from Mary Dick and Tom'. Putting the message into writing draws attention to letters, words, the direction of script, all of which are reading too.

It takes time, like all things that need practice, and, strange as it may seem, the other kinds of practice that go on at this time, in play activity, in acquiring other skills, indirectly help the idea of learning to master the complex behaviour of reading and writing. Riding a bicycle, swinging without being pushed, swimming, winning at marbles: all of these move forward a little at a time. Our patience has to be the child's patience when he becomes frustrated; our confidence is his assurance when he most needs it.

Mastery is always rewarding, but achievement of it takes time and often means giving up other enticing activities. Our children have never known a world without television; their culture is loaded with its conventions and assumptions. They are practised viewers if not discriminating ones, and many of

the perceptual skills and language uses that reading demands
are quickly learned by watching television in early childhood.
The dialogue of modern stories, the modern author's ways of
telling are modified by the fact that children now expect stories
to move quickly. If a book does not whisk them into the action
as rapidly as the visual image plunges them into narrative, they
complain of boredom. We book freaks may deplore it, but it is a
fact of life. In return, let us admit, television has promoted the
sale of books in a quite spectacular way. Most programme
makers behave responsibly to reading: many have been devoted to discussing reading problems and reviewing books. A
complete literacy service for illiterate adults was sponsored by
the BBC. Some children's authors are household names as
the result of the adaptation of their work and its appeal to
adults as well as to children. The problem is, should children
be made to feel that if they are going to read well, they should
expect to watch less television? Is that part of the partnership
bargain with school?

To read takes time and effort; to watch television is easier,
for adults too. The child between the ages of five and seven
needs to discover that there are as many good stories in
books as on the box, and that some of the best serials they see
began as stories in books. Adults can organize time in a way
that children singularly fail to do. A going-to-bed read needs
a parent's initiative if it is to supplant the 'just one more'
programme on television, especially for school beginners.
The book at bedtime lets adults put their feet up and many
children's books are better than mid-evening viewing.

Even when they have made a good beginning and are
clearly going to be successful literates, children nowadays
find reading and writing are indoor, anti-social activities.
Even the bedtime story is a doubtful pleasure in the long
summer evening when the voices of older children are
ringing in the street outside. Advice to take reading books on
picnics, to the beach and on journeys in the car for long waits
in traffic queues is sound enough, although one draws the
line at Reading Book Three making its appearance with the
sandwiches. We want to make reading seem natural—the

paperback in the pocket, and so on. Yet we can overdo it, especially when we are offering advice rather than behaving as readers behave. Sometimes, on the caravan site or stranded by the roadside or abandoned at an airport, there are other children, just as fretful as yours. Read to them and see if yours will listen. As a child it is easier to tolerate your parents' concern when their attention has moved a little off centre for once.

Assume, then, that these are some of the activities that fall to the supporting adult as part of the partnership in literacy that we have with our children and their schools. One important thing remains. If the teacher is giving the bulk of her attention to reading instruction, individually or in groups, organizing reading promotion in the library and in the school bookshop, and selecting books for reading to the class as a whole, she will expect a supporting adult to exploit on behalf of a child all the resources outside school. If you can do only one thing for your school beginner, when work absorbs your day and visits to school can be only on the official occasions, concentrate on finding, borrowing, begging or buying books for your children.

Choosing Books for Fives

When school reading begins many parents feel that it is now the teacher's responsibility to select suitable books for the children in her class and the parents' role is to accept her choice. In fact, no children read enough in school to become readers. They all need a different kind of help outside school; they need *time*. To sustain their efforts in the year after their fifth birthday, whether they can read well, a little, or not at all, children want adults who will read to them so that they can discover as many different kinds of books as possible.

They have to find out what the language of books *sounds* like because it is both similar to and different from the speech they hear round about them all day long. Above all, they need time to practise reading for themselves, and that means reading to someone with the patience to listen while they try out the tune on the page to find the voice of the author as well as the words they know.

Children also need time to choose what they want to look at or to read with an adult. Quite often parents cut this choosing short so as to get down to the business of reading aloud even when they know that part of a reader's satisfaction is the anticipation that comes in browsing. From their earliest days of having books and looking at pictures most children express preferences that are clearly important to them. You see them walking about with books held close, or they point a finger at 'that one' as a definite statement of choice. They may select a favourite book on sight or single one out after a long deliberation. Choosing a book is a subtle business so it is important that there should be plenty of books to choose from, certainly as many as you would expect your child to have if they were toys.

The best books to choose for your child are, as always, the ones you can enjoy together. I don't mean only those you already know you like, but also the new ones in which you can both find something of meaning and value, where you can share a good story or a joke. Remember that, for the good reader, reading is always something of a game. So you need to make a collection of story and picture books, not the teacher's kind, although there is often a wide overlap between the real books in school and those that children like to read at home. Families whose children have outgrown their early books will often pass them on. Don't disdain any of these, especially not the books with worn covers. These are the favourites. Collectors of really old children's books tell us that the ones that survive intact were either expensive or unreadable in their day. The best are very rare, and always dilapidated.

Not every family lives near a library, and good children's

bookshops are few. Sometimes you have to encourage your local stationer to expand his stock of paperbacks. If you can find other parents who want to make more books available locally you may discover that they too are keen to extend the reading their children do at home. The needs of parents who are far from a ready supply of books and want help in choosing them led to the founding of a magazine for parents, *Books for Your Children*, now edited in partnership by Anne Wood and Jean Russell. This in turn led to the foundation of the Federation of Children's Book Groups —an organization for parents who want to find out more about children's books and spread their influence. If you write to the Federation at 22 Beacon Brow, Horton Bank Top, Bradford, BD6 3DE, West Yorks, England, you may find there is a group in your district.

Puffin Books have their own Puffin Club which runs a magazine, *Puffin Post*, full of competitions and activities for its members. There is a junior section with its own magazine, *The Egg*. Your child is never too young to be a member. Write to the Puffin Club, Penguin Books, Harmondsworth, Middlesex, England, for details. Both of these organizations have flourished as a result of the enthusiasm and energy of those who know the kind of pleasure and profit children gain from books. If there is a Puffin exhibition within walking or driving distance be sure to go to it for there you will see the scope and diversity of the topic you are embarking on. Whenever I feel downhearted about the dreary writing tasks children are given at school, I think of the verve, inventiveness and imaginative variety of what I regularly see at Puffin exhibitions.

There is really no short cut in choosing books for children of any age. You have to like them enough to read a lot, and the more you read, the better choice you make. Some of the best stories in the world can be bought in paperback for the same price as three bottles of lemonade, and the effect is much more lasting.

There is no need for anyone to tolerate poor reading material nowadays. The wealth of books for children starting school is quite amazing. Whether your child can already

read or not, take as much time as you can to look at the work
of outstanding picture book artists. You will recognize the
distinction of Edward Ardizzone and Maurice Sendak who
are in the great tradition of Randolph Caldecott and Kate
Greenaway. Begin with the best and you will choose confidently thereafter. But styles also change, and a short list of
contemporary artists of merit would have about fifty names
from Britain and a representative international survey might
run to two hundred. Look for books by Quentin Blake, John
Burningham, Pat Hutchins, Shirley Hughes, Faith Jaques,
Errol le Cain, Charles Keeping, Krystyna Turska, Helen
Oxenbury, Gerald Rose, Brian Wildsmith. See how a child
responds to the fascination of *Anno's Journey*, a wordless
picture book by a Japanese artist, and you will understand
that by looking for the tiny traveller in the midst of Europe's
major masterpieces the reader learns to focus on significant
detail—the skill he needs to decipher print.

At one end of the scale, the art of Maurice Sendak derives
from a deep exploration of his memories of childhood which
emerges in images of great universality. *Where The Wild
Things Are* and *In the Night Kitchen* are both wholly diverting
for young readers and powerfully significant. At the other
end, Celia Berridge's *What did you do in the holiday?* shows how
the child's everyday world becomes the matter of his own
creative imagination when he understands that he too can
draw pictures and tell a story. We cannot explain to five-
year-olds the nature of dream imagery, the hauntings of fear
and guilt or why it is possible to believe that the Gingerbread
Man is real. Nor can we discuss adult foibles or the
complications of our multicultural society in ways that the
young can understand as debatable issues. But they can *feel*
an adult's frustration if he is Raymond Briggs' Father
Christmas on his rounds, and a picture book by Ezra Jack
Keats—*Whistle for Willie*—will make the point about children
whose skin is not white. Anthony Browne's *Look what I've got*
is saying that imagination is worth more than possessions.
The picture book lets the child's mental imagery entwine
with the artist's so that both become fused in his memory

and mental pictures, what we still call 'the mind's eye'. Good readers develop this habit of carrying pictures in the head as well as that of recognizing words on a page. In the young child both are equally important.

So even if you think that because your child can already read he should push on to more text and fewer pictures, take care in case he should miss the best of real literature for children. Some of the most important learning a child does comes from looking at pictures which hold, as a single image, the complicated ideas that are both his knowing and his feeling. Fluent readers and absolute beginners both need picture books as the beginning of thinking.

If your child can read when he goes to school, don't be too anxious to demonstrate his progress by making sure that his teacher moves him quickly through the reading scheme. She may even give him less attention because she knows he has an early advantage. You must take care to confirm his first pleasure in reading by going back over his favourite books, talking about them as something still important because you both know he can now read other books. Encourage him to make up new stories from his wordless picture books, or to discuss John Burningham's *Would you rather* ('be covered in jam', 'have a ride on a pig'). Nursery rhymes and traditional stories can be re-read in different editions. Even more than the reading ability they foster, Old Mother Hubbard, Dame Wiggins of Lee, Jack and Jill are *possessed* in a special way by young readers. Find a copy of *A Nursery Companion* by Iona and Peter Opie and you will understand as you read it with your child the joint nature of reading pleasure at this stage, for young and old.

A successful early reader is sometimes perplexed by school reading books. If this is your problem let him see how books come in series or in collections other than those of the reading scheme. He will enjoy looking at the works of a single author, Beatrix Potter perhaps, because the attraction of these books lies partly in their size, or in a good series that beats the reading scheme at its own game, like *Happy Families* by Allan and Janet Ahlberg. *Breakthrough to Literacy* has a small number of books arranged in levels of reading development. Many of them have too little text for really fluent readers, but those who are just beginning to find their feet can race through the first lot to discover that the difference between school reading and doing it on your own at home can be more apparent than real.

If you still think your child needs 'stretching' beyond the confines of the school's view of reading, then let the extension of his skill come from hearing you read to him, rather than from his tussling with tougher sentences at the end of a busy school day. Sensitive editors, like Sara and Stephen Corrin, make collections for parents to read with their children. Their *Stories for Six Year Olds*, and *Stories for Seven Year Olds* mix traditional and newer stories very well. This is the time when family traditions begin, and parents' recollections meet children's needs, in Kipling's *Just So Stories* for instance, *Winnie the Pooh*, and in the best tales of the Old Testament. A quick survey of the children I know produced clear recollections of Leila Berg's *Little Pete Stories,* Dorothy Edwards' *My Naughty Little Sister* and Barbara Euphan Todd's *Worzel Gummidge*. Every family must collect its own favourites. The adult reader and the young listener are caught up together by the verve of the storyteller. I doubt if I could ever explain the feeling of pleasure as well as, I guess, you remember it.

If by now you're thinking, it's all very well for those early readers, but my five-year-old is just beginning. What do I choose for him? Does he not need more of the kind of reading he is doing in school if he is to catch up? Try to be reassured that there is no absolute time scale about learning to read, and no firmly fixed ladder up which the young reader has to climb. If your child is just beginning, then it is even more important that he should have a wide range of books or else he really will confine his view of reading to the books in school. Don't worry about his getting the words off the page until he has had a good deal of experience of handling books and looking at them. Go back a little in this book and read again what was said about picture books, rhymes and stories. He must have his full measure of these, otherwise his view of reading will be locked into the school book, the reading scheme, which I am never tired of saying is a series of books written by no one for everyone. The lesson of abiding importance for beginners is that book language sometimes seems to be like speech, especially at the start, but, in fact, it is its own kind, and real readers know that.

You will hear debates about whether it is better to write books for children in language we know they use (the Ladybird reading scheme is based on this idea), or to repeat words they ought to know. The fact is, we still don't really know what helps children to recognize words on a page. If they already use them, that must surely help. But every confident reader knows that his vocabulary increases by reading words he doesn't know, especially when they are used to explain and explore new experiences and ideas. You can see how important this is for children learning English as a second language who need to learn how a story *sounds*. The test for adults reading to children who are beginning to read for themselves, even if only a little, is to discover if you can bear to read aloud the story, the poem, the account of an incident more than once. The fewer words there are on a page, the more the author will have weighed them in the balance. Many a would-be writer of children's books has begun with the idea that short texts are easy to write because the readers are relatively unsophisticated and discovered that genuine simplicity is an elusive quality, sometimes best left to the real experts. Do not choose a book because it is handy, cheap and has few words, all of them easy to read. Children find for themselves the popular comics and stories that abound in supermarkets—*Mr Men* and *Topsy and Tim*. There is nothing wrong with these; they are sometimes the first material on which a child will 'go it alone'. In the same way looking at comics is not a bad thing to do, especially if in so doing the reader discovers what a joke is like in print and pictures.

Young children spend a great deal of time laughing. They find humour in pictures as soon as they begin to look at them in even the simplest systematic way. They are not constrained by the necessity of logic, so they detect humour in

situations, characters and words. Children see the incon-
gruities in *Funny Bones* (Janet and Allan Ahlberg) and the
Corrin collection, *A Time to Laugh*. I like David McKee's
Not Now Bernard in which the boy hero tries to tell his parents
he is turning into a monster but they take no notice. The
only problem about humorous books for children is that
adults are sometimes less patient with them than they should
be. If you want to be properly critical, distinguish the
books that have a sense of humour related to childhood and
those where adults are having a joke at the child reader's
expense. I wish there weren't any of these, but there are
some.

Sometimes, talking about choosing books for young readers I find I am encouraging parents to be less *teacherly*, less
like me, in fact. I know that if a child has to go to hospital, to
the dentist or on a long journey, it is good to talk about the
prospect beforehand, especially if you think you can dispel
any likely fears by reading a book that shows how the hero or
heroine gets better or arrives safely. My instinct is to say that
books on delicate subjects are sometimes best read *after* the
event is safely past and the child is already coming to terms
with the consequences—if any. I am convinced that a book
about a single-parent family, adoption or divorce, must be
introduced with care. In the same way, the very familiarity
of some situations: going shopping, helping to wash the car,
looking round a street to see how many people walk in it, and
so on, means that children don't always need to find them in
books. In our enthusiasm for reading we have to take care in
case our zeal runs away with us. Books called 'I can *read*' and
'I can *count*' are all very well, but when they stop being play
and become school-at-home, some of the fun goes out of
reading too.

Sometimes you will hear reading experts expounding
theories about how big (or small) the print in children's
books ought to be. Clearly, it seems to get smaller as
readers develop, but unless you have some anxiety about
your child's eyesight, you need not worry too much about
the actual type size. Publishers are alerted to this problem

and the picture books for five-year-olds are almost standardized so that there is plenty of space around the words, especially in hard-backed editions. You should avoid books where the coloured pictures are overprinted with text; that makes the words difficult to decipher. Sometimes, as in *A Wet Monday* by Dorothy Edwards, the author, illustrator and publisher try to make sure that the line of the text can be seen as a whole at a glance; a good reading strategy. But in the end, the reader invents his own rules about how he will make his eyes go to the words he has to read. Book designers are still experimenting with 'visual array'—the way the words and pictures are designed to go together—to see what influences the way the reader reads. No one has yet devised a way to design and print a book so that a reader reads in spite of himself. The author and the artist have to spin the magic that keeps the reader's eyes on the page and the reader has to be drawn in. You will soon discover which publishers take greatest care with the standards and the variety of the books they produce. Our children are very lucky. The supply of fine picture books seems to be unending and the general standard is high. They are not all story books, and you may find many that extend an interest your child has developed from what he has seen on his walks or in school—*Truck* by Donald Crews, for instance, or some of the Dinosaur publications that deal with everyday events. Even if we do not have something as outstanding as *Where The Wild Things Are* every year (and every year it gets harder for artists and authors), there are enough goods books available to make a reader of every child who has just gone to school.

If your child is just beginning, try to believe that, with your help and some good books, he will catch up those who look as if they have been reading for years. They haven't; they are just confident that they know what reading is all about because they choose what they like. Do not worry if your child likes books that you think are too babyish for him. He may have missed these earlier and he will grow out of them soon. There is no reason why a child who begins with books at three should think reading is a pleasure, while one who begins at five has to think it is work. Unless the five-year-old discovers what it was that kept the three-year-old going he may not want to continue.

The main difficulty for parents and others who want to choose books for five- to seven-year-olds is that the reading scheme, with its built-in 'levels' and 'readability', looks like a more scientific piece of apparatus than the apparently haphazard choices of the reader or the parent. Try not to let the reading scheme dominate your idea of reading development. You know that your child learned to talk in ways that were quite distinctive and individual. So will his reading be, and his taste in books. All children older than four who have any experience of books are bound to be at three stages of reading *at the same time*. First, they return to the books they know well, reading the text to themselves or turning the pages, looking at the pictures and saying some of the words. These are *the books they go back to*, again and again. Next, they read *what suits them best at the moment*. Some of these will become established favourites; others will be left behind when they have widened the reader's scope and his experience of what stories are like, whether about animals or humans, funny, happy or sad, realistic or fanciful, prose or verse, long or short. Then, readers know they can look forward to *what they will read next*. This anticipation can be spoiled by both parents and teachers if they rush ahead too fast. We make wise choices when we let our young readers return to the security of what they know well, extend the range of the present selection, take time to wait for the next stage as it comes in its turn. You may well find this advice again in this book as it applies at every stage.

If you are worried in case your child has arrived at school and you think he may have missed out on some vital reading experience, don't be dismayed. There are plenty of books, if you will take enough time to read them together.

Questions at Five

My child goes to an infant school with vertical grouping: that is, there are some children in her class who can already read and others who seem to have no idea what to do. Can the teacher deal with them all? Should the class not be all of the same age when they are beginning to read?

We are so used to counting the development of young children in weeks and months that we forget that reading progress goes in jerky stages over a long time. One month shows a great step forward, then there's a period of marking time. Within the two years of the vertical grouping class there are children at every possible stage. To make progress they need not only instruction, but also practice. By reading with children who are slightly better than they are they will be stretched, and by reading with others who need their help they will practise. In fact, children in vertically grouped classes often have more time for reading, and they learn to read in a way that is not always based on the test of reading to the teacher. If you are worried, talk about it. Check on your child's readiness to read things other than class books. Her keenness is all-important. If that gives way to anxiety or boredom, then a visit to school is necessary.

What is an 'individualized' reading scheme?

At its simplest, it means choosing the most satisfactory book for a child at the stage of reading she has reached, then following it up with another, different book at the same stage (confirmation), or one that enlarges the reader's scope (extension). If we can match a child's stage in reading with a number of books that can confirm what she can do by giving her more practice, and then give her a book that will help her on to the next stage, we are usually very pleased. To do this we try to know the interests and abilities of each individual child and the level of difficulty set by the books. But we can never be absolutely certain of either. The interaction of the child and the book settles the child's stage. The best known and most carefully researched series is that of Cliff Moon. He agrees that formal reading schemes are unnecessary, although he uses some of the scheme books in his stages, from picture books (Stage 0) to general fiction (Stage 13), and that talk between teacher and reader about the book is the best guide to the child's understanding of what she is reading. Copies of his booklet can be obtained from The Reading Centre, The University, Reading, Berks.

When is a book too difficult for a child at this stage?

The Bullock Report talks about the 'frustration level' of a child's reading and teachers have adopted this phrase because they recognize the anger and dismay when a text will not 'come right' for a reader. If your child says something clearly inappropriate more often than one word in every eight, then the book is possibly too difficult. But children often read quite difficult books if they know the story and they are not 'sight reading' something they have never seen before.

Why are children's books so full of talking animals?

A long tradition, passing through Aesop and Leonardo da Vinci, brings us this literary convention. In fables, story animals such as crows, elephants, storks and foxes are endowed with a single recognizable trait when this is important as part of the action. The subtlety of *Jemima Puddleduck*, for example, depends on the reader knowing something of the old fables and the characteristic behaviour of foxes. In their earliest encounters with stories, children want action, happenings and events they feel they can control. Real people are usually larger than they are and can do things they are not yet able to do. Most animals are smaller; they exhibit the charm of the small of all species and they do things children would like to do.

My child is five and four months. She has been at school for eight weeks and still asks: 'When will I get a reading book?'. We read with her at home and she says that the library books and the picture books we buy aren't 'real reading books'.

Discover if by 'a real reading book' she means the kind of

book that has been given to others in her class. Some children who can nearly read are not given the very first books of a reading scheme. There is no need for them to have one. But if your child won't believe that she *can* read, then you might suggest to the teacher that she needs her reading skill confirmed in a way that makes her confident. Meanwhile, let her see that she is a reader when she reads with you. Don't switch to reading the school book at home. Explain to her that 'real' reading books come in all shapes and sizes, not only in school. Check up on the school's next stage for good readers and enlist the teacher's help.

A picture book without words lets the child make up a different version of the story every time she reads it. In a book with sentences the words stay the same. Will wordless books make a child think that she can say anything she likes when she reads?

The pictures in a wordless book allow some improvization, certainly. They also let the child say a great deal more for each picture than she will read in her first story book. The idea of the story is all-important at the very beginning. Then in the books with a little text the reader begins to match what she says with what she sees. She also extemporizes to explain the picture. When she knows she must look at the words, she begins to exclude from her matching all the other explanation she has offered. She knows reading is reading the text. But she also knows the story is more than the words. If you are in doubt about this, look out for films on *Beginning Reading* shown on TV. These demonstrate it very well.

Are girls always faster than boys at learning to read?

No. But if teachers expect girls to be faster they may push them on. The boys then see that they are expected to be slower and make the most of the time when attention is away from them. Our culture encourages girls to read and discourages boys. When we hold to the idea that reading is unmanly we restrict both boys and girls.

My child's teacher says I shouldn't teach her capital letters. Is the teacher right?

In the end the child will learn to distinguish and to write both kinds of letters, and even different ways of writing the same letter. To avoid conflict, help the child to see that there are many kinds of letters. If the teacher is adamant, ask the child to show you 'the school's way' of describing or writing capital letters. If the teacher is really telling you not to interfere, don't make this a battleground. You will think of other things to do until the matter settles and the child can handle both sets of letters.

In a talk to the parents, the headmistress talked about 'psycholinguistics and reading'. What does that mean?

Psycholinguistics is the study of language in ways that relate it to the development of thinking. It is not a method for teaching reading, but a way of looking at what a reader does that throws light on the process. When they learn to read, children are already experienced talkers, so researchers such as Frank Smith and Kenneth Goodman show us how children use their experience of language learned in talk to understand that reading has to make sense.

My child is lazy. She won't read for herself. What do I do?

You know your child best, but sometimes children become oppressed by the idea that reading is so important that everyone must do it well and get it right. Some children would rather not risk failure and so hesitate to read to a parent. Take the first step in reading with her. You will have to do most of the actual reading until her confidence is established that she does not have to prove herself worthy of your attention. When you are reading something together, pause at a separate phrase, or some small unit of conversation. Then say, 'That says . . .' and tell her what the words are. When you come to this phrase again, let her say it. Gradually increase the number of words for which she is responsible but keep the telling of the story foremost in the activity. Give her time to pause to insert her words. Let her feel pleased if she succeeds. Make sure she does more of the work each time.

Should I read her comics? She likes that.

Why not? Especially if you both like it. There are many books that look like comics: *Tintin*, for instance, or a good shared joke like Briggs' *Father Christmas*. It isn't possible to read a comic unless you are both looking at it, because neither the words nor the pictures tell the story on their own. Gradually comics come to be the child's own reading matter, and all the better for that. Then you can read something else to her.

How long should I practise with my child each day?

Go gently. If reading begins to seem like the worst kind of repetition, the fun will go from it. Try not to look at the clock. A story at a sitting is a better way of judging the amount. Concentrate on the wholeness of the experience, not the time spent or the number of words read.

4

Seven Is Important

The first years of school pass in a flash. As soon as they find their place in the classroom and the playground, children become working members of a real community, for school is the society of children. In Great Britain, primary schools are sometimes divided into infants and juniors, so that children are told about 'moving up' at seven, the first of several transitions in their school career. There are also first schools, which cater for children from four to eight or nine, followed by middle schools and high schools. Whatever the pattern, the general assumption is that reading and writing will be firmly grounded by the time children have passed their seventh birthday, and most parents expect them to be able to read *on their own* shortly after that.

Children and parents are aware of a subtle change of emphasis in the lives of seven-year-olds, at home as well as in school. The seven-year-old is growing fast, assuming responsibility for things in the adult world, the dustbin or the washing up, his animals and his friends, and he is developing a distinct personality. Great leaps in learning are visible from day to day: tying shoelaces, doing jigsaw puzzles, remembering what it was like to be younger, and joining in grown-up discussions about holidays to come, moving house, or about what life was like when grandmother was young.

Confident cycling, team games, crossing city roads, helping with 'real' work have all begun. The seven-year-old knows what adults do in their free time and may join in: going to the cinema, dog racing, football matches and concerts. First visits to the dentist are over. He may know about hospitals and have asked the early searching questions about babies and dying. He distinguishes 'the way we do things' as a family on Sundays or at festivals, from the way others do them, and he knows, not always consciously, but as part of the pattern of his life, how those who care for him expect him to behave, at meals, for instance, and when people are silent. He is learning the value of money, and that certain lessons are important. School is now 'my work'.

We know that we convey strong messages to children about the kind of lives we want for them. We often hope that they will have chances we didn't have, or didn't take advantage of. So that they do not miss certain opportunities, we want to make sure that whatever has to be learned early, should be learned now. This means we are sensitive at this time about giving children special kinds of scope to develop. If we think we have a potential ballet dancer or musician in the family, we arrange extra lessons in their 'free' time, such things as early grade examinations in music, the voice trial, gymnastics or the special times at the skating rink or the junior tennis or football club. Most children respond well to invitations to try new things. The problems arise when these special activities develop into individual striving or competitive endeavours, and then parental pressure increases. But, for the moment, we assume that home is still where the child is most himself, where he develops in his own way because the adults care about him as a person, and will give him a chance to explore new possibilities. Success in any one of these performances affects the child's view of himself and leads to other successes. The apparently timid boy who shows himself to be a lion-hearted goalkeeper begins a new life in the classroom on the day of his first splendid save. The girl who stands up to a bully who says she can't play football even when she is clearly better than most boys earns a new kind of respect. Many of these activities are optional throughout school life, but reading is different. Children have to be good at it, yet it is also such a common accomplishment that even the most persistent exertions and striving may pass unnoticed. In reading, only success will do. Learning to read is what everyone does, so that when their children are seven, parents' concern increases.

A junior school can be distinguished by the significance and the importance it gives to the activities and interests that support a child at home. A good teacher is aware of these. But now the individual differences of children, even the things that are the powerful roots of their growth in understanding, their very distinctive characteristics, are modified by the social organization of the classroom. Reading is now 'reading in class'.

By the age of seven everyone has learned some formal school behaviour. The casual walking about to see what a friend is doing, the spontaneous talk and reporting, are often less in evidence and sometimes even discouraged. Teachers seem to bend down to the child's level less often. A class and a teacher enter into a kind of tacit agreement that work will be more systematic and the day more structured. Lessons may now have names, like history and geography. 'Topic' work will gather up activities and centres of interest. Specialist teachers of games, music and art are distinguished from those who concentrate on mathematics. An extra reading lady may also appear. The books in the classroom are suddenly full of information rather than stories. Work and play are more clearly distinguished.

The mornings are taken up with maths, reading and writing, while the relaxed afternoons are reserved for modelling, painting, music and games. This is not an accurate picture of all junior schools; it is a travesty of some of the best. But the sketch is accurate enough to be recognizable. The children are mostly busy and cheerful, and, on the whole, accepting of their lot. Apart from occasional outbursts of frustration from children whose endeavours outrun their patience, British primary schools have very few discipline problems. But children know each other very well. They also read signs that adults believe they have concealed. They know there is a 'best' reader in the class and they are beginning to notice that some children do not succeed in the tasks they are set. Until he comes to school the normal child has no notion of 'failure', or of not being able to do something. He has always been encouraged to try. He knows that it takes longer to learn some things than others, but he doesn't think of himself as not likely to master whatever he attempts. Reading is one of the first school tasks at which it is possible to fail.

Therefore parents who meet each other at the school gate eagerly discuss their child's reading progress. Literacy is the world's yardstick for children's learning and every first school is expected to serve the expectations of the society that pays for it. What was once a shared pleasure at home, is now an individual accomplishment within a public setting, with degrees of success measured by books of progressive difficulty and teacher's praise and standardized tests.

Parents and children recognize the good reader at once. He is fluent, omnivorous of all the print he encounters, confident and skilled beyond the risk of failure. Above all, he is secure and relaxed because he can make sense of meaningful text. He grows in confidence each time he can read a story for himself, or decipher pictures and captions and talk about what he sees. Some early confident readers can also write well and spell accurately. Very soon, the achievements of the most successful become the standards by which the slower children are judged.

We know that many early readers are 'bright' in the school sense but there are also many very intelligent children who find reading difficult. We wonder, and do not really know, why some children need no lessons while others struggle for a long time. Unlike speech, reading does not come 'naturally', so we think it has to be taught in the terms of the adult's understanding of it. This is where we confuse ourselves. The point we have been slow to understand is that the child needs formal instruction only in so far as it helps him to learn, but really to learn he has to read for himself, as good readers do. I am absolutely sure that the child learns because he wants to gain what reading offers him—and that a great deal of his learning should come from his responding to encouragement to behave like a reader. If at seven he still hasn't 'got the hang of it', what has gone wrong?

Successful teaching and learning occur where the child's

expectations and the information given by the teacher mesh together. When the child knows what it feels like to turn words on the page into a story or how a story goes on, then he expects the words he sees to be that story. Even if the words he actually says aloud are not exactly those on the page, he is reading well if the story makes narrative sense. When he knows how to do that, the child turns the teacher's instruction into something that accords with what he is already doing. If the child has no idea of his part in the activity of making the story, he tries to do what he is told with the words on the page whether or not he understands the instructions he is given, and then things go wrong. His view of reading is not to make sense, but to get the words right!

The seven-year-old in difficulty can be recognized by his attempts to do what we know he must stop doing if he is to be fluent and successful. He is often hurt by the impatience and disappointment caused by his performances. He makes 'mistakes' and is anxious. His eyes slide away from printed materials that pose a threat. As he pronounces one word at a time in his reading book he does not know that he is to remember what he has said or how to think ahead of what he is saying. Usually he is looking for the message in a sequence of letters in a way that cannot release it. He may have had no experience of seeing what he says in its written form, and perhaps no one has helped him to write. If you find this difficult to believe, think of an occasion when you tried to read the handwriting of someone you didn't know without any clue as to what the message could be about. The fluent reader knows he turns sentences into meaning; the hesitant seven-year-old seems to wait for the book, or someone, to tell him what they say. Very soon, when adults watch his attempts to read, he hears phrases like 'learning difficulties'. His parents may monitor his performances in ways they never did when he was learning anything else. The powerful message is beamed to him by the adults around who, despite their encouragement, are tacitly saying: *he can't do it*.

Most children at seven are somewhere between the early fluent readers and the slow ones. They are going about their learning at their own pace, with different kinds of help from the adults around them. The good readers have their abilities augmented by a constant flow of praise. The slow readers have their lack of success demonstrated almost daily. The middlers think they will make it, and, for all that they attract less attention and should have more, their confidence is their best guarantee of success. We may think that the good readers will manage well on their own, that the slow readers must have help, that the moderately-paced readers will be safe, but slower. In fact, all three kinds of reader need help in school and at home from those who can enlarge the scope of the confident, confirm the moderates and make sure that the slow starters are firmly set on the way to fluency. Essentially, we must not now become impatient with the speed of any child's progress as long as he is trying to read on his own. If we support them all with a little more understanding of what they are doing, then they will all succeed. As Margaret Donaldson has said—in a fine book, *Children's Minds*—it is our very knowledge of what they have to learn that 'blocks the realization of precisely what children need to be helped to see'.

Learning to read and write at seven is no more and no less of a problem than learning at any other stage, with one difference: the learner's view of himself now dominates the process. If he thinks he is a failure, in need of 'remedial' help, then he has begun to believe that he is somehow different from other children. If he thinks he is slow, he may well become slower. If others around him seem to know the secret that eludes him, if, in some mysterious way, they do what he cannot do, he may think it is because he is not as other children are. We have to avoid, at all costs, the possibility of giving the normal seven-year-old the impression that he now needs *different* skills, or special techniques, to be as good a reader as those who began earlier or were successful sooner. What he needs, above all, is more genuine reading experiences, a purpose of his own for reading and confidence in his ultimate success. If these lessons do not come at school, they will have to come at home.

Watch carefully for signs of growth in the slow starter. A positive step forward comes when a child who has hitherto shown no interest in reading picks up a book of his own accord. Ask yourself if he is enjoying the experience of reading. Is he keen to carry on? If he is, then encourage him to predict his way through a story you have already read to him and he has enjoyed. Don't insist on every word being exact. Encourage him to tell the story as he reads it. Let him choose a book he thinks he can read and help him to come closer to the text in each re-reading of it. Sometimes it is easier to let a seven-year-old read to his toys than to his parents or his teacher. Encourage him to tell the story in his own way if the 'calling back' of the words is too painfully slow to make sense.

When a seven-year-old's difficulties are severe and seen to be prolonged, or if success still seems far off, it is tempting to believe that the child has some physical or neurological deficiency. True, partially sighted children or those with impaired hearing have special problems, but these handicaps affect other skills as well. There is no evidence that reading is so particular that it uses parts of the brain or the senses in a way no other activity does, but poor reading can be the most prominent symptom of other problems. Some children want to be taught to read so as to prolong their right to an adult's individual attention, for instance, and would rather keep on pegging away at a beginner's book, provided an adult is there to be reassuring, than take on reading as something to do on their own.

Other seven-year-olds want to run with the gang, for that is where their main interest lies. You may have to wait for the holidays, for a rainy day or the time in bed with measles before you can do much reading at home. It is difficult, however, to bide your time if you are anxious. The weeks slip by and another birthday comes round. So at all times we have to let children know we will help them to get the enjoyment that reading brings. We rarely make reading easier by discovering a new method to teach it (all methods are centuries old), although a change of process is often a

good thing to try. But doubt, guilt, threats of the consequences of illiteracy are best kept away from a child learning
to read. He picks up these instead of the pleasure we want
him to have. Remember, at home we see him as a whole
person and we know how reading fits into his life. Many a
busy gang member is a story enthusiast at bedtime for all
that his teacher may find him boisterous and rarely still for
long enough to read successfully in class.

Most parents of seven-year-olds are helping their children
in some way or another towards literacy. In the distinct gap
between school ways and family ways of doing things,
children come to understand *teaching* as something different
from helping, and they tell their parents about school
reading behaviour. Consequently, parents worry in case
their attempts to help in fact confuse their child who is being
taught according to a particular method. They also fear that
the teacher may resent interference. Some schools do indeed
tell parents that reading should be left to the experts.

It is very easy to bamboozle a child with too much
instruction. Many children think that reading is doing what
the adults say because they know how reading works.
Orders, hints and rituals come from those at home, while in
school there are cards, boxes, word machines as well as
books to help the process along. It is all called 'reading'. The
teacher's operations are the most persistent and backed by
other kinds of authority—marks, stars, places in class, praise
from the head of school. The problems arise when the child
cannot match what he is told to do with what successful
readers seem to be doing, or when he is told at home to read a
book, to 'do' reading, and at school he has a specially
selected scheme of cards and boxes. Parents worry because
reading, like mathematics, seems to be taught differently
nowadays. They wonder about methods and materials, but
they know that, in the end, the successful child manages on
his own. If the beginning doesn't go well, what should they
know about the way their child is being taught to read? How
can they help the child without usurping the teacher's role?

If there were one infallible way to teach reading all

teachers and parents would follow it. All the evidence shows that there is no such method, no set of books or piece of apparatus that guarantees success. A good teacher with quite poor materials is more likely to help children to literacy than an indifferent teacher with a supply of the latest resources from the reading industry. The quality of the personal relationships between teacher and taught makes the difference. When they come together to read, the child must know what the instructions mean, or have enough confidence to ask questions if he doesn't understand. The teacher needs to know how what she says fits into the child's frame of reference for the words she uses and the questions she asks. Parents and children share a common frame of reference. Teachers and children have to establish one. For example, a teacher may hold up a card with *peg* written on it and ask:

'What does that word say?'

'Where you put your coat,' replies the pupil.

'No,' says the teacher.

Having mistaken the intention of the exercise, the child thinks he is wrong. The teacher's 'no' is part of her hurry to move on to get the right answer. In fact, the child's response is a good one. This is how confusion begins. Teachers are often unaware of the repressive effect of the negatives because the 'right' answer, in their terms, is part of the lesson plan. Bamboozlement results from misunderstanding rather than from ignorance.

When the child mistakes the teacher's intention and the teacher chooses not to hear the child's replies, the teacher begins to expect 'brightness' from those who correctly grasp her meaning, and 'slowness' from those who seem not to. Sometimes teachers assume classroom intelligence in children from very little direct evidence. They believe and state, for instance, that children from bookish homes read well. But there is a wealth of evidence that they are often wide of the mark about the nature of children's lives out of school. The presence of books in the home is no more guarantee of a child's reading success than the lack of them can predict his failure. Only a sense of a child's personal worth is relevant. If his teacher shows that she values all children as individuals and provides for their needs, your child is safe.

Whatever the teacher's private assumptions about the children may be, her explicit expectations of seven-year-olds are these: fluent, connected speech in response to questions; well-established primary reading behaviour, such as holding a book and turning the pages properly; the signs of fluency that are present when a child knows how to follow the direction of print—to expect a message from the words, to have some strategies for tackling a new set of sentences with unknown words. Teachers also expect the child to have had some reading experience, to be almost, if not wholly, independent, whatever teaching 'method' used. They look for a certain ease when children are writing short sentences, although their views on handwriting and the formation of letters may vary.

In many schools seven-year-olds are given a reading test. Sometimes this is for the school's benefit, to see who may be in need of extra coaching, called 'remedial' lessons. (I shall discuss these later.) Occasionally there is a public monitoring of standards in the local areas as a whole, to see if the general level of reading is satisfactory. At present, government agencies are trying to standardize new tests because the old ones are no longer reliable, so your child may be selected for this national testing. The school's private test may be nothing more than a list of words to be read aloud at sight; the national test may be a continuous narrative from which some words have been deleted. Neither an old test nor a new one gives a *predictive* result about any single child. It cannot accurately tell you what kind of a reader your child will be at ten or eighteen. If you find that your child is worried by it, or you want to know more about it, ask his teacher or the head of the school.

Usually the result of a reading test is given in terms of a 'reading age'. This is a number which is supposed to indicate a child's reading standard in relation to his chronological age. In fact it should be regarded with great suspicion as it

can become the most inhibiting factor in the whole process of
learning to read. If a child of seven learns that he has a
reading age of 6.5, while others in his class are recorded as
8.6, he begins to feel it is useless to go on trying. Instead of
helping teachers to understand children's reading difficulties, these tests simply give insecure teachers a misleading
idea of any one child's capabilities. A test does more harm
than good if the teacher believes the result tells her what the
child will always be like. Good reading teachers say: if you
need a test to tell you how well a child reads, you don't know
him well enough. If you really know him well and what his
reading is like, the test will tell you nothing new. All children
know whether or not they can read. From a test the good
teachers get a boost they don't need, and the poor ones are
confirmed in their awareness of their lack of success.

The most important factor in a seven-year-old's school
reading is his teacher, not a test result. What goes on in a
reading lesson is significant, and what the child is given to
read tells him then, as earlier, what adults think of his
reading. The teacher is now the focal point of his learning.
The more you know about what goes on in her classroom and
what seven-year-olds should be able to do, the more easily you
will form a working partnership with her. To help you
understand what you may discover on your next school visit,
here are three typical classrooms. Don't expect others to be
exactly like them, but you'll recognize the outline as soon as
you begin your conversation with the teacher.

In the first, the teacher believes that 'real' junior school
learning, the kind that depends on looking at books, collecting information and writing 'projects', is impossible until all
the children can read well enough to work on their own. So
she organizes planned reading instruction at the beginning
of the year to make sure that every child's reading is 'secure'.
In her well-ordered classroom the children are given books
at the top end of a number of reading schemes to complete
before they are 'free' to choose their own reading material
from the class library collection. The procedure is understood by the children who believe that they can read when

they no longer have to read aloud to the teacher. Some are 'free' in a few days; others never seem to be released from the 'little books'.

The teacher says she uses a 'mixed' method to teach reading, implying that she is not convinced that a single set of teaching strategies will help every child. She is dismissive of the infant school's habits, which she calls 'look and guess', and insists that children need 'word attack skills', by which she means phonic sounding and blending. The reading books go home with the children, and parents are expected to hear the children read what they have done in class and to prepare (i.e. read ahead) the passage for the following day. A card inside the reading book records the numbers of the pages the child has read successfully to the teacher. Parents are usually relieved when a school library book replaces the reading scheme, but they are also reassured that the scheme has been used and the skills 'taught'.

Children in this class are expected to 'decode to sound' unfamiliar words that they meet in a text, that is, to enunciate the letters in turn. They are taught the alphabet as a series of letter names and expected to repeat it in order. From time to time, they are given word lists to learn for spelling—first the words which are 'regular' in that the letters and the sounds are expected to match (*nest*, *best*), and the 'exceptions' (*put*, *suit*). The teacher places great emphasis on this letter-and-sound correspondence, and on the repetition of common segments of words, like 'ing', 'tion', 'ed'. The children are constantly told to 'sound out the letters and put the sounds together to get the word'. Those who have experienced this procedure understand what this means, although to others it seems like an empty ritual rather than a true reflection of the sound system of the English language. I have already noted in the discussion of beginners' problems how the spelling rules and exceptions can confound the learner rather than help him. But by the time the young reader is seven, emphasis on phonics may increase because it looks like a pattern of rule-governed behaviour which the

learner can operate. He can, but only if he neglects what else
he knows about how language works.

There is no doubt that there are observable, learnable
correspondences between sounds and letters. Our writing
system was devised from this principle. But English spelling,
as it now stands, cannot be taught as a set of formal units, nor
can we tell how a word is likely to sound if we don't know the
word. (A child trying to decipher a word beginning with *ta*
had difficulty if the word is *tall*, *take*, *tank* or *tail*.) It is difficult
to write good English text in words that embody so-called
phonic *rules*, although the Dr Seuss books, *The Cat in the Hat*,
Fox in Socks, probably do most to help simply by making fun
of the whole business.

The greatest danger that comes to young readers who
learn too well from phonic instruction is that the strategy
dominates their learning and becomes all-pervasive. It
is then the only way some children tackle unknown words.
For all that teachers say they use a range of methods in
teaching reading, their pupils do not vary their approach to
new words. They do not use a variety of tactics to get at the
meaning. Instead, they stick to sounding and blending.
They rarely trust their understanding or read ahead because
they have been told to 'use the rule' and to 'get the word
right' without guessing.

Most children survive the phonics instruction and its accompanying reading scheme because most teachers are inventive
and disinclined to stick for long with what doesn't work.
Children are experts at turning adult instruction into sensible
behaviour. Generally, it is the early stages of learning to write
that sort out the relation of sounds to letters, for in writing the
child attends to the sequencing of letters in a way that is
naturally systematic because it is part of the process. I have
never seen a reading teacher, even one who discouraged
guessing, who insisted on the phonic rules being followed
where patently they could not be. For some children this is
doubly perplexing; they wonder how the teacher, and other
children, know when the rule applies and when it doesn't.
That's the unasked question in every class that has a phonics-

based programme for reading and doesn't let the children write soon enough.

The sad fact about a reading scheme, or any other programmed learning material, is that it costs a great deal of money and must be constantly in use to justify itself. Once the books and kits are bought, teachers feel they have to use them. They are safe, tested like washing powder. Once these materials are in use, the teacher feels she cannot be blamed for the child's failure because she has given him tried, expertly made materials. An even sadder fact is that many children become dependent on this reading matter, believing that it has within it the vital clue to success.

If your seven-year-old is in a classroom where reading is taught formally from a reading scheme (it will have more books with longer sentences than the beginner's) by means of phonic practice and 'word attack skills', and if he has developed a notion that real school reading goes on only in these books, you must build a bridge from there to real reading. Find the Ahlbergs' *Happy Families* ('Mrs Wobble was a waitress') or their hilarious *Burglar Bill*, or look for another story that could be within his grasp of understanding. Judge the amount of text by his normal staying power. Don't think that a picture book is too babyish; some demand a sophisticated sense of humour. A traditional tale in modern dress is a step forward, such as Grimm's *King Grisly-Beard* with Sendak's pictures. Read the story through to the end for the fun of it. When you read it again, suggest that your child helps with the telling by joining in where he knows the words. When he has done this on several occasions, stop and say, 'You go on now; it's the bit about . . .' and here you tell him what follows. He may resist, but be firmly encouraging. 'You know how it goes . . .' If he tries, be patient. *Don't* help him this time. See how long you can wait when he comes to something he isn't sure about. Watch carefully to see what he does, and then you will know what strategies he is learning in school to make meaning from the words on the page.

If he stops entirely, suggest that he goes back to the beginning of a sentence he can read and runs up again to the sticking point. Encourage him to guess the word he doesn't know so that what he says makes sense. If his guess is nonsense, he isn't thinking about the meaning. Help him to put phrases together: 'over the wall', 'on the mountain', instead of pecking at each word separately. Encourage him to read a whole page on his own without stopping. Point out clues in the pictures. He is bound to remember what is happening and he will discover that the meaning of the words is predictable from other parts of the context as well as from the word itself. You will probably find that he relies a great deal on the clue of the initial letter. If he is anxiously sounding and blending, tell him the word and then ask 'Can you see why it is that?' and let him give his explanation. The most important thing for you to discover is what kind of a clue to meaning he thinks is significant. He needs to have his strongest perceptions confirmed; that is, whatever really works needs emphasis, and he should be steered away from useless nagging at syllables.

In classrooms where reading lessons are formal page-by-page exercises, there is rarely enough time at a stretch for children to read a whole book and to reach the end of a story. If your child has no time for 'real' reading in school, he now needs it all the more at home.

In our second classroom there is a teacher with a special responsibility for reading throughout the school by virtue of her extra qualifications or special experience. While it is true that recent research has enlarged our understanding, it has also produced a great deal of reading matter to be used in teaching reading, not all of it helpful. A wise reading teacher knows which of the new resources, including special machines, are worth the trouble of maintaining. Books are actually cheaper than other things. Most of the new devices were produced in response to the teachers' pleas for time to help individual children when there did not seem to be enough teachers to go round. Now they are mostly used in 'remedial' lessons. But it is just possible that you will find your child is not reading a book, but working on a 'reading laboratory' for most of his lesson. This is a series of cards with reading exercises specially graded for 'readability' or 'textual density', to give children the illusion of progress by letting them monitor their success in the accompanying tests. The child works independently at a level he finds he can manage with material he can handle.

It is a strange irony that in some schools which take reading very seriously and where teachers are most anxious to increase the reading ability of their pupils the activities performed seem almost to be anti-reading. Sometimes the glamour of the devices, electronic or otherwise, have increased the teacher's status rather than the child's inclination to prolong reading by machine for his own pleasure. It may be neither convenient nor helpful. A reading laboratory rarely lets a child be challenged by a story, a topic or an idea as a way of thinking or telling. Getting the right answer on the card, or gaining a higher score on a reading test may increase the child's confidence, but it does not necessarily augment the number of children who read for the reasons that real readers know. Answering a question in order to get a mark creates a new reading problem; it actually discourages the very thing reading gives a reader time to do—to stop and think, for most children soon discover you can answer the questions without reading the passage more than superficially.

So if your seven-year-old sees reading only in terms of 'getting it right', you are bound to extend his view of the process by reading with him even after he seems capable of doing it on his own. He must make the leap from school exercises to real books or else he will stay at the word-calling stage. Children who have not read continuous text for their own satisfaction suddenly find that their sounding out of words no longer seems to serve them because they have never done what readers do. *This is the crucial time.* When you visit your child's school, do not be too impressed by the mere presence of unusual reading materials unless the teacher's understanding of these includes the idea that the seven-year-old should dispense with them as soon as possible in order to read real books.

The atmosphere in our third classroom may strike you as too casual for there are no reading schemes and no formal lessons. Except for music and games and other special activities there may be no timetable. Yet the class is full of books and children reading. Here it is even possible for a child to read for a whole day at a time. The teacher's view of reading includes storytelling and writing. A child who has a story to tell but cannot write at the speed of his thoughts has the teacher for his scribe, and then he uses his own text as his reading material, just as I suggested that parents could do for the first stages, but at greater length. You may find the teacher choosing a book with the fastest reader, or listening to one of the few eight-year-olds who needs more school practice for his reading than the others.

It is difficult for parents who visit classrooms based on the pattern of the 'integrated day' or who see reading taught as part of other activities to be reassured that all is well when there are no formal reading lessons. You may see children engaged in a study of Africa, for instance, where one group is discovering the size of each country compared with the British Isles and the languages spoken in it, while another group listens to a folk tale on a cassette. The teacher has joined a group that is finding out about a recent election (the current TV news item) from materials she has prepared for them. The children are asking about voting. In one corner a boy is reading about motor cycles and a girl is finishing her special project about triangles. We are surely reminded again: never underestimate what children can do.

The teacher here says she bases her approach to reading on the child's experience, involvement and interests. She knows that there are at least five children who should read better than they do, but most of the others can put their reading to work for reasons of their own devising. The books in the classroom are for that purpose, and they range from adult books with pictures, borrowed from the school's main collection, to stories in paperback from the school bookshop. Everyone has a book to read if his writing and other work is complete. The teacher has a record of each child's reading and an individualized programme for all the children who still need confirmation of what they have already learned. The teacher has her own scheme of reading for the class, one which gives the children freedom to learn and to take pleasure in books. She has one outstanding support: the school has a skilled, qualified and accomplished teacher-librarian who has turned all the books in the school into a fully used resource for teaching and learning.

Only skilful teachers organize their classes in this way so that reading is a pleasure in its own right, especially at storytime when she reads to the children the books they are not yet able to read for themselves, but which they can understand. But here reading is also the tool of thought and learning. From a class where reading and writing are powerfully linked to his intentions and concerns, a child comes home keen to prolong the activity for the same reasons, so there is little difference between reading at home and at school. Help is natural and continually available; criticism of reading performance is rare.

Even mistakes are regarded as sources of understanding and are called 'miscues'. For example, the teacher may hear the child read the sentence 'where he wanted to look was round the corner', as if he thought 'where' always introduces a question. As he reads the sentence aloud the reader suddenly changes his question 'tune' or intonation when he discovers that he is reading a statement. The teacher notes this as a successful move in understanding. A simpler example; if a child reading aloud comes to the word 'truck' and says 'lorry', he is going for the sense of the passage and so it is easy at the end of the section to teach him 'truck'. To stop him in mid-flow to 'sound it out' distracts his attention from the real point of his reading. Clues such as these are now being investigated as ways of understanding children's reading behaviour and the sources of their difficulties.

Once the graded reading scheme is abandoned, reading is constantly used as a means of increasing a child's experience. A wide range of books must be on hand in the classroom collection, the library and the bookshop. The teacher encourages the children to read at a stretch, long enough to go beyond the information required so as to give it a context in their imaginations and in their experience of life outside school. She helps them to define their purposes for reading and writing and to carry them out.

Parents wonder if this approach, lacking as it does the structured procedures of phonic instruction and the reading laboratory, is sufficiently precise for each child's needs. In fact, it is closer to real reading. This teacher's problem is not to give a pupil reading instruction, but to see that he gets enough time to do enough reading with the kind of help he needs. She knows that sentences are easier to read than words, paragraphs easier than sentences, pages easier than paragraphs, so she encourages stretches of reading, especially for children who have too many intrusions on their time when they are at home. Her trust lies in skilled authors who write for children, and her greatest worry is that children may not have their full share of all the splendid books that are written for them.

What people sometimes call the 'basic skills' of reading are only part of the process of being absorbed into an activity that lasts over a period of developmental time from looking at books at the age of two or three to writing final examination papers, whenever these come. Short sharp bursts of drill may alert the plodder to the possibility of going faster, but, by themselves, reading exercises do not make competent and fluent readers. A teacher who promotes learning to read in conjunction with reading to learn usually offers herself as the model, sharing delight, new books, new discoveries and, especially, new stories. In reading to her class a good teacher can edit a whole novel into a five-part serial (on the basis of the BBC's *Jackanory* programme) so that the pupils hear ten new stories every term and are reassured that they can read them too.

To structure a child's reading development it is necessary to discover what a child can do, to encourage him with well-chosen material and sufficient relevant help for his sticking points. He will go ahead for reasons that seem good to him. If the teacher lets the pupil understand that his life outside school is also relevant to his learning, then reading, talking and writing come together. Does it seem too haphazard? Should the child not have his 'miscues' corrected? Yes, he should, but by correcting them himself because he needs to make sense of what he is reading and not simply get the words right to please the teacher and his parents.

If your child is in a school which has an integrated day, no formal reading scheme or timetabled reading lessons, you may be worried about 'results', reading age, and his overall competence compared with that of other children. You should discuss these with his teacher. You can also watch to see if the child reads willingly at home. Does he, for example, want you to read stories with him or to collect material for the school project? Does he show signs of independent reading? Can he use an index? Will he go to the library on his own? This is the time to show him how a reference book works. Choose a fine big dictionary, the giant atlas, the real *Britannica*. Look up something together: the speed of light, the distance to the moon, the Battle of Waterloo, not as a homework chore, but in the context of something you have already begun to discuss.

Some classrooms that appear to be comfortable, and even casual, are hives of industry. Others may simply be casual and your concern about 'sloppiness' may be well justified. Some excellent reading teaching is concealed in purposive reading. (Some classrooms are too haphazard.) If you need to be reassured when you visit the school, ask your child's teacher how she monitors his progress. There should be a quite specific answer to that question. If there is not, then you should ask the teacher to see you again at the next half-term so that you can compare notes on what you have been doing to help your child and to see if you can resolve his problems together. You will find that your interest, provided it poses no threat, will focus her attention on giving your child more of the help he needs.

*

If a child is having severe difficulties in school, or even if he only says he doesn't like reading and avoids it on all occasions, it is not easy for parents to be cheerfully helpful at home. Some solve the problem for themselves, if not necessarily for the child, by paying for extra coaching help out of school time to ensure the individual attention that the child may need. If you decide to do this, find out if your child is actually doing enough reading in class, or whether he gets out of reading there by saying 'my other teacher will help me'. If a class teacher knows a child is having extra lessons she may feel that she can relinquish responsibility for that child and concentrate on the less fortunate.

It is not necessary to find extra tuition for slow readers, but they may need more help than a class teacher can ordinarily give them. Most good primary schools have a special teacher who gives attention to children with reading difficulties. The effectiveness of this help depends on how the child regards it. Some children are glad to be excused the hurly-burly of the classroom, and so will prolong their extra reading lessons in order to escape. Others will worry that they have been classed as non-readers. The important inquiry to make if your child is having special attention is whether or not the school calls these lessons 'remedial' sessions, implying that something has gone wrong which needs to be put right.

No child of seven (or nine, or twelve, for that matter) should need 'remedies'. Either he can read or he cannot, and if he cannot he needs help to learn rather than relief, repair, or a kind of reading dole. The use of medical jargon has been singularly unhelpful in the development of good reading teaching because it has encouraged teachers to believe that, as most normal people can read, a child who has had only little success could be retarded or abnormal in some aspect of his growth: his hearing or eyesight, for instance, his left-handedness, his speech, his spatial perception. Remedial exercises, designed to strengthen these deficiencies, are sometimes given to children in the same way as people are taught to walk after a severe injury. Sometimes the exercises are successful, and after a series of confidence-boosting sessions the child returns to his classroom 'cured'. But my experience of remedial classes in schools is that they hospitalize children, letting them think that they need never encounter the real difficulties of learning to read because they have an alibi for not trying. A good 'remedial' teacher is one who makes herself redundant as quickly as possible.

If your child is withdrawn from his class for extra help, ask his class teacher exactly what is happening and how long the lessons are likely to continue. If she is unsure about this, try to make her commit herself about the kind and the duration of special help. Children cannot remain confident about the chances of reading normally and well if they are faced with the prospect of indefinite clinical attention. Before long, the child who cheerfully accepts extra reading lessons begins to see himself as a poor reader, and again, his class teacher gives him less attention if he is having more elsewhere. The view the child now gets of himself as a reader is the one that stays with him. A responsible head of school will explain in detail what is the school's policy about extra reading lessons, and be prepared to arrange a meeting for you with the reading specialist. Again, be wary of and not intimidated by test results. If the extra lessons are not increasing the child's confidence and inclination to read on his own, it would be wise to have a consultation with all his teachers. When reading becomes joyless there is no progress. It may be hard, or challenging; indeed, it often should be. But if the child notices no difference, if he is only back on another reading scheme or a different set of exercises, you should ask about this. No child improves by being given more to do of what he has already failed to master.

If you do seek out the reading teacher, pay special attention to what she says about *writing*. If the written work is only filling in blanks on cards and copying, ask if your child can read what he writes. If he does no writing, then resort at home to writing books for and with your child in the way I have already described. Children who are making a

slow start or slow progress are the ones who benefit most
from discovering the power in their own production of what
they want to say. The slowest children have most difficulty in
recognizing the words that others have put on a page, and
least difficulty in recognizing those that they put there.
David Mackay (who pioneered *Breakthrough*) says:

> With the Sentence Maker children compose texts of varied
> content from facts about home and school to fairy stories,
> from a long imaginative story like that written by one
> child about 'The Crocodile in My Bath' to the stark little
> statement of a child awaiting transfer to a special school,
> 'I will not think about what I cannot do'.

Learning to read at seven, the watershed time, is important because the child will begin to judge whether or not he is
going to be a reader. He cannot make a conscious decision,
except in so far as he is willing to imitate the behaviour of
readers he knows and admires, and to the extent that he has
discovered what is in reading for him. Thus, it matters most
if he likes and trusts his teachers. If school makes him feel
inadequate about reading, his parents must step in. The
child's chances are best where the partnership of the adult
outside school and the teacher in lessons is complementary.
What, then, is the role of the outside adult besides that of
taking an interest in the school's arrangements and not being
overwhelmed by the teacher's expertise?

First, it is to maintain the child's sense of his own worth.
As reading extends into more activities as he moves up the
school his teachers will assume that reading has been taught
and learned. Therefore the child should feel competent to
handle what he needs to discover and to know as part of the
school curriculum. Next, it is to understand that children are
very self-critical. There is often a period when the child
realizes that, although he has been making progress, reading
is a lifetime affair and there is still a long way to go. He may
simply look at a newspaper or an adult book he is interested
in and suddenly feel he will never succeed. Be especially

encouraging at this time. Then there is the child who feels that reading is too much of a hassle, that too much fuss is made about it, and the one who is so passive that he waits for all the initiative to come from adults. Both of these need help: the first needs less pressure and more encouragement, the second more challenge to get moving on his own.

No standard pattern of a seven-year-old reader emerges from any studies. When we concentrate on their samenesses we miss the essential thing, the different ways in which all children approach their learning. If he likes his teacher, if he has a natural inclination to find things out or to master skills and crafts, a seven-year-old will become an autonomous learner by learning to read. Most children of this age, especially those who have had too long at the reading scheme, need to be encouraged to argue with what the text says rather than to sound it out, to discuss what the story is about, rather than to get a page 'done'. The good readers are those who want to be treated as readers. It would be easier if every stage of reading had its own milestone, but it has not. Only increasing fluency and understanding, independence and response are signs of progress. The best role for the supporting adult outside school is that of a resourceful supplier of reading matter or joint reading activities, a senior partnership in reading.

Choosing Books for Juniors

Between the ages of seven and twelve, as their fluency increases, children need a wide range of books, stories and pictures. Some they will browse through—a skill well worth encouraging—some they will read again and again, others they will skip over once for pleasure on a given day and never look at again. From their eighth year onwards, children have at least three ways of coming to books. They know what they have already enjoyed: the picture books, the stories that first pleased them. To these they return for comfort, remembered pleasure and the confirmation that they can read. Then, there are the school books which engage them at work, at the level of their present skill: the class library book, the information book they can handle, the topic books on subjects of emerging interests and the stories that are within their grasp to read at one gulp and in great numbers. Beyond that is the challenging reading, the books the teacher wants them to read, the next stage of independence. At home you will see all three ways of reading. It is especially important to go on encouraging the reading of stories—at the very time when schools expect an increase in reading for information—for this reason: the length of narrative texts, the demands they make on the reader to find out 'what happens next', engage the child for longer stretches of time, and help to build up the staying power of the good reader and to familiarize him with the varieties of the written language. When they leave the infant school most children read silently at the same rate as they read aloud. As the eyes take over entirely from the voice, longer books should be read. In children's novels, the episodes and chapters keep the reader going for many pages at a time. In non-fiction books with illustrations, the text is often still no more than caption length, not enough to ensure fluency or to build up the relationship of one episode to the next. The adult's problem is: how do I know what my child can manage to read? The answer is: he will soon show you when you read with him.

Many ingenious schemes have been devised to rank books in their order of difficulty or 'readability', such as codes of colour or marks attached to the books themselves. I am sympathetic to the problem, but hostile to the idea of colour coding because, in the end, the child knows that he is being given a pink book because it is easy, or he avoids a blue book because it is said to be difficult. The best support systems are not readability charts, but the help of those who are specially interested in books for children; the Children's Book Groups, Margery Fisher in her magazine *Growing Point* and reviewers of children's books in the local and national press. The titles I have listed at the end of the book are only some examples of the range of books available. There is, I fear, no short cut for any of us, teachers and parents alike. We have to know the books and the child to match them in terms of the complicated individuality of both. Once you get going you will find it easier than you think.

One sign of reading advance that parents notice is the shift in the balance between text and pictures in what a child reads. But this is too simple a measure because some of our most resourceful artists are also accomplished writers, and many fine books are the result of a successful author-artist partnership. The child's understanding of the interaction of text and illustration is a skilled form of literacy because it involves a shift of images from words to pictures and back again. Many picture books for older children also have subtle visual and verbal humour which the reader can examine in detail. I have already mentioned how, quite early (as in *Rosie's Walk*), the reader shares the joke with the storyteller. Now this can be extended to include verbal wit and crazy incidents that have credible links with real life so that the reader learns that the story is something made up and *well-made*. Look at *The Church Mouse* by Graham Oakley (there is a cassette too); *How Tom Beat Captain Najork and his Hired Sportsmen* by Russell Hoban and Quentin Blake; John Burningham's *Come away from the Water, Shirley*, and Michael Foreman's *Panda's Puzzle*.

Comic books like *Asterix* and *Tintin* have helped hundreds of children to read, not only because of their excellent draughtsmanship, but also because they teach their readers the nature of the in-group literary joke in which, as in the best cartoons, words cannot be separated from the pictures. This is another example of our *un*-taught reading skill. To understand the illustrated stories of Raymond Briggs, *Father Christmas* and its sequels, *Fungus the Bogeyman* and *Gentleman Jim* (possibly not a children's book), the child has to do much more than read the words and look at the pictures, but he is often given very little credit for the subtle reading these books demand.

A possible next move is to the illustrated story where a longer text is supported by the pictures where before there was a shorter text interacting with illustrations. Some are in series, like Hamish Hamilton's Gazelles, others are singular and special examples of the art and craft of storytelling, such as *The Battle of Bubble and Squeak* by Philippa Pearce. In this group are many family stories, animal tales or the modern derivative of the fairy story, where witches and magic abound. The best have a definite individuality that characterizes the theme and the writing: *Clever Polly and the Stupid Wolf* by Catherine Storr, *Jeremiah in the Dark Woods* by Janet and Allan Ahlberg, *The Iron Man* by Ted Hughes, *Mrs Pepperpot* by Alf Prøysen, *Jacob Two-Two meets the Hooded Fang* by Mordecai Richler and *The Castle of Yew* by Lucy Boston. All of these can be read again and again if the story and the pictures appeal to the child. When you read stories like these, you will understand why many people are so enthusiastic about children's literature.

But there are other, more ephemeral, stories that can be read easily and quickly, and these also help children to become fluent. There are paperback collections of stories that are enjoying current popularity because of a television series (*Dr Who*, for example) or because the author has become famous in another sphere (Frank Muir, Spike Milligan, Clement Freud and Jim Slater have all written books for children). From the easily read paperback children discover reading-as-idling, or the running-in of new interests, or simply a kind of peer-group currency for swopping in the playground. There is nothing wrong with this reading in bulk. Think of how many adults still look at strip cartoons, read detective stories, horror tales and love stories. Children have to learn to discriminate. They do so when they have to cope with both the thought-provoking aspects of literature and the books that do little more than exploit the most banal literary conventions.

The best-known author of books for children, Enid Blyton, does precisely this. Whenever parents, teachers, librarians and other interested people meet, her books claim attention. Parents report that their children read an average ten titles without hesitation or difficulty. Children's literature experts, on the other hand, describe her books as 'unreal', 'slow poison', 'totally divorced from life'. Teachers acknowledge that children who will read nothing else and are content to carry on with Enid Blyton have to be weaned to more significant stories. Clearly, any book that attracts children as much as the tales about the 'Famous Five' has to be taken seriously.

Most attacks on Enid Blyton suggest that she makes reading too undemanding, a sloppy escape from both real reading and real life. The worry is not that children read these books, but that they may be inclined to read nothing else. We have to look beyond the books to the part they play in the individual development of each child. If an adult says, 'surely you aren't still reading that rubbish?' the effect is twofold. The child may lose confidence in what he *can* do, and may resent the adult's suggestion that this is not good enough, just as he is finding satisfaction in being a fluent reader who can cope with the conventions of a story. 'Do you want me to read or not?' is the obvious answer.

Once you know what your child is capable of you will soon find something better for him than this. But you should also read at least one of the books that 'hooks' him. (Don't be seen taking too curious an interest. Children are suspicious of adults who stoop to them.) You will then appreciate the distinction between reading more books with satisfaction and some books with more satisfaction. A young reader, like an inefficient cyclist, wants to exploit his skill, so he goes at reading, fast, when it is more important to confirm his ability than to extend it. From Enid Blyton he learns how a formula tale works, how to distinguish villains, villainesses, heroes, and heroines, satisfactory endings, and other literary things, such as episodes and chapters, cliffhangers and climax, and the moral patterns of right and wrong as the book portrays them. This last, the standard of values, the falsehood of the characters together with the undistinguished writing, the stilted and unreal dialogue make those who care about literature moan and groan. Yet the very aspects that Enid Blyton's critics abhor: the class snobbery and dubious motives and reactions, make inexperienced readers feel safe in a limited world of predictable encounters and familiar words and phrases. We may never want to give such books to our children (I certainly don't) but they will find them, and we may have to put up with them as we continue to offer others to replace them. If your child is stuck in a particular series that seems to have little to commend it, do not forbid him to read what he enjoys. Quietly, distract him just as the series is beginning to be too predictable. He will learn to discriminate by contrasting one kind of writing with another, and the good will begin to supplant the indifferent.

There are some stories, however, that no child should miss: fairy tales, folk tales, legends and myths. After the nursery rhymes, fairy stories are genuine children's literature, and we know that there are deep and abiding links between the childhood of mankind as preserved in these stories and the early life of each of us. If I go on to say that traditional tales are exactly right for children, I do not mean that throughout all of their childhood they should devote their reading to the exclusion of all else, and I know for certain that, round about nine, between their enjoyment of fairy tales and legends and before even sophisticated readers move to the genuine myth, there can be a period of indifference to these stories. But on the whole, the fast-moving plots, essential spare dialogue, big open characters which the reader inhabits as in a play role, the explicit action rather than a motive, are what most children want. Catastrophic events are heralded, they happen and are gone, or are changed into happy endings. If your seven-year-old does not know any of the Joseph Jacobs' collection, begin there, with *Tom Tit Tot* for example.

Magic and fantasy are part of children's thinking at this stage. 'Let's pretend' is a serious game by which they extend the limitations of their smallness and weakness in the face of adult power and authority. How big is big? What is the farthest a plant can grow? If there were a magic mountain and Hobbits lived there, what would their name be and what would they do all day? This naming and patterning is the way children make a whole of their universe which is still a

confusing collection of parts. They know the uncertainty of
their fear. As a giant or a wolf it can be named and seen. At
this stage the inner world of imagination and outer world of
the here and now are the same universe for the child; both
are equally real, and both need to be ordered. Stories make
this possible, especially fairy stories, because the characters—Snow White, Jack and the Beanstalk and the rest—are
busy changing the world by acting in it. This is also what
children do. If we want to give our children reading matter
that will initiate them into the kind of *meanings* that reading
makes possible as the extension of 'let's pretend', they must
have fairy stories.

Not all fairy tales, however, are suitable at the earliest
stage. Hans Andersen, for example, should be kept until
later. Concentrate on the well-known stories like *Cinderella,
Jack, the Giant Killer, Snow White, The Fisherman and his Wife*
and explore the great collections of K. M. Briggs. When you
read them with your child you will soon discover which he
likes. Do not be too anxious about the masculine and
feminine roles of the chief characters. Boys are caught up in
Cinderella and *Red Riding Hood* as much as girls; but if some
fairy stories seem to outrage your feminism, find a list
called *Little Miss Muffet Fights Back* or *Clever Gretchen and
other Tales* retold by Alison Lurie. Look for good retellings
of old stories, and good new editions of devoted collectors.
Read Tolkien on fairy stories as well as *The Hobbit*. Compare
Philippa Pearce's *The Squirrel Wife* with her retelling of *Beauty
and the Beast*. Reading fairy stories is one of the best acts of
collaboration between adults and children, because the tales
belong to them both. Read together the stories of the
Brothers Grimm. Remember, they were scholars who knew
how easily the oral tradition could fade, and who, virtually,
made our children the inheritors of a great deal they might
never have had otherwise.

Next comes the legend, the story of the hero and his
friends. At one time the heroic deeds of Arthur and the
Knights of the Round Table were known all over Europe.
They have survived long enough to become a musical

comedy (*Camelot*) and a comic film (*Monty Python and the Holy Grail*) in our day, but the quests, the chivalrous exploits, the forests where paths spring up, where knights rescue damsels, and Arthur is finally tragically beaten, are more than tales for children. They are a total sensation of the numinous—a kind of holy dread and inspiration that lasts until joined by *Lohengrin, Parsifal, Peléas et Mélisande* and *Bluebeard's Castle*. Elizabeth Cook, who has made a study of myths, legends and fairy tales in the lives of children, is certain that children who are never told of legendary heroes are, in the genuine sense, deprived. She also makes it clear that, in common with television, these stories have strong visual images which remain in the memory as a sensation as well as a story:

> In reading the story of Jason one is not listening to the verbal thought process of a single human being, or sensing half-verbally the emotional interactions of a group of individual characters, one is seeing a space between a whirlpool and a monster, or a witch and a warrior standing beside a tree and a serpent coiled round it and a golden sheepskin hanging from it. Some parents are hesitant about fairy tales and legends and report that children are made anxious by them and have nightmares. It is difficult to reassure those who are persuaded of this, but, in fact, the opposite should happen. Unresolved or unnamed fears are threatening; stories bring order to the disorder of our emotions.

Another important source of stories for children at this time is the Old Testament. Those tales that were once the backbone of morning assembly in schools are now a problem of teachers' consciences. Once removed into the classroom or to home storytelling, Daniel in the lion's den, David and Goliath, Jonah and the whale can come into their own again. Look at Peter Dickinson's retellings in *The City of Gold*, a remarkable book by any standard. In addition, children have the folk tales of their classmates whose culture is not theirs, yet whose traditional tales are as riveting. There are good books of Indian, Islamic, West Indian, African and Chinese stories. We shall understand our multicultural society better if we know the stories people tell their children. We may have to trade our imaginings of the dark European forest for the parched plains of India, but we shall learn to do this and then begin to see the many ways in which folk tales are a natural way to help children to be at home in the world.

It is difficult to put this more simply, because it goes to the root of reading and learning to read. If children have never entered the life of a story where there are giants and monsters to be feared in safety, younger sons to be admired for their wit and enterprise and heroes to be imitated, how can they fully know about wishes fulfilled, promises kept, testing times, dark days, and, above all, chance—that idea so hard to grasp in childhood, but so all pervasive in our lives.

Round about the age of nine when we have forgotten that learning to read was ever a problem, we watch our children striding out on their own. The fairy tale or the modern equivalent may go into a kind of eclipse, especially with boys, although there is no reason to discriminate between the sexes on this matter and every generalization will be only half true. We see all children becoming indefatigable fact-gatherers, both at home and in school, so that reading to learn now seems to take over from learning to read. *The Guinness Book of Records* beats all others at this time. Again, the parent's role is to confirm what absorbs the child and to extend the scope of the search for information. My general advice is: look for good information books in the library, but don't underestimate what the child can know or handle.

You may have to see which topics are of passing interest (and there should be many) and which are more lasting. Browsing, looking at books by turning the pages and reading bits here and there, is a good habit, but it has to be balanced by a more prolonged involvement if a topic book is to be of any significance. So you may find yourself explaining *Whitaker's Almanack*, books of first aid, timetables, football records and a dictionary in the course of discussing everyday happenings. Be sure to let your child see that *you* need books to keep abreast of events. It is wise not to be too enthusiastic about facts you want your child to know before he wants to know them. When my children asked questions at this age, they suffered from my over-conscientious didacticism. This led them to be circumspect about asking for explanations: 'Is spring in Australia in March?' they might ask, adding 'Don't explain it, just say yes or no'.

We have to remember that real history, exact geography and science begin as a kind of looking and checking, rather than as a book to be read. A craft, like knitting or painting, a leisure pursuit like fishing or collecting wild flowers, is usually begun in apprenticeship to someone who enjoys these things and practises them. Books extend and deepen new interests, usually after the interest is aroused. Be careful not to insist too much on your child reading a book about young musicians just as he is beginning to play a tune. A stamp catalogue is a great help, but only once you are well launched as a collector. In our anxiety to link reading with all the interests our children show, we may overdo things if our enthusiasm outruns their accomplishment.

Sometimes parents are so keen, especially at this question-asking time, to give their children the key to all knowledge, that they think only an encyclopedia will do. A good encyclopedia is a great book, especially in settling arguments about the size, strength, power, number and time of every-thing from the hanging gardens of Babylon to the latest oil rig. Only a very few children actually read these books as books, however, because television programmes offer infor-mation more accessibly. Children look up topic books when their interests are self-generated. Otherwise they are content to be amazed at the flick of a switch. It is always wise to let a child's interest in a topic prolong itself for a little before you buy many reference books. Here the library comes to the rescue again, for the problem about information books for children is that they deal mostly with the beginnings of things, a stage quickly passed by any child who has more than a cursory interest in the topic.

When our children begin to ask questions on a variety of

subjects we know that their interests are being stimulated at school. Sometimes a parent's expertise is brought right into the classroom, when a nurse comes to talk about her work, a computer programmer helps in a maths lesson or the reporter from the local newspaper writes a page of news with the class. Some children know well where their interests lie; others have to be helped to discover that they can become interested in a topic they once regarded as 'boring'. Teachers differ in their approach to work in what are called 'content areas', and the amount of involvement they expect from each child. It is possible to fulfil the class requirement and still read and write very little, so it is wise to keep abreast of what is going on, again, not to usurp the teacher's role or to take over the child's learning, but to make sure that your child's involvement in the 'Romans in Britain' is more than a few copied sentences and some cutting and sticking of pictures from a Sunday colour supplement. The child won't thank you for the books you bring from the library if he is expected to do extra homework for you as well as his teacher, but you may be able to prolong his interest or to promote new reading. In the child's fourth, fifth and sixth years in school he learns to link his reading and writing with many new ways of talking and thinking about the world.

The quickest way to discover what children's information books there are for this stage is to offer to help in the library or the bookshop. You will discover that, unlike children's fiction, topic books are often of poor quality in both information and presentation, but they are cheaper and there are more of them. Information always looks like knowledge, although most of the topic books in junior schools are rarely read by either teachers or children; they are simply there to represent learning rather than to promote it. Sadly, schools spend much less of their book allowance on stories than on indifferent collections of miscellaneous facts. The best libraries have good collections of humorous books, anthologies of short stories and poems, fine art work and spirited true tales of adventure and heroism. The worst have undifferentiated series of specially packaged information which rarely comes alive because the author has no interest in the reader. You still have a search on your hands when you are allowed to accompany your child as he now makes his way independently about the library.

Look for Isaac Bashevis Singer's *A Day of Pleasure* about his boyhood in Warsaw. Here is a writer who knows what children like and are like. *The Puffin Book of Magic Verse* and *I like this poem* are good to dip into. By this time your child will have met the dinosaur, the beast that has all the enchantment of legend and the actuality of pre-history. There are scores of books from all sources. Charles Clarke's book on Everest, with its fine photographs, will show you what a good and gripping adventure book can be, while it is not too soon to be interested in politics with *So You want to be Prime Minister* by Des Wilson. There is only one hazard: never underestimate children's interests or ability. I have seen eight-year-olds handle the AA reference books with assurance in pursuit of what they really want to know, and others find that the world is full of exciting wild life, nature study, history and the apparently endless marvels of science and technology. Children can become experts in a range of subjects because TV quizzes and puzzles stir their natural inclination to enquire. The problem of the TV is its flickering from one subject to another, but from time to time a real expert, someone who has made a topic his own, fires a child's imagination by the quality of his involvement and sets him on a path of genuine discovery.

To make the most of the rich resources of knowledge that come to them in books children need help to match what they know they are looking for with the way the material is ordered so as to be read. This takes time, patience and an ever-widening range of reading skills which cannot be taught in isolation but have to be acquired by the child's determination to find out what he wants to know.

Parents can help in three ways when reading for learning begins: by finding helpful books, by helping the reader to find in the books the information he needs to satisfy his curiosity, and by talking about the aspects of the topic that link what the child already knows to what he is finding out. This is the crucial feature of the reading-to-learn enterprise. The author of a book on bees or water or dinosaurs cannot know how to link what he has to tell with each reader's experience. The reader is often too inexperienced to select what he wants, and so may copy out great swathes of text into a notebook in the hope that some of it may be relevant or useful. Often it is not looked at again, nor read by the teacher on whose behalf the exercise was done. So the information passes from one book to another without forming part of the reader's experience: a complete waste of time.

The child's difficulty in handling books of information extends beyond the mere acquisition of information. Books of facts, especially facts about the modern world, are organized by adults who know how these facts are viewed in the world—something the child does not yet know. The facts about oil wells, modern farming and transport are checked against what actually happens. But the presentation of these facts to children is never value-free; the author's view of ecology, people from overseas countries and the exploitation of natural resources also lies in the choice of pictures and the statements made. Choose a book for children on a topic you know something about. When you have read it, ask yourself: is this the account I want my child to have of this subject? My special anxiety is the latest craze in books for children about European countries where the inhabitants are portrayed in fancy dress and eating strange food. The very best books are by experts who want the young to become apprentices in their subjects and who write with enough care to invite new young minds into their field and to share a particular enthusiasm. Look at Niko Tinbergen's *Tracks* and Richard Mabey's *Street Flowers* to see what I mean.

The hardest thing for supporting adults to understand is the effect of invisible attitudes to children's reading, at home, at school, and in the books. At the risk of boring you with repetitions, I say again: you don't have to be super-intelligent to read well, or rich or learned, or to have special coaching. We need reading experience, deep and satisfying at an emotional level, or as a support for our curiosity about the world itself and the lives of our fellows, what they invent and do to promote, conserve and change life as we know it. At seven the child is beginning to form his view of reading, the one that will persist. Seven is important.

Learning to read in the later stages of the primary school is a varied and exciting affair for those who have learned how to make books serve their purposes. It is also the time when a number of children are deciding that their interest lies elsewhere, and some are still threatened by print and reading lessons. Children who can read and still don't, have no idea what they are missing. Those who have still no confidence in themselves as readers because they had too little practice in the early stages will read less and less, and every year it becomes more difficult to catch up. Between seven and eight children seem to decide, even if unconsciously, whether they will make the effort that will eventually make reading effortless, and their decision is influenced by the view of reading that is presented to them. The supporting adult still has a good chance to make it a rich and satisfying source of experience.

Questions at Seven

My child's reading teacher says she cheats.

I wonder what she means. If she thinks 'guessing' is cheating, then I expect we all cheat sometimes. Could you ask your child to explain exactly *when* the teacher says she does this? Some teachers are suspicious of children who read to the end of the story, or who look for clues in the pictures, nearly get the words right and always get the sense right. The serious aspect of the allegation is the lack of trust between the teacher and the child. A talk might clear the air.

She says the teacher says I have to know about 'silent e'. Are there any other things like that I should find out about?

It might be helpful to discover what the teacher expects the child to know. If your child already knows about 'silent e', then you needn't worry too much. Keep in mind the teacher's way of teaching, but don't necessarily imitate it. Your child may have over-learned the language of instruction without necessarily getting help from it.

If you are hearing her read, let her explain what she does when she comes to a word she doesn't know. If she is 'sounding it out' without success, help her with some of the re-run strategies we have listed on page 122. If you don't want to do any of these things, examine: *hat*: *hate*; *pin*: *pine*; *bit*: *bite*; *at*: *ate*. The 'e' at the end is 'silent', in the teacher's terms, but the rule doesn't always work, in *axe*, for instance.

What are word attack skills?

The difficult part of reading is to know what to do about a word you don't recognize at once. Whatever you do to 'make it out' is to 'attack' it. Some teachers think there are 'skills' for doing this—like knowing the first letter, discovering the sound of the middle vowel, and so on. The best strategy is simply to know what word might make sense, but many teachers think this is too chancy and they make lists of other 'attacks'. Mercifully children soon discover which strategies work best for them. Watch your child reading and you'll discover what she does. If you want to know what the teacher means by this phrase, borrow the introductory book that goes with the reading scheme.

Surely, the one thing that is difficult for young readers is to read a word they don't recognize at once. Is guessing it really good enough? Should they not have some rules or skills for tackling unknown words?

The most difficult thing of all about reading is for the literate adults to believe that individual words are less important than they seem in getting meaning. It is actually easier to grasp the meaning of a sentence or a passage than to read it word perfectly. Also, a child may be perfect at 'sounding out' and still not grasp either what the word is or what it means. (Try *minute*, *dawn*, *knot*.) Many children read aloud quite badly yet understand what they are reading very well. Fluent readers rarely stop at an unknown word. They guess and go on, looking to the rest of the passage to confirm their guess. If they go wrong, they go back and try again. They develop their own rules for dealing with unknown words. Guessing is never 'just guessing' but *getting meaning*. Poor readers are often those who believe they *have* to 'say' every word in their heads or aloud. They become bogged down in the rules, because they never know if the word they are dealing with is governed by the rule or the exception; whether *bear* is the same as *bare* or *beer*. It seems a pity to offer a child a set of rules she can't trust, and remove the idea that the context will help. The child's natural rule is 'what is that word likely to be . . .' and she sorts it out for herself. The initial letter is a good clue. Better than all the rules is the confidence that comes from reading a lot and talking a lot. Try to believe that children learn phonics by reading, not reading by phonics.

My child of nine reads slowly and accurately. She worries that it takes her twice as long as anyone else to read the passages set in class. What would help her to speed up?

Discover first how well she understands her own problem. She may still read to herself as if she were reading aloud; she may even say the words to herself.

It is not necessary to read everything fast. But children who have read a great deal aloud in reading lessons tend to develop a single rate for all reading. Encourage her to read silently even when she is reading with you. Urge her to discover something about 'what happens next'. If you read aloud to each other, take turns and see if you can encourage a more natural rhythmic speaking than the word-by-word utterance of the slow reader. Read dialogue as in a play.

Encourage her to look ahead, not to stop for mistakes unless the sense is wrong. (Everyone who reads aloud makes mistakes.) She needs to take more risks and know that she will still be safe. A psychologist says: 'Rapid reading represents an achievement as impossible in theory as it is commonplace in practice'.

Is it not the case that children of nine and ten should have given up babyish books and be concentrating on more adult books such as 'Alice in Wonderland' or the novels of Dickens?

In choosing books for children, the difficulty is to avoid their coming to separate literature into 'books I like to read' and 'books I have to read'. Naturally we feel that there are some 'great' books that our children ought to read. If we press these on them before they are ready, they may read them to please us and have done with them for ever. *Alice* is a book to share. But it may need a run-up through *The Wind in the Willows* or *The Borrowers*, and these too may need adult support. Dickens, and indeed any writer before 1950, writes in a manner that produces quite 'dense' text for a child in the eighties. Be patient. Let the child pace herself a little, and find for her the modern books that distinguished writers produce for children of her age, and read your favourites with her when you both have time to enjoy the expansive writing that authors produced in the days before television.

I think my child reads too many stories. She is lost in fantasy most of the time. Do children's books indulge children in unreality?

It is difficult to be sure what goes on in a child's head, but most evidence about children's conceptions of the world suggests that junior school children need imaginative literature as a means of mapping their thoughts, knowledge and feelings about the world. Unless your child is giving up being active, playing with other children and talking to you, I think you have nothing to worry about. Sometimes children escape into books as a way of avoiding unpleasant encounters in real life, but when this happens, life outside the book needs attending to.

5

Round About Eleven

By the time they are eleven, most children can read. We no longer worry about them as we may have done when they were five or seven, and we have seen the last of the reading scheme so long ago that we have forgotten about it. We rarely hear our children reading aloud now, but when they do, they are fluent in the way that shows us they understand the meaning even when they trip over unexpected words. Do we need to pay any more attention to their reading? Haven't I said, throughout this book, that good readers can read on their own? Books written about reading that deal with eleven-year-olds are either commentaries on children's literature or studies of reading failure. Competent readers at eleven are rarely a cause for anxiety or special study.

In contrast, this chapter suggests that the supporting adult's role assumes a new importance at the time when a child is moving to secondary education. The reading scene changes dramatically, even for good readers. The familiar, domestic atmosphere of the primary school gives way to the highly organized, bigger community where lessons and timetables are structures of great complexity and the library is a formidable institution. Life is suddenly less predictable because teachers and children roam about, singly or in droves, across what seems to the newcomer to be acres of field and playground and down miles of corridors.

The confident reader who is undaunted by the textbooks and worksheets that are distributed in each new subject classroom now calls on all his reservoirs of self-reliance. His earlier success in reading and his belief that any text can be made to yield sense and meaning now stand him in good stead. But he knows he is expected to perform well. The less-than-confident reader may be more uneasy. He sees at once that being able to read is now taken for granted. On his first day in the new school he may meet as many as five new instructors, all of whom assume that his reading ability is equal to any task they may set him, so he may dread the first reading homework from an unfamiliar book. Both the confident and the more timorous pupils know there is a new reading hurdle, often an invisible one, and both may again feel at risk for at least the first few weeks.

Most children arrive in their secondary school accompanied by a record card that gives details of their reading ability: a reading age, a test score, or a comment from the primary class teacher. Some secondary schools begin at once to sort out children who read with less confidence or skill. They may do this by noting the primary school's report or by setting a reading task or a test and then grading the children according to the results. Those who make mistakes or are diffident or slow may be given extra reading lessons, right from the start. Many teachers in secondary schools think they are essentially teachers of their subject, so that in all lessons except English (where reading is still, strictly speaking, *taught*) the children are expected to take class reading material in their stride. When they cannot, they may be withdrawn from lessons to go for some kind of supporting exercises with a reading teacher, on the principle that reading skills can be strengthened and sharpened. The expectation is that when this is done, the pupil can catch up with the rest of his class. The notion—that reading can be taught apart from what is to be read—is prevalent in secondary schools, and children are often very anxious in case their lack of tip-top reading success will separate them from their fellows or leave them in 'the remedial stream'.

Round about the age of eleven, children's reading skills and their tastes in reading matter are at their most diversified and individual. There are some very skilled readers who can tackle most books with success. As in the infants' school, teachers tend to latch on to these readers because they will learn quickly from textbooks and keep themselves supplied with reading matter. There are some 'inexperienced' readers who have found their life experience outside of books. They are often very wise in ways that are not bookish. But many schools do not know how to value what they bring from life to lessons, and as school marks are directly related to reading and writing, a 'non-reader' attracts an undue amount of the attention of his teachers. Other middling pupils adopt and perfect a technique for getting by in secondary school so that they are noticed no more than is necessary. They read only as much as will secure their freedom; they can read, but mostly they don't. The question now is: what can a supporting adult do for a secondary school child beyond giving general encouragement? Does the child's literacy now become a matter for the school alone? Certainly no eleven-year-old wants at home another regime of school instruction when he comes to do his homework.

In most children of this age there is a general move towards independence and this is reflected in their reading. You see it in the performance of the really competent eleven-year-old who makes either a wide-ranging choice of reading material or who has an absorbing interest which he pursues in all his spare time, in books and elsewhere. Everyone knows the child who looks at all kinds of books, from those about rocket-launching to pictures of Tudor schools and the Canadian prairies. He seems to have a quick active curiosity that tests out what he reads against what he observes. He can skim and skip over pages and pounce on relevant details in ways that no one admits to having taught him. In fact, he learned these skills from watching his teachers, his parents and other adults and from a secure belief that books exist for pleasure and use. There is a confident economy in his approach to books. He reads as much or as little as he wants to, and, to the surprise of researchers, watches a fair amount of television as well.

I have spent a lot of time asking children of this age what makes reading easy and why they enjoy it. Their answers deserve attention, for when they discuss the matter, especially with their peers, they become more explicit about their reading than any test ever shows. They talk a great deal about their early pleasure in books remembered in some detail. Most clearly they talk about something that they call 'being taken out of yourself', or 'being in the book as a kind of invisible watcher'. They say that they like best to read in bed because no one can then ask them to do something else and the telly isn't too near. It is important to them to finish a book in order to know how a story ends because, they say, 'you see the beginning differently'. They know how one episode in a story links with another. Sharp criticisms are made of authors whose characters do not seem to behave as 'real' people would, and there is praise for writers who can 'see the funny side of things'. They understand suspense in a narrative, and are prepared to sympathize with a villain while agreeing about the necessity of retribution that befalls him or her. These, and a growing awareness of the author's tone of voice, are some of the literary abilities of eleven-year-olds that characterize good readers. I doubt if these things were ever overtly taught as lessons. They emerge in the course of the discussions that readers have with each other about shared reading pleasure.

In pursuing these inquiries I discovered that good readers had quickly learned how to escape from reading lessons. They learned to 'perform' reading aloud to satisfy the teacher but they never believed that was 'real' reading. They could even say that they could read aloud without ever making a mistake and yet have no idea of what the passage was about. They used the time that remained at the end of each school task to get on with the story they were reading for pleasure—a possibility in a junior school that disappears in senior schools when bells segment the day into lessons in different rooms. They taught themselves how to tackle all kinds of texts because they were in search of information they needed. They admitted that they could read and understand words they didn't know how to say. One boy remembered the recurrence of *determined* which he pronounced 'deeter-mined', while *picturesque*, *misled* and *diarrhoea* were seen but never spoken. But no one was anxious about making reading mistakes. They all said that when they expected a text to make sense, it usually did, especially a narrative.

Asked what gives them most difficulty, competent eleven-year-olds are quite clear: it's the problem of 'getting into' the story and not giving up too soon. The beginning of a new book is always a challenge. Anything written before 1940 assumes that the reader has time to be led into the setting, or to become accustomed to the author's tone of voice, that wholly distinctive thing about a writer that literary critics call style. Modern novelists grab hold of their readers in the first paragraph with some arresting dialogue. The best first sentence I know is from E. B. White's *Charlotte's Web:*

'Where is father going with that axe?' asked Fern one morning before breakfast.

Other writers keep their readers waiting for an explanation, setting the scene with care, or telling the end of the story first, so that the reader is keen to read on for the explanation. Eleven-year-olds understand the problem of tuning in, especially if the writer tells the story in the first person.

If you look at the first paragraph of *Huckleberry Finn,* a book that teachers often recommend for children in their first year in secondary school, you will appreciate some of the skills required of the good reader.

You don't know me, without you have read a book by the name of *The Adventures of Tom Sawyer,* but that ain't no matter. That book was made by Mr Mark Twain, and he told the truth, mainly. There was things that he stretched, but mainly he told the truth. That is nothing. I never seen anybody but lied one time or another, without it was Aunt Polly, or the widow, or may be Mary. Aunt Polly—Tom's Aunt Polly, she is—and Mary and the widow Douglas, is all told about in that book—which is mostly a true book; with some stretching, as I said before.

If this opening is to pose no difficulty, the reader has to tolerate the uncertainty of his ignorance about Tom Sawyer, Mary and the widow Douglas. (He may have read *Tom Sawyer,* of course.) He knows that *without* means 'unless'; he understands 'stretching the truth'. He would not expect to write in class 'that ain't no matter', so he listens and waits for the narrator to explain more to him. He is untroubled by the grammar mistakes, as he understands the storyteller's use of dialect, unfamiliar at first, but recognizable by all who have seen American films. He is not puzzled by the truth or falsity of the author's account of events, but he is prepared to believe him for as long as his art makes the story a good one. He may remark on the fact that Mark Twain is really telling this story too, and so enter into what Tolkien calls 'literary belief', the way we let storytellers have their way with us. Above all, he knows that, by simply going on, he will sort out the conventions on which the story rests.

Every skilled adult reader takes all of this for granted. But these things have to be learned. Evidence shows that they come into regular use in competent readers round about the age of eleven as the result of a wide range of reading experiences and practice based on enjoyment of stories.

A more elusive skill, which is difficult to demonstrate in a short space but absolutely central in a reader's development, is the bond between the reader and the writer that comes from being together 'in the know'. It rests on a sharing of value systems, of reading background, of a common cultural experience, of a knowledge of the patterns of written language that makes possible allusions and references. If you want to understand this in the way that your child will be expected to understand, here is an example from a little further on in the story of *Huckleberry Finn*. Mark Twain is playing a subtle game with his reader in order to show what a down-to-earth character Huck is compared with Tom Sawyer whose imagination is fired by what he reads. Tom has turned his friends into a marauding gang and promised them that they will set upon a 'whole parcel of Spanish merchants and rich A-rabs with two hundred elephants and six hundred camels and over a thousand sumter mules, all loaded with di'monds'. Huck takes up the story:

I wanted to see the camels and elephants, so I was on hand next day, Saturday, in the ambuscade; and when we got the word, we rushed out of the woods and down the hill. But there warn't no Spaniards and A-rabs, and there warn't no camels nor no elephants. It warn't anything but a Sunday-school picnic, and only a primer class at that. We busted it up, and chased the children up the hollow; but we never got anything but some doughnuts and jam, though Ben Rogers got a rag doll, and Jo Harper got a hymn-book and a tract; and then the teacher charged in and made us drop everything and cut. I didn't see no di'monds, and I told Tom Sawyer so. He said there was loads of them there, anyway; and he said there was A-rabs there, too, and elephants and things. I said, why couldn't we see them, then? He said if I warn't so ignorant, but had read a book called *Don Quixote,* I would know without asking. He said it was all done by enchantment. He said there was hundreds of soldiers there, and elephants and treasure, and so on, but we had enemies which he called magicians, and they had turned the whole thing into an infant Sunday school, just out of spite. I said, all right, then the thing for us to do was to go for the magician. Tom Sawyer said I was a numskull.

Good readers do not stop for the words they don't know: 'sumter', 'a book called *Don Quixote*', because they are in pursuit of the action of the tale. The meaning emerges from the pattern of relationships. This way of knowing develops in the reader and becomes clearer as the story goes on. The real skill lies in seeing the double trick of Tom Sawyer's saying that magicians had changed the Spaniards and A-rabs so that they looked like a Sunday school picnic and recognizing Huck's irrefutable logic: 'the thing for us to do was to go for the magician.'

Allusions, images, being in the know, these are exclusive literary skills that come from a literary culture. They are exclusive in that inexperienced readers do not share them and are puzzled by them. They are not taught in exercises or practice. They are part of the author's way of telling his story and sometimes a teacher draws attention to them if she thinks the pupils have not understood what is happening. She does not lay bare all the subtleties to eleven-year-olds. Young readers learn to expect them as part of the pleasure of reading stories when words seem to mean more than they say. But, above all, the good reader's confidence lets him neglect what he feels he will come to know all in good time if he needs to, and he presses on with the story to find out what happens next to the characters whose fortunes he is caught up in.

It seems important to explain this at some length because these aspects of learning to read are taken for granted by those to whom they become second nature, notably teachers. They show up in class in response to tests of *comprehension* in some English lessons, where, again, they are expected to be part and parcel of a reader's ability. The questions the teacher asks ('Why was Huck Finn disappointed in Tom Sawyer's games?', for instance), give the good reader a chance to shine, but they never teach the other pupils how this knowledge is acquired. Good readers are just expected to be 'bright'. Very little attention is generally paid to the way in which *what* they have read, the range of stories, poems, plays, books of information, newspapers, secret searches in adult reading matter, contributes to these reading abilities.

If your child is acknowledged as a competent and sensitive reader, you may never have to worry about him as teachers will always confirm him by their approval of his bookishness. Have an eye, however, to his tendency to read everything at top speed. Some books need a slower pace. Do not urge him on too fast to read acceptable books approved of by adults. An eleven-year-old reading *Robinson Crusoe* is enjoying the story, not reading it as an adult does. I have known many children of this age who have been undaunted by *Nicholas Nickleby* and *Oliver Twist*, but they are, in fact, following the fortunes of the younger characters in these books by dint of ignoring what does not concern them. This is fine, but it is sometimes better for an eleven-year-old to read a stretching book for the young than to pick a partial way through the most accessible of the classics. The two need not be mutually exclusive occupations, but I am always very sorry when parents announce with some satisfaction that their eleven-years-olds have left children's books behind and now read only 'real' literature, implying that there is more quality in any adult novel than in all of those specially written for children. The opposite is true. Many a book for the young has a standard of craftsmanship lacking in accessible adult books because the authors have chosen their audience and shaped their work accordingly. Look at Alan Garner's *Stone Book Quartet* and you will see how apparently simple yet how demanding children's literature can be. To read these four short books is to enjoy a literary experience of a quite distinctive kind.

Good readers need imaginative teachers and indulgent parents. The teachers sometimes have to admit in the pupil a deeper understanding and love of literature than they may possess. To put the next book into the child's hand is a challenge; to be the trusted friend of a good reader is a rewarding experience. Librarians are often their allies. Parents are no longer the source of all book wisdom, but they can offer humour and tolerance and, above all, book tokens and talk. Of the many good, instructive ways of helping children, the subtlest lies in leaving them alone. Their ability and confidence reflect the trust you show. It is worthwhile understanding that this activity needs time and the patience of adults who are sometimes worried if their children constantly have 'their heads in a book'. If this is the case with your child, resist the temptation to send him out into the sunshine or on an errand.

You will be most aware of the good readers if they are *not* in your family and your child reads very little. Perhaps he watches television, or is active in sport or with his friends, and regards school as a place where his gang goes about its own affairs, with a reasonable acquiescence in what the teacher proposes for a lesson, but no great enthusiasm for extra-curricular learning. Perhaps he does not read or write as well as you think he should. What, if anything, should be done to turn him into a reader if his days in secondary school are not to rush past with little effect on his learning?

Asked what they think about reading, a fair number of secondary school children claim that they 'don't see the point'. Strangely, they may all be reading something, usually in paperback, but they do not see this as relevant or related to reading in school. At best, reading is for the times when there is nothing better to do. Here is an eleven-year-old writing about books:

> Books to me are boring. I can never get into the story. In school I don't mind reading. In school it's different, it's not so boring. You've got to sit down and shut up. I think I can get into it more in school because there's nothing else to do like looking over the wall to the Park for mates or raiding the biscuit tin. When we read in school if the story aint so good I usually get in a bad mood or I get a headache.

Reading is an anti-social activity for most eleven-year-olds. They have to go away from where the others are milling around or shut out the noise of play and conversation.

This writer goes on to relate a significant reading experience:

> There was one moment I remember most. This was in the fourth year of my Junior School. It was the first day in my new class and the teacher wanted to hear us read. My stomach turned and I was getting hotter. There was about 20 people in front of me. One of them couldn't read well and Miss said Well, Well, now we know the people who can't read. I was next after Leigh and I felt as though I was burning up. It was my turn nothing would come out every word I said came out with a quiver. Even very easy words wouldn't come out and she stopped me. I was never so imbaraced in my life my face was turning bright red as

the teacher was saying how bad I was. She didn't seem to
understand how I felt and that I was a good reader really.
She seemed to be like a robot with no feelings.

There is a hint of toughness in this, and the suggestion that
she has recovered from the blow to her self-esteem. But the
writer gives us a clue to the way a teacher's behaviour may
defeat the very purpose it is expected to support.

Indifferent readers at eleven lack stamina and good
models. They usually read too little because they do not, by
themselves, initiate reading activity, but wait until there is a
school reason for doing it—to answer homework questions
or to complete a worksheet in class. A significant amount of
evidence shows that, in secondary school, although teachers
state that reading is important, they rarely give class time for
it, and a great deal of 'looking up' and 'learning' is done at
home; some of it is never followed in class. It is possible to opt
out of reading if it doesn't appeal to you. Very few London
eleven-year-olds believe, as an absolute article of faith, that
they have to be literate to be employed. They know too well
that this is not the case. So, as soon as they think they are no
longer unable to read, they may well give up the activity
altogether. Sometimes even their parents do not know that
this has happened, and their teachers may not take action in
time. The next crisis comes the year before the examinations,
as we shall see in the next chapter.

Parents need to know that the secondary school day is
packed with activity of widely different kinds, and that
information and learning are made available and possible in
many media, from film loops to cassette recordings. Reading
and writing take time, and, to be effective, need the accom-
paniment of talking and listening. The reading done by
many children is not inadequate in style or skill; it is simply
short-winded. They do not do enough of it. In addition, there
is a school view of reading and writing that turns these
activities into getting information from books in the shortest
possible time and making the copied sentences into some
kind of 'report' in order to get a mark in a subject. Specialist

teachers do not all agree with the findings of the Bullock Committee which laid on every teacher the responsibility for the pupil's literacy in that subject. In some schools, children who 'don't see the point' in reading and writing can get away with doing very little.

The difficulty for parents of children who evade reading and writing is that they can no longer entice their offspring into shared activities as they once could. Very few families naturally sit down to read to each other. The active eleven-year-old has a world of scorn and contempt for all that keeps him from his social life. He says 'it's boring' in a way that brings adults, parents and teachers alike to near despair. The worst effect of television is to suggest that every activity has to be both simple and diverting. Good teachers and supportive parents are those who help children to survive the challenge of something that engages them more fully for longer stretches of time. Reading is one of those things, playing a musical instrument is another. We are just beginning to see that the hundreds of children who now perform in orchestras, where only tens were active before, have been encouraged by those who gave the activity a social setting and group support, beginning with what the children wanted to play and making it possible for them to try.

We haven't yet tried to make good readers of all the indifferent ones because we insist on ignoring what children are prepared to read and on not giving them time to do it. Then, when the situation seems serious, many secondary schools step up their use of reading laboratories, tests, special exercises and special books. What the children really need is a great deal more time to read and write for their own satisfaction. This means more books, a wider selection of titles and different kinds of writing. In a very few schools, a certain length of time is set aside each day for uninterrupted silent reading when the teachers read too and the pupils can read what they like. I have referred to this before as 'reading in bulk'. It is still a necessary part of the development of a range and diversity of skills.

Just before adolescence takes over, children are still

influenced by the models set by their parents, so I have to repeat that there is no point in nagging your child into reading if he never sees you doing it for yourself. Admired adults are still the strongest factor in the reading business, and, in the same way, a child will never learn to write unless he has both occasion and encouragement. By this time, teachers have long expected more than a few sentences for 'composition'. They have seen the powerful fluency of those who enjoy composing. But if your child sees that reading and writing (letters, notes, lists) play no part in family life, he will think less of the tasks when they are solely connected with school.

If you think your eleven-year-old should read and write more than he does, you must see that he has the space and time to do these things. First, check on his bedside lamp. Can he read comfortably? Has he a surface where he can write without having to clear away other people's clutter? (He may have to clear up his own.) Can he put his own books in a place where he is pleased to have them as his possessions? If he makes a collection of writing implements don't suggest that one pen will do and that he needn't spend any more of his pocket money on notebooks. Writers need tools as carpenters do. When magazines about cars and motor bikes pile up on the floor, don't complain unless you have a suggestion about where they can be kept. Many things connected with reading are part of a wider pattern of behaviour linked to making literacy a meaningful state.

When you think there is too little evidence of reading and writing being done at home, a talk with the class tutor or year head is called for. You should be able to see evidence of what is being done in school and to ask about the kinds of reading and writing that are expected of the pupils in their first year. It does no harm to ask what kind of help parents are expected to give, and what amount of time is set aside for continuous reading and writing in school. If anyone expresses dissatisfaction with your child's reading and writing, try to extract as clear an example as you can of what is causing the unease. Ask to see who is taking any responsibility for help. If there is no one, then arrange an appointment two months ahead with whoever drew the child's weakness to your notice and see if there is any progress. If you are to help by buying books for your child to read at home or getting them from the library, be sure that you are shown a sample of material that is thought suitable. Make notes on the spot. Before they reach home, most parents forget what the teacher told them.

The chief difficulty for an eleven-year-old in reading a book of information, or a subject textbook, is to discover the relationship between what he knows in real life, his 'action' knowledge, and the way that same information or experience is represented in a book. For instance, many eleven-year-olds are keen on football, so teachers pile football books into class libraries. The reader has to link the information about the rules of the game, the history of clubs, the reminiscences of goalkeepers with the vitality of the action and discussion that crowds his weekends. It is not an automatic transmission. Many a teacher has been bitterly disappointed because a pupil's avowed interest has not been related to any classroom activity. Not surprisingly the pupil may want to keep to himself his knowledge of racing cars, horses, sailing, as the part of his life that he inhabits in his own right. He may read to satisfy curiosity, to gain information relevant to those out-of-school activities, without necessarily wanting to write a project about them. So you may see a fair amount of reading being done at home in connection with interests which are never pursued in school. If you feel you have only a limited scope for influencing or supporting your child's reading interests, I suggest you provide the desired adult book for the out-of-school activity, and help, but only when you are given a lead, to turn the action knowledge of your child's experience on to the textbook presentation of subject matter by talking about it.

The skill which all children need to learn in secondary school is to *interrogate* a text. Too often those who 'don't see the point' of reading imagine that books are simply full of information to be transferred in some mysterious way into their heads. They rarely believe that you can disagree with what an author says if your experience contradicts his assertions. This questioning works in two ways. A child can be stimulated by a book, especially those now available with fine pictures of wild life, travel, cities, cars or aeroplanes, to look at something that intrigues him. The book alerts his curiosity so that he checks his findings from the pictures or what he already knows against the explanation in the text. The confident reader looks again at the text to find the reason for any difference between what he reads and what he knows. The indifferent reader pursues the matter no further than scanning the picture. You can help to stimulate a better kind of enquiry with a newspaper and television. Encourage your child to see that the same event is not always reported in the same way in both. The following up of written accounts of events is good support for the kind of enquiry he is expected to pursue in school. In learning to find his way about a newspaper by regular reading at home he will do more to help himself than in the one-off 'newspaper lesson' in school.

It is now the time to discuss the public print you both see all around you, instead of simply reading it. Natural caution and healthy in-built scepticism keep most people from buying all that they see advertised, but the eleven- or twelve-year-old is at his most gullible. He is more or less accustomed to taking adults at their word, so that advertisements look like promises. Arguments about which cars go faster, whether a robot can do things on its own, how a calculator works or if a five-pound watch is better than a four-pound one need not result in lengthy library searches, but suggest where you can, together, begin to seek out what he needs to know. Then the important point about reading as something related to real life begins to be made. It is the time to explain licences, savings banks, manuals of instruction, and possibly this is the best time to read the Highway Code. These reading experiences can be acquired at home because there they come up naturally in the context of use, as will the words of the pop song and the teenage magazine. It isn't easy to persuade 'turned off' readers that they do read quite a lot, especially if they are determined to shun the reading model proposed by school and demonstrated by those whom they regard as stuffy adults. The best way to confirm the reading habit in your eleven-year-old who is less experienced as a reader than you would like him to be is through those interests that absorb him for longer than he reads in school. It may not always be easy to read with him, but you should seize any occasion that offers.

One significant lead comes from television. I may have given the impression that television and reading are usually in conflict, but sales of books show that whatever appears on *Blue Peter*, *Book Tower*, *Jackanory* or as a TV serial is widely read, or, at least, widely bought. This is another manifestation of the security offered by 'known text'. The events in the serial film about Grange Hill School caused more discussion by children than ever before about the issues that affect their lives. The book that followed the film is not a school story in the old-fashioned sense, with dormitory feasts and the like. Instead it explores the relationship of the young with those in authority, the ambiguities of what is fair, the problems of the hurt child and racism in schools.

Many children genuinely can't 'get into books', not because the words are difficult or because they do not find themselves pictured within, but because they have not been helped to find the relevance of what they read to their own deep and pressing preoccupations. Adults want to believe that children need not be worried by street violence, the effect of the nuclear bomb, and their possible role in the world, and so they often play down these problems. But where children find books that genuinely speak to their condition they read them with passion. The trouble is, parents are not now the best people to give them books, not even books about parents, such as Louise Fitzhugh's *Nobody's Family is Going to Change*. But another trusted adult could well do that. In any case, there will always be some popular paperback titles making the rounds, what teachers call 'literature under the desk'. You may not like what your child is reading, but to be tolerant is to be trusting.

A non-engaged, casual, inexperienced eleven-year-old reader worries his parents and his teachers. In school he needs help to cope with texts that assume he can deal with the beginnings of logical relationships in his thinking. In books about submarines, volcanoes, making crystals or the medieval monastery, the organization of the material is now more generalized; less of it is in the direct narrative form. The reader is expected to understand the relationship of cause and effect: if this happens, *then* that happens. School is the place to learn to deal with this logic in detail, but you should now see the beginnings of it in your child's conversations and arguments. Don't insist that you are always right. Give him ample scope to organize his reasons and encourage him to complete his ideas. Interrogation of text on a page—that most necessary of all reading skills—begins, I fear, with the questioning of the authority of all adults.

The toughest problem is still *time*, time to read, to talk, to write. These processes now become much harder as thinking is spelled out in words, and more patience and stamina are needed. Eleven-year-olds will persevere with what interests them, but they fool about a great deal, and it is easy to be impatient. One kind of help that pays dividends is to give them the support and scope they need to finish whatever they undertake, from the washing of the car to reading to the end of a library book. You may well be able to help your child to finish a story when the book is due back at the library. That is better than returning the book unread.

You may hear people say that children who can read and don't want to are 'reluctant readers'. I am not convinced that this is the case. Children are never reluctant to do something they have mastered and enjoy. Usually they have not yet discovered what's in it for them, either because they don't read well enough or because they have had the wrong kind of books, or too restricted a choice. Inexperienced readers need more experience. So we have, again, to promote the books they can enjoy and master, with whatever other support systems are available, beginning with the things that interest them. If your child doesn't want to read, he must lack time, means (the bedside lamp again), encouragement, books, skill or, simply, interest, and there is no short cut to supplying these. You have to ask yourself, first, if you have the will to *help over a period of at least six months*. It's no good saying one Saturday afternoon in the bookshop or the library will do till Christmas. The common factor in disaffected readers is the lack of adult support at the time when it was most necessary. So don't think that some day in the future he will turn to books. Perhaps he won't.

What then of the eleven-year-old who has, clearly, very little acknowledged reading skill? How will he fare in his new secondary school?

If you think your child is in this position you must be vigilant right from the start, especially in all the decisions that are made about how he is to be taught. With luck, he will not be placed in a remedial unit straight away. Most schools now recognize that the hospitalizing effect of putting 'poor' readers into small groups separated from the rest of their peers is more serious than the slower growth of reading ability in an ordinary class. They usually have a 'withdrawal' scheme where children have special lessons to give them more attention, although the remedial department of the school may still be responsible for these lessons. The plain truth is that *very* few children have only reading and writing difficulties. If these have been prolonged or severe, then many other aspects of a child's learning have been affected, especially in subjects like history where books are the lesson tools.

Every non-reading eleven-year-old has an individual history of why he cannot read. He also has a story which he tells himself about his failure, and more often than not, he has a satisfactory explanation, usually validated by his family, as to why he is not so good at reading as his friends. You will know why your child cannot read, and he will accept those reasons as sufficient. The real question is: can he, will he learn, and what can be done to ensure that he is successful?

What follows is not a counsel of despair nor a warning, but it is important to realize that the longer a child puts off learning to read, the longer the learning takes. If a pupil who has had six years in school still cannot read, then this fact must be known and some steps must already have been taken to change the situation. In my experience no child of eleven is without any reading skill whatsoever. Most children know what reading is about; they vary in their inclination to engage in the activity. Some want to avoid it altogether because they think they cannot do it. Every child who really *wants* to learn to read, can learn. A very few really don't want to, and they pose special problems. Most inexperienced non-reading eleven-year-olds don't know if they really want to read because they are not sure if they desire the consequences of literacy which, in many schools, look not so much like freedom as more work than ever. To stay in the remedial stream is undoubtedly less demanding, and some children hide there for all their time in school. If your child wants to read, and can't, then he needs collaborative help to learn. The trouble is he may be having reading lessons, which are not always the same thing.

So far, I hope the tone of this book has been positive, encouraging and realistic. Nothing is gained by shirking the issues. Now we have to confront the fact that an eleven-year-old is able to make some decisions for himself, and he may have to decide to learn to read, and to stick with the consequences of the decision. This may mean nearly two years of quite hard work to bring him within sighting distance of his fellows. This isn't easy for parent or child, and you may decide you need help. Let me explain what is involved.

First parent and child must face the fact that reading and writing won't just happen. It's too late for that. On the other hand, the eleven-year-old is no longer a baby. He knows the score; at school he will confront his failure every day. Do not try to shield him from it, but don't rub it in. His resentment, truculence, rebellion and despair are fuelled by remarks about his stupidity. He needs success and help so that he can see himself getting better, not worse. Three kinds of help pay dividends. The first is to treat the situation as a job to be tackled, with as little emotional blackmail as possible. For this reason parents are not always the best teachers, yet they can give help if they can do so without communicating their anxiety. Visit the school and find out what is happening there. Do *not* repeat at home what you have learned, but let the teacher know that you are keen to be supportive. Try to make this partnership a genuine consultative one. Secondly, expect the child to behave like a reader. If he goes for errands with a list, take time to tell him what is written down. Explain what he is to look for, if it is in a supermarket, and when he comes back show how the words are printed on the bags and boxes. Extend this into the same kind of looking at public print that might have gone on when he was very little. Poor readers need constant reminding that there are things they *can* read. Very often they distrust whatever skill they have and think it irrelevant to the great amount of reading that they are not doing. Assume that he will behave like a reader, and expect him to. I have never met an eleven-year-old who could not read correctly 'Push' and 'Pull', 'Fire exit', 'No admittance', 'Ladies' and 'Gentlemen'.

The third kind of help is the most demanding and the most effective. You have to discover if he can bear to become fluent. The many non-reading eleven-year-olds I have met (not because there are many, but because I seek them out) have just as many strange views about reading, most of which are unhelpful. They read slowly, word by word, in a strange one-toned voice, like a beginner typist punching keys. They read a whole page like this, and collapse exhausted at the end. If you ask what happened in the story they can't tell you, yet they got every word right. Quite literally, they have to change their tune; first, by telling themselves the story, silently, and then by reading the page aloud as if they had written it. They have to go fast, taking risks that they may get some words wrong, but hunting down the meaning through their understanding of it. That is, they have to behave like readers, when their whole experience and expectation tells them that they can't. When they fail, they want to give up. This is when it's really hard. They have to keep going. The only reason they will is that they want to succeed *and* because what they are reading is worth taking trouble over.

When people first began to look into the problem of the older, slower reader they discovered that very little had been written that took account of undeveloped reading ability and pre-adolescent interests. When, under pressure, publishers began to produce books for 'reluctant', 'backward' or 'poor' readers they took the reading scheme as their model, and so we had books about family life and working teenagers, a kind of social realism in short sentences that was supposed to match the concerns of the so-called 'non-readers'. This was a great mistake; only real books make real readers, especially at this stage. You can imagine what it feels like to a slow or inexperienced reader to be given yet another book that proclaims his position. If you want to make a reader, you have to find a book he can enjoy, one that makes him believe you think he can be a reader, and then you must help him to find his way through it. Involve him in the library search for a book you can both enjoy, then turn the pages together.

You will now begin to learn two things. The first is about what the experts call *textual density*, how tough the prose is. There are two kinds of 'thick' writing you can recognize: a page of closely packed print that has no pictures or long sentences with many ideas related to a central theme. Beginners find both of these daunting. So when you are choosing books, select them according to the topic that will interest the reader, and spend as much time as you can turning the pages, looking, talking and then reading. If you don't find a book that the reader wants, a Sunday colour supplement will do—even the cartoons and the advertisements for Rolls-Royce cars and French perfume. Behind these ephemeral productions there is an awareness of how to produce reading at everyone's level, from single word captions to packed layers of comment and criticism. You will soon discover which kind of text your child can *interpret* without your help. Go on assuming that he can find his own level. Let him be the expert on the topics he knows about.

Then, you will begin to realize that reading over a stretch of text demands that the reader follows the cohesion of the narrative or the argument. This means that the reader has to keep in his head the sequence of thought, so that words like *he, she, it, they, who, whose, which, that*—words not difficult in themselves—refer in the text to what has already been mentioned. No one can learn to read from captions only, and so a restarter, someone who has still not learned to read, needs good stories, so well written that he not only gets the tune of the author's style but learns how the action follows. (The best story I know for this is Ted Hughes' *The Iron Man*.) Your help is needed to smooth the reader's utterance so that he can read the page faster, making the story into something he is telling. He won't do this at first sight. You will have to read it to him. But he has to *feel* what it is like to be fluent. This is hard, like violin practice, but the slow reader has to begin to 'chunk' the meaning into natural sounding sequences where once he thumped out single words. The secret of this success lies in your finding what can honestly be praised, what needs more practice and how to encourage him to do most of the work without despair.

Successful teaching of slow-starting eleven-year-olds means keeping the balance between reading-as-a-job-to-be-done so that an ability may be mastered, and enjoying-reading-for-its-own-sake. The subtlest and perhaps the most difficult thing for reading teachers to do is to adjust their expectations to the pupil's performance. To let him off too easily is often a relief at the time but a source of anxiety later. ('She's given me an easy book so that I won't make mistakes and then feel better. But I hope I can read something tougher than *that*.') The child has to feel that he can make an effort and be successful, and at the same time have a realistic but not intimidating view of the task ahead. It's hard. But frequently we underestimate children's resilience and their respect for an ambitious undertaking.

The inexperienced eleven-year-old reader also writes with little confidence, again because he has written too little.

Everyone knows at a glance the difference between handwriting that has been worn down with use and that of the hesitant user. Many fluent writers begin to change the style of their handwriting at this time, so it is not insulting to suggest that your child has some practice. New pens and pencils are an incentive: rough work books are encouraging. But again, you must not expect quick, painless improvement. Think about your mastery of anything and how long the achievement took, and your patience will stretch. When you are exhausted with trying to encourage the stumbler to try again, recall your own experience of receiving encouragement to persevere. Remember, too, we all have our off days.

One minor warning: if neither you nor your reader is enjoying this encounter with books and reading, it is better to stop and seek help elsewhere. If your best endeavours are increasing your child's frustration, do not feel guilty or believe that he is sick or stupid. Consult his teacher again to see what can be done to increase his desire to read and to lessen your anxiety about him.

My lengthy experience of poor readers in the first years of secondary school suggests that they are not hampered by lack of ability, only by lack of desire, confidence and reward. They just don't know what fluent readers get out of reading books. They have no idea how the author becomes a companion, that writers want them to understand rather than to be perplexed. They know the words, but lack all knowledge of the rules of the game, especially the ones that are not taught in lessons, because they have so rarely been invited to play, and the champions are all around. A small but significant number of children cling to extra reading lessons as a means of securing attention. When they learn to read they no longer need it.

It is difficult to tell you that to be helpful you have to share the reading you do with a child in such a way that he gradually takes it over. That's what happens; easily said, very demanding to do. You cannot supplant this with any special teaching method, reading scheme or organized material because, in the end, the child has to be reading the real thing, a story book for his own pleasure, or the class text to learn his lessons.

Can a parent ever really help a slow reader? Yes, indeed. The best are those who themselves enjoy reading so much that they cannot help sharing the activity with their children in an interested but relaxed way. The worst can be so threateningly didactic that the child cannot hope to learn for fear of failing. Assume that your child *will* learn, and treat him as a reader with real books. With the right kind of attention, increasing effort on his part and enough shared time over a period of about a year, all will be well.

Choosing Books at Eleven

The confident eleven-year-olds know what they like, find what they want, and latch on to adults who can provide surprises and suggest new titles. In these days of mass production of books for children it is difficult to say what any child ought to have read. Ask around and you will discover that your best-read friends have skipped some celebrated classics or made good excuses for having passed over a well-known author or two. I should have to know a child well before I offered *The Water Babies* because I know most children read no further than the first three chapters. Many a boys' school leaves the selection of modern children's fiction to parents and opts for class discussion of *The Thirty-Nine Steps* or *The Memoirs of a Fox-Hunting Man* which eleven-year-olds can read if they have to. If you take time to read children's books, you will find that there are many you can enjoy with your children. Buy some that the rest of the family can share; borrow some till you know what will be read again. Increase all pocket money at this time with books in mind. Don't censor the selection, however.

I should be sorry if able readers passed over the tales that have the qualities of endurance that guarantee new editions in every generation: *Little Women, Alice, The Secret Garden, The Hobbit* and *Black Beauty*. These appear in all lists and surveys. You may not know the more recent books that spark off imagination and discussion: *The Wizard of Earthsea* and *The Blue Hawk*, for example. So the problem is to promote the well-tried and to keep abreast of the new. A good school will have a 'Book Night', perhaps in collaboration with the public library and a local bookshop, or some special activity in connection with Children's Book Week. The pity is, children read books all through the year while exhibitions appear infrequently and other good book activities come in great explosive feasts followed by months of famine. Parents can do a great deal by sharing expertise, or asking publishers of children's books to speak at PTA meetings when there is no national event in sight.

Book lists are essential. The National Book League has many; the School Library Association has others, mostly compiled for those who have to order for libraries and collections. *The Good Book Guide Selection for Young Readers* offers roughly the number of titles an enthusiastic reader can cope with in a year. *Signal*'s lists include a selection of poetry and another of humorous books that can be consulted with profit. Other sources are: *Children's Books of the Year, Books for Keeps, Books for Your Children*, and the lists produced by the Youth Libraries Group of the Library Association. Most local libraries have special lists. Newspapers like *The Times* and *The Guardian* and the bigger Sunday papers are conscientious about reviewing books for the young. Again, Christmas and summer holidays provoke a flood of reviews, whereas most parents want to know, on the spot or at a wet weekend, or just as a new hobby takes up their child's enthusiasm, how to capture the moment of interest.

The central problem is: how do you choose? Are there undisputed criteria of what makes a good book for children? I think there are, but you may not be so interested in my ways of choosing as capable of making your own. Generally speaking, commentators on children's books are in fair agreement about those that are worth reading. There are some demarcation disputes, but there are enough avowedly 'good' books for children to keep even the most voracious reader happy. You choose because you know the child, his interests, his staying power, his enthusiasm, or his lack of these things. You are not really helped by my saying that Emma Smith's *No Way of Telling* is a superb story for eleven-year-old girls until you know about the story and the girls.

What makes a good children's book for this age? Many things, including the standard of its production. There is a crafted quality in the writing and an awareness that the book is a whole world for the reader and the writer to inhabit. If you think you know what a good story is, then you will find that a great book for an eleven-year-old is a good story, well made, in which the elements of story and telling are so fused that the reader responds to an experience that both confirms and extends his own. Part of the making is the author's use of language, part is the quality of the author's imaginative force. There is a uniqueness about great children's books as there is in adult literature of the serious kind, a high quality of particularity that lets the reader feel the general application of what the writer has to say in his offering of a singular situation or event. Those who know this quality are keen to promote it; those who have made no contact with it cannot understand what fires enthusiasm for books like Rosemary Sutcliff's *Warrior Scarlet*, for instance, Mary Norton's *The Borrowers* or Alan Garner's *The Stone Book*. No adult novel is of quite the same kind. Behind them lie the author's satisfactions with myth, folk tale and the long tradition of English literature bound up with a realization that children see things very clearly. There are other concerns, about moral values, idealism, the relationship of the book to the child's known world and the social concerns of the day. But in the end, a children's book is crafted and brought into being by the creative imagination of a writer who wants it to be as it is because, for his audience, he takes trouble to make it well.

A useful way to identify the books our competent eleven-year-old might enjoy is to read the collected works of one author. You may know C. S. Lewis's Narnia stories. Try next a new author: Robert Leeson, for example, or Nina Bawden or Penelope Lively. You will see that, for all their undoubted and continuing appeal, the Narnia books carry the values and social awareness of an earlier age. Newer writers are challenging the unquestioned acceptance of earlier standards while exploring new problems that were not part of the world of the children for whom C. S. Lewis wrote. But the Narnia stories still appeal, and rightly so, because the author took his audience seriously and believed that a children's book was a special way of saying something important.

Once a reader 'gets into' a story, he knows before long what kind of a place he has come to. If the characters eat breakfast, catch buses, talk to their friends, worry about money just as we do in the course of a day, we recognize the story world as the same as the one outside, and as we go on reading, we know the conventions or rules by which the real world becomes a story. You can change a family's fortune by a win on the football pools, or even by digging up treasure, but not by waving a wand. The popularity of realistic tales with children is based on the fact that they find a place for themselves in the action. They recognize characters as people they know, and the issues that the author deals with are their concerns too. A school story is now about a comprehensive school. Realistic stories confirm and extend the experience of the reader in a way that relates directly to social life—the family, school, housing, adult jobs, holidays and the like.

As society changes, so do the plots and settings of these stories, and the attitudes of the people portrayed in them. It is no longer acceptable to show girls as fulfilling stereotypical roles in the home, for example, and the white middle-class family of *Janet and John* is no longer the typical one. Language, clothes, and social habits seem to change as fast as the books are printed. In Robert Leeson's adaptation of the television school story, *Grange Hill Rules OK*, the relationships between the adults and the children are not those of the Chalet School stories published in the thirties. The sources of pleasure, pain, loss, joy and disappointment are different. The way people behave in these stories, the motives for their actions, are judged by what people do now, and by the standards of values that are practised *and debated* in the world outside the book. Yet you will see the connection between the old and the new *as stories*.

Inside the book, the narrative style, the dialogue of the characters—including their swearing and their slang— and the moral system implied by the author are organized by means of a set of literary conventions. Young readers understand the nature of the hero or heroine, whose fate they care about, and they are capable of subtle distinctions in judging the villain, who threatens the stability of the system. They expect to tell good from bad. These things are part of their growing literary competence. Some writers have been carried away by the notion that children should meet the 'real' world in books, either so that they may empathize with the less fortunate or confront the facts of life. Read as widely as you can on behalf of your eleven-year-old, because in these books their experience will be different from yours at their age. Take special care with books that deal with childhood disasters. I am not convinced that the young want to read about divorce until the pain of their experience of it has subsided somewhat, and I doubt if they are consoled for a death in the family by reading about another.

You may not be too happy with books about one-parent families, drunken or feckless parents, or terminal illnesses. But television has made the young especially aware of, if not always better informed about, a whole range of subjects which their elders once believed should be adult secrets. Remember, children are moved, if not logically persuaded, by the way people and events are presented. The topic is important, but the treatment of it for a young audience is crucial.

One particular example that shows how the child is

advancing in reading is his gradual understanding of the first person narrator, the story told as 'I'. To the inexperienced reader this is a puzzle: who is talking? He takes on the 'I' story as he begins to realize that the characters not only talk but tell. The arrival of this awareness coincides with a number of other instances of the child's attempts to see a situation from several points of view. The books that need this skill include those with an autobiographical flavour: *Huckleberry Finn* (but not *Tom Sawyer*), *Black Beauty*, *The Treasure Seekers* (a very special one because the narrator sometimes refers to himself by his name) and *Treasure Island*.

Eleven-year-olds have a clear notion that some stories bear a relationship to the world they know outside the book while others do not. They know the literary rules for stories where they can expect the laws of nature to work as in the everyday world, and know too that they are different from 'fantasy'. It is no accident that 'fantasy' offers authors scope for experimental storying. *Alice* is the archetypal book in this category. To read books of fantasy the child needs his earlier experience of myths and sagas, and fairy tales, for these all have modern, derivative forms. A well-read eleven-year-old knows, instinctively if not consciously, that in a folk tale a woodcutter can be as worthy as a lord, but in a legend he would be a prince in disguise. That is, he knows the rules of the game. By the time they are eleven, good readers know how many different kinds of games are played in storytelling.

Less experienced readers need to learn how fantasy stories work. Some can be enticed into books where the authors suspend reality by letting magic breathe into the world they know: in the ghost story, for example. Many an indifferent reader will give this kind of tale, and others that play tricks with time and space (see *Dragonfall 5*), a chance to enchant them. Then they discover what the experienced fairy tale reader already knows: the world *can* be changed. All scientific advance was a fantasy once. When the young reader inhabits the fantasy world of a book, he can contemplate not only the unity of the universe as seen in myths, legends and folk tales, but also the *nature of possibilities and their results*. So do not think that if your child is not a high flyer he should have only books about ordinary things. On the contrary, he should be invited and encouraged to take on the possibilities of human experience in the story world that a good author has made. Boys who are expected to reject the imaginative are in fact enthusiastic inhabitants of Middle Earth in the Tolkien sagas. *Dr Who* is television's answer to a deeply felt need for make-believe that shows us what the world could be like, and produces for the young the even-handedness of justice and the consolation of a happy ending.

If you are making your first dip into the sea of children's books on behalf of an eleven-year-old, do not draw back too soon. Judge the storying power of your child and match it with the length of the book. Better a good short one finished than a long one left, reproachfully, half-read. If you think your child can read very little, do not begin your search by asking for books for 'reluctant' readers. Look instead for a story that has well-written dialogue. Inexperienced readers cope with this best because television has taught them how it carries the action of the plot. If you are not sure whether the book will urge the reader on, read the first chapter with the child to see how long he takes to become involved in the tale. If he is still with it after four pages, the chances are he will read to the end.

When your child rejects a story book and wants something more 'real', a book of information, you have to find more than one book on the desired topic. The world of information books for children is vast, especially now that television stimulates children's interest in the physical world and the wonders of technology. There are Observer books, spotters' guides, star gazers' manuals. Some are beautiful films transferred to pages with captions. Others, like David Macaulay's *Castle* and *Underground*, show how the intricacies of social living are reflected in the networks of engineering and architecture. You can pick your way successfully through this incredible supply of non-fiction if you look for the books that encourage children to ask their own questions and then help them to find the answers. All good non-fiction books *must* have an adequate contents list, an index and directions to other books. The lesson every child has to learn about books of information is that they offer only *selections* from all that is known about the main subject, and therefore two books on the rabbit, electricity, the world's rivers, the fauna and flora of England are always better than one. Part of the reading task for a real reader is to pursue the topic from one book to the next.

It is difficult to believe that eleven-year-olds who cannot read well should share the books easily read by those who can. But this is the case. If the helping adult does more of the reading at first and gradually lets the learner take over, less confident readers begin to change their view of what they can manage. Ideally, to be sure that a child has the best possible chance in his secondary school, his parents need to help his teacher to maintain and extend his reading and writing in his last year in primary school. But if this hasn't happened, parents must now raid the whole range of children's books in search of what will help. Begin with what the child wants to read. Extend it to a new interest for you both. Don't be ashamed to read the comic writers (look at Raymond Briggs' *Gentleman Jim*) or to moan gleefully over *The Old Joke Book*, (Allan and Janet Ahlberg). There are others in the book list on p. 243.

Powerful literacy brings to the young unbounded freedom. Those who care about this are never at ease until they have made time, help and books available to provide wide and deep reading, and to show a child how he too can become an author by writing stories to match those he reads. The child at eleven needs to range over all kinds of reading matter. He should also possess, on his shelves, *and in his head*, a number of books that let him know what real reading is like.

Questions at Eleven

Is there no such thing as dyslexia?

For some few children of undoubted intelligence learning to read is a slow and painful process. Some famous authors have recorded their early struggles; it is claimed that Yeats and Flaubert were handicapped at first. Many people who say they have suffered from this disability have written about it. Eileen Simpson's *Reversals* is an account of 'victory over dyslexia'. If you are bright and cannot learn to read it is undoubtedly a relief to be told that you are suffering from a neurological handicap; your failure is then no longer attributable to your want of effort. In the case-studies of dyslexia we find these common features: a poor beginning of learning to read, early failure, blame, very little patience on the part of the teacher and violent reactions on the part of the child, no pleasure in what is read, endless struggles with small segments of text. All the features of failing children are concentrated in those who say they are dyslexic (or dyslectic, the American form).

Interesting features of the dyslexia debate are these:

* those who take it seriously are vocal middle-class parents of failing children.
* there is nothing in the teaching of dyslexic children which is specific to them. The best remedies are good teaching practice for all children. The teachers adapt their understanding and method to suit the child. There is no special material which can be used only with these children. However good the games, the exercises, the machines, the children are readers when they can read (as anyone else might) a text that is written to be read.
* poor readers get better when they are encouraged to respond in their own way and to analyse their responses. Individual teaching helps. Children are prepared to be called dyslexic because it is a relief. They no longer feel guilty or ashamed as they did before the diagnosis. (We all prefer to be sick rather than to be considered stupid.)

* doctors offer dyslexia as a medical term for learning
  disfunction. Teachers who want to teach the child to
  read can do so without this description.

Those who, like me, are unwilling to talk about 'specific
development dyslexia' are not concerned to remove this
description from those children or adults to whom it offers
comfort. But I would rather encourage the child to discover
more about reading and confirm her in readerly behaviour
than subject her to the kind of 'cure' offered in a clinic or a
hospital. The best place for reading teaching is where it
makes most difference, in the ordinary run of school and
home life.

Are gifted readers ever held back in school?

Gifted readers are, by definition, those who usually need very
little help. They need a good supply of books, someone to talk
with about them, and just as much encouragement as anyone
else. They could be disheartened if no one took care of them, or
showed interest, or offered them a book worthy of their ability.
Otherwise, they usually find ways of pleasing themselves. No
one would dream of stopping a gifted reader from reading.

My child's spelling seems to get worse and worse. What can I do?

Be assured that it can improve. You may be able to
understand the problems and wait for the moment to help.
Read Mike Torbe's book, *Teaching Spelling*, and Margaret
Peters' *Spelling: Caught or Taught*. The writer can learn to
proof-correct her work. She can go over the first draft and
learn to look at the places where she knows she might be
wrong, then check with a spelling dictionary. (The Collins
one is helpful.) Encourage someone of her own age to help
her. Discussion is best. It is difficult to persuade the young
that adults who read what they have written are not simply
on the lookout for mistakes but adult readers are sometimes
distracted by poor spelling from considering the ideas.
Anything that turns this problem into an interest in *why*

words are written as they are is a bonus. Try to steer a middle course between worrying the child so much that she gives up writing in case she makes mistakes, while at the same time not letting her think it doesn't matter. As examiners consider how to mark English compositions more fairly, they tend to insist that what should be right, must be right. It may be some consolation, but no excuse, to know that some famous authors were, and are, atrocious spellers. The best spellers begin to be careful much earlier than eleven, but most poor spellers improve with care and encouragement.

Should there be a set time every day at home for reading practice?

This is a more difficult decision that it seems at first. If you insist that the book comes out every evening after five, then the child resents the intrusion of school tactics into home life. If you have a special shared time with a book you enjoy when the reading is also shared, this is practice, but pleasure too. Avoid at all costs the bad compromise where the child knows you are being teacherly but pretending to be jolly about it. Let there be a good agreement between you, and a book you both really want to read.

Should I cut down the amount of time my child spends watching television?

I have never found simple prohibition (switching off) actually made a child do something else at once, but it is helpful not to let the decision to switch the television *on* rest with the child. Once engrossed, the watcher is hard to unbind from the spell. To try to interest her in something other than endless TV is a good idea. Do you know what she watches? Is any of it related to reading and writing? Cut down television viewing time by helping her to choose what is worth watching. Discussion-and-choice is a good rule. But I have also noticed that those who watch television plays and dramatizations of books become quite proficient at understanding the conventions of narrative and the many-layered thing that a story is. So my answer is, choose, discuss, and add other stories to those she sees.

My child's teacher doesn't give her reading lessons. She just marks her work with 'good' if she has copied enough from a book.

A great pity. If your child can read fluently, she will no longer need specific reading *lessons*. But in many classrooms children are not given explicit enough help in understanding how to approach a text that is new or a subject that is unfamiliar. Where teachers only mark exercises, the supporting adult has a special responsibility for discussing what is read, not as an inquisition, but as a shared interest in the subject matter. Read a new book together, preferably one that stretches the reader a little in content or form.

I have tried to interest my child in reading something worthwhile but she just shrugs me off and reads the pre-teens magazines I don't like.

It is difficult for parents to know where and when they are entitled to make suggestions about reading. Some children seem to be totally acquiescent, agreeing that the adult's view is one that necessarily prevails so it is better to go along with it. They read the books suggested by the teacher and their parents and are accounted virtuous. Others rebel; they want to choose for themselves. The best aspect of your daughter's reading is that she is determined to assert her right to choose. She is also practising for the next stage, in a still uncommitted way, and is curious about being a teenager, but still safely not there. If you object to the magazines you will, of course, commend them to her all the more. (Magazines are partly a school cult.) If she is a reasonably competent reader, let her experiment. Encourage her to buy and collect books. A special pocket money supplement helps. She might also change her children's library ticket for an adult one if the librarian agrees.

My child is a very poor reader for her age. Her teacher tells me so and her friends laugh at her yet she doesn't seem to mind. I have been told for three years that it will just 'get better' but I doubt it.

I doubt it too. Help is clearly necessary. But before you rush into anything, discover, as exactly as you can, what your child can do. For example, can she read the labels on boxes and packets in the kitchen? Who judges how *poor* she is? What does the teacher say? What should she be able to do that she cannot manage? To say that a child is 'a poor reader' is to say nothing helpful. At this age some poor readers are those who never want to open a book. Some children who want to, can't read. Decide first which is the case for your child. Next, find out what she can read and will read willingly if helped.

Do not believe she doesn't mind. This may be bluff. Show her that *you* mind, without frightening her. Offer to help, but don't transfer your anxiety before you have made it clear that you think she could improve. Begin again, together, if she will let you. If she won't, you may have to look for extra help at school. The teacher must arrange it. Be casual at first, but the fact that you care will give her hope.

Where can I find out about reading tests?

If you really want to (remembering how poor tests are at *predicting* an individual child's reading ability) you can read about them in a book: *Reading: tests and assessment techniques* by Peter D. Pumfrey. I advise going no further, because every book about testing is soon out of date. Most new tests are devised on the basis of *cloze procedure*. The teacher will explain this and show you what is involved.

My children's school library is full of old books they are expected to read. I'm sure their teachers don't know about modern children's books. We haven't enough money to buy a lot and a school bookshop isn't really possible, as the children are scattered over a wide rural area. What can we do?

A small beginning would be to ask for a chance to see new children's books at a parents' evening. This shouldn't meet with disapproval if the parents take on the responsibility of setting up an exhibition and making a list. Paperbacks are really excellent value at less than £1, and children soon discover how to exchange them amongst themselves. I think the sight of children sitting and reading new books in school when there is an exhibition is one of the strongest moves towards a change in the reading policy. The National Book League exhibition, *Children's Books of the Year,* can be hired. Choose a summer's evening when parents and children are more disposed to linger.

Is there any harm in an eleven-year-old reading all of the Nancy Drew mysteries, or does what you say about Enid Blyton apply here too?

I'm always in danger of saying two opposite things at once with regard to these stories. (N B the boys' equivalent is the Hardy Boys series.) I'd never ban them, or despise them. I don't care for them. But I've seen scores of young people who have been brought to reading by having worked through them. You may take some consolation in the fact that Dickens was well-read in their Victorian equivalent. Usually, both boys and girls are only too eager to have something else offered to them. Try *The Ghost of Thomas Kempe,* or any story by Betsy Byars, or those in the book list on p. 240.

You haven't said anything about racism or sexism in children's books but we know it is there. What should parents do about it?

Read and think, all the time. I am worried by the fact that some commentators fail to distinguish between the deep roots of these problems and their surface presentations. The mere fact of a heroine performing masculine feats is no guarantee that the author's values are sound, and the shift of focus to the problems of a Pakistani hero does not automatically produce a well-written story. I suggest that you consult the National Book League list, *A Wider Heritage,* where you will find not only a well-selected list, but a distinctive contribution to the discussion which must continue about these issues.

6

A Lifetime's Pleasure;
or the Lost Adolescent?

The good reader at fourteen

Everyone who writes about teenage literacy is worried about it. Parents wonder if their children are reading enough, or too many indifferent books, or not at all. Teachers strive to find riveting narratives for classrooms full of lively bodies too vibrant to sit still unless spellbound. Keepers of the public conscience seek out evidence of prejudice and unreality in books for the young adult. Writers wonder what others are writing. Critics who are aware of adolescence as a cultural barometer debate the existence or non-existence of the teenage novel. In addition, we all know that opportunities for employment and extended education depend on reading and writing so we feel constrained to see that our children grow up in a community that takes literacy for granted. We believe that reading in adolescence is important because the habits that are laid down then seem to last for a lifetime.

When professional readers and writers, whose literacy is the source of their fame and income, report on how they behaved in their teens, we learn that some read constantly while others gave up reading altogether as early as twelve and did not begin again until twenty or later. From a persistent search to find out what makes readers and keeps them reading I can say only that readers and writers are made, in adolescence as in childhood and middle age, in response to a discovery that these activities offer a sanctioned pleasure. Those who read for a lifetime are caught up in the activity as others play musical instruments, sail boats, create gardens, watch football or collect stamps. In all of these things a degree of passion accompanies the doing of them, and enthusiasts seek each other out. Most students who read well say that one of their teachers or another influential adult made them keen by sharing their bookish pleasure with them.

The adolescent book-worm has not been studied as a rare species, but some of his characteristics seem to run counter to general expectations. From observation I can report that he reads widely, indiscriminately even, often unwisely and sometimes in fragments and snatches. He bolts through books that adults deplore. In ways that remain mysterious he discovers the books that relate to his current concerns, even when these are not the books that are written to deal with these concerns. He makes ambitious choices of reading matter, and wrong choices. He backtracks to earlier satisfactions and can be found reading *William* on the eve of O-level examinations. He reads unpredictably and may sneer at books loved by his elders. Wise adults keep out of his way until it is time to clear out the mice that nest in the piles of film or car magazines, or to rescue *The Rachel Papers* in response to a card from the library, or to offer a book token. Such a book-worm may appear in a family that has never had one before, and his parents may take some time to get used to his solitary habits and the withdrawal from social life that reading entails.

Do we need to worry about the adolescent hooked on certain books? Will he not find his way to literature all in his own good time? Sometimes we feel we have to take a hand and hear ourselves saying, 'Surely you're not still reading *that*?' or 'Don't you think it's time you moved on from *Jackie*?' I believe that it matters what young people read and reject the idea that as long as they are reading something all will be well, but tact and patience are needed. We relinquish whatever hold we have on our children's reading progress if we disparage what they choose. It is better to share what we like with them than to reject what they may read as a kind of rest from the world of school texts. Adolescent reading enthusiasts thrive on challenge and encouragement. If you have an avid, if indiscriminate, reader in your family you may have to get used to some unfamiliar reading matter. In the lifetime of most parents there has been a great increase in the kind of books which match the changing social experience of the young. We are not always able to understand *how* a teenager chooses a book or how he reads it. My intuition is that many of them are looking for the books that they, in their turn, will write.

You would think that if a young person and the right book come together the alchemy of literature would produce the indissoluble marriage of true minds. It does happen, and then adults are advised to withdraw from the scene. My experience teaches me, however, that these occasions are not so frequent as we hope, and that most young people need help to find their way to the books that could attract them. Unfortunately, many would-be readers are turned away by domineering and urging adults, parents and teachers alike, who want to make readers according to a pattern. Parents still hanker after that undefined 'general knowledge', the vague sense of being 'well-read' that lingers from pre-television days. We betray the unease of our generation when we note that our children know the distance of the Earth from Saturn but not the date of the Battle of Waterloo, and when we suggest that people are thought well of in terms of what they have read. Teachers believe that a boy or girl who willingly reads history books is 'good at' history. But this reading may come from the encouragement that being thought good at history gives to their reading. We also have to admit that there are great gaps in our knowledge of how young people learn to tackle more difficult texts. W. H. Auden said that many people who learned to enjoy reading did so when they read a book suggested by someone they admired, even if they had to pretend at first that they liked it more than they really did.

What distinguishes the good teenage reader from the less competent one? First, he assumes that he can read what most adults expect to read: newspapers, for instance. He can cope with the range of his school books, from English novels to science texts. When he is interested in a special subject or a hobby he has additional facilities. He may be moving towards longer books, such as adult novels. His staying power is increasing and he can read for an hour at a time, skipping without guilt and matching the rate of his reading to the matter he is dealing with. A story takes him smoothly along; a book of information makes him cast back and forth in the text until he checks what he has learned. He predicts how a story will unfold and he can modify his expectations in the light of events. He links one episode with another and he knows how to evaluate the author's point of view. In a text that offers him information or ideas he is now learning how to relate the main thrust of an argument to the supporting details and the modifying conditions. He does what you are doing now, because he has learned how to as part of his reading experience. We know that to be well-read is to be able to do these things and that they are not taught, in any lasting way, apart from reading with the intention of finding out what happens in the text being read.

Does the skilled adolescent ever have reading difficulties? In the chopped-up day of the secondary school he has rarely enough time to get into a book unless he persists. He is not always sure that his friends approve of his reading so he may appear more casual than he really is. He may pick up whatever print is nearest him when he is too tired, lazy, or indifferent to seek out something more ambitiously literary, and his parents will show their disappointment when they see him reading yet another detective story. He often needs help to bridge the gap between the books he likes to read and those he is expected to read, between *Dr Strangelove* and *The Catcher in the Rye*. The answer is not always *Animal Farm*. He finds that novels with adolescents as heroes, *The Lord of the Flies*, for instance, are not always novels for teenagers. The literary work set for the examination may be reduced to a heap of textual breadcrumbs in the very class that should inspire him most. These and other hazards may well turn him away from reading if he finds them too strenuous to overcome.

Parents who want to help are inhibited by their uncertainty about what the young will let them do. Teenagers challenge the directions and models offered by even the most trusted adults about all the new ways in which their world is expanding. If parents let reading count as a significant activity, even if they do little of it themselves, they will at least make space for it in the household. To treat a reader's books with respect and to let him go on reading with encouragement are both important things to do. On the occasions when you are invited to share a reading experience or asked to suggest a book, let it be known that you think this is worth careful thought and discussion. We are often critical of adolescent self-regard, but we must take care not to say things like 'Are you going to sit there all day with that book', if we really want the reading habit to grow.

The more usual problem with avid readers is, should they really read anything they want to at this stage? Many parents are worried by what they think is undesirable reading matter and would like an X certificate for books as for films. But censorship in both only increases desire, and a banned book often becomes a best-seller. Unwholesome books abound and the young will read some of them, even if the libraries reject them. Parents have no control of the literature that is passed round under the school desks. My sympathy is with those who, like me, are sometimes over-whelmed by the representations in stories of adolescent traumas: drugs, rape, maladjustment, alcoholism, molest-ing, racism and violence of all kinds. Competent readers soon pick out and reject the authors who exploit the feelings of their readers. (I was alarmed when *Skinhead* made its appearance in a class I taught until I realized it was there chiefly to alarm me.) The discerning young soon tire of junk when something better replaces it. Essentially they are looking for *their* book. Once I saw a whole school reading *Kes*, indoors and out, as the result of one lesson with one class.

If you have confidence in your young reader let him look for his fantasy reading where he wants to, and trust that his prurient curiosity will soon have its day. Meanwhile, if you read biographies or autobiographies of men and women whose youth was turbulent you might share them with your children. It is often easier to talk about the genuine concerns of the young at this stage as if they were problems affecting some eminent or famous person who survived them.

Although we recognize the keen young reader whom teachers and librarians are only too anxious to help, we are not really sure what fourteen-year-olds *ought* to be able to read. On the whole we regard fiction as less important than the reading that is undertaken on behalf of the school curriculum, and in that we are wrong. Adolescents need stories as much as younger children. If they do not read, they go to films. If this looks like relaxation, not being serious, remember that narrative, especially novels, provides the habit of reading for longer at a time.

School textbooks are a strange species. Despite changes in book production and studies of what makes books 'readable', they are still fairly unattractive as sources of reading pleasure. But a pupil who wants to know something will tackle with enthusiasm, skill and understanding a book that might seem too dense in terms of vocabulary and sentence structure compared with what he normally reads. Good teachers understand that part of their job is helping their pupils to read and write within the disciplines of their subject. When they set reading for homework, they review what the pupil has understood and make sure that the learning goes forward in an integrated way. A history lesson is where pupils learn to cope with more than one source of information for a topic. Geographers teach map-reading, mathematicians make plain the significance of graphs as text. I have said many times that the 'skills' of looking up words in a dictionary, or information in an encyclopedia are learned only when the context for the use of these skills is significant for the learner. School reading becomes more flexible and economical as the pupil puts it to work on behalf of something he needs to know or to think about. What are sometimes called 'comprehension' or 'higher order reading skills' are in fact the ways in which a reader *thinks* about what he is reading, not as an exercise to flex his reading muscles but as a means of making judgments and generalizations from experience.

The best way to help a fourteen-year-old with books he has to read is to discuss the topic. If you have no specialized knowledge of the subject, there is no harm in letting the reader initiate you. His learning takes on a new relevance when he has to explain it to someone else. If he asks directly for help, don't say you have no idea what the topic is about. School books are usually arranged so that the main points are clear, and an experienced reader can always help to unravel the necessary information in most school subjects. Ideas worth thinking about cannot be taken in quickly, and even the most skilled reader at this stage has to learn to go slowly sometimes. Do not be dismayed, however, if some homework reading tasks are speedily despatched when your child finds and copies out the answer to a question. A great deal of school work is done in this way.

You will hear even the most competent pupils asking two questions about reading and writing: 'What's the use of it?' and 'Why is it so boring?' The first means 'What is this study contributing to my interests, my development, my knowledge in a way I can be helped to recognize?', and in the second, *boring* means 'the ways in which teachers want me to read and write are never ways that engage me as myself and what I care about'. Parents may not always be able to help good readers to read, but, mercifully, they are still the adults who can be encouraging when the whole business of reading in school seems to run counter to real living. The root of the problem of making young people more committed to reading lies in the fact that there is only a limited space in school for learning initiated by the pupils. But wherever imaginative people, inside or outside school, share their interests with the young, invention and discovery flourish, and literacy becomes a powerful tool of thought.

It is not possible to cover the whole range of reading abilities or touch on all the problems that beset school pupils at this time. Part of the trouble comes from our unwillingness to examine in exact detail what we want our children to be able to do. No one ever tells a literate fourteen-year-old that he can now read and write better than his grandparents could at that age. Many children who try to fulfil their elders' expectations find that they can never reach the golden apple of success. National surveys threaten teachers whose pupils are considered failures, yet no one listens when teachers explain that the reading habits of adolescents are as different as their faces. For all the reading research we have financed we are certain only that good readers pick their own way to literacy in the company of friends who encourage and sustain them, and that a large supply of paperback books and the enthusiasm of a trusted adult can make a difference.

Here, again, is a check list of what the good reader can do that the less accomplished reader finds difficult. It is meant to give you some idea of what can happen without formal lessons: encounter with significant books is the source of all these skills.

The experienced reader is confident he can read and he expects to understand. He makes guesses about what is not at first obvious or explicit, knowing that if he reads on more will become clear. He has read a fair amount, even a great deal, in bulk and depth, and he changes his reading style to suit the reading matter. (To the inexperienced, a book is just a book.) The confident reader moves beyond the information given to ask 'What does the author mean?'. He embarks on long reads, accepting the uncertainty of the first page of a novel, for example, and understanding how the ending helps him to reconstrue the beginning. He detects the author's tone of voice, and comes to recognize irony or sarcasm. The events in the book are matched against the reader's experience; he can recognize jokes, allegories or puzzles as well as authoritative statements backed by evidence. He models his writing on authors he knows well.

The most obvious difference between the skilled reader and others seems to be in the diversity of their abilities, the amount they read and the satisfactions that follow. It seems unfair that excellent readers need so little practice once the habit is established. Their awareness that they can read anything is difficult to trace to its roots, but it is undoubtedly connected with early satisfaction and success. Margaret Donaldson's assertion that 'the *process* of becoming literate can have marked—but commonly unsuspected—effects on the growth of the mind' is powerfully relevant at this stage.

Clearly, all the questions about literacy raised at the start come home to roost at this crucial point in the secondary school when good readers begin to specialize in the subjects they do well, before last-ditch remedies are sought for non-readers and poor spellers, or pupils are allowed to drift, quietly or noisily, to the end of their schooldays. There is no simple way to talk about the reading habits, needs, expectations or prospects of fourteen-year-olds. We can say that we want to diversify their reading experiences to match the growing complexity of their lives so that they will be able to understand the world and their place in it. But we are often at a loss to say how we might do that for more than one child at a time. If *your* child is a good reader, be glad, give encouragement, space and time for all his reading, and keep him well supplied with writing tools.

The indifferent reader

It is fairly certain that fourteen-year-olds, even the most addicted, read less in their out-of-school time than they did at the age of ten or eleven. School work increases every year; social life is paramount. Drawing on nothing more than my own experience I once said that expert readers at this age were bound to be myopic asthmatics whose afflictions (both in my case) condemned them to long, sedentary days on their own when their more fortunate classmates were on the playing fields, in the swimming pool, or just going for walks with friends. Teachers and reading experts sometimes speak of the young who read 'reluctantly', but I have never found a pupil who showed this particular attitude to reading out of school. If they have a choice, children either read or don't. Reluctance is the result of having to read when you don't want to, a feature of school reading. The young we are now concerned with are those who can read fluently enough, but on the whole, choose to do other things. Our anxiety about them stems from our awareness that to give up reading too soon is to miss its greatest rewards. Is there anything we should do to promote reading to those teenagers who see it as playing little part in their lives, the ones who are genuinely indifferent about reading?

There is, but with at least one proviso. Committed, enthusiastic readers have great missionary zeal. I know I want the young to discover that reading is important as a means of continuously encountering ideas, as the fuel of the imagination and the satisfaction of curiosity. It promotes the habit of ongoing intellectual endeavour. It is also useful for finding out the times of trains and the telephone number of a plumber. But I have had to realize that there are many people whom I greatly admire who do not find reading as important as I do, yet their understanding is greater, their social sense more acute, their sympathies broader, their ideas progressive and their children as literate as mine. Their wisdom comes from a pattern of social and personal relationships. In the same way, some young people look to the world for their experience before they seek it in books. When they say of reading they can 'take it or leave it' they are not critical or disparaging of the bookish. They simply look for understanding in the world first.

The fourteen-year-old still needs experience to promote his understanding, and we have already argued that books give life in its abundance. So I think parents and teachers are right to worry if the reading habit, the natural turning to books for what books can do best, is not established firmly enough in indifferent readers who still have at least two years of full-time schooling ahead of them. It is worthwhile taking stock of whether your teenager doesn't read because it is a laborious and tedious activity, or because he has too many other interests to pursue, so that reading has to take its turn as one of them, again, usually in bed.

Most adolescents read a fair amount within the culture of their peer group. This means they swallow the kind of print that may pass unremarked by their elders: football match reports, magazines on every topic from aeromodelling to yoga or Zoroastrianism. This culture puts up clear 'no entry' signs to adult interlopers who then take revenge by insisting that reading of this kind does not really count. The reading habit is more widespread amongst teenagers than most surveys show, because much of this kind of reading matter wins no approval and little validation from those whose professional job is to ensure adolescent literacy in the 'higher' rather than the 'popular' spheres of culture. It bears the same relationship to literature in the eyes of some teachers and parents as pop music does to the classics.

Reading avoidance, doing as little as you can get away with, is different from this indiscriminate swallowing of ephemeral print and can be distinguished from pop reading. Signs of its presence are: increasing dependence on television for information and diversion, no contact with books, unless for a brief glance at pictures; homework hurry, no more library visits, and little inclination to put a book into a pocket, not even the most obvious teenage story of romance, science or detective fiction, supernatural, spy, or war tale.

To keep the reading habit going in an adolescent who is gradually getting out of it you must avoid panic and confrontation. It may be only temporarily in abeyance. If you see magazines being read frequently, or notice a certain preoccupation with pop songs, you may also find that school lessons are based more and more on reading and writing and that these things are now *work*. The whole string of O-level preparations, the choice of new subjects, and that vague threat of future shock that creeps into the voice of even the best teachers, all these things serve to step up attention to books in school. Some youngsters just need a rest at home. Remember, too, that this is the age when they criticize your behaviour most sharply. You may be brought up short by their 'rudeness' in saying: 'I can't see why you keep on about reading when you never do it'. When they are five, children notice books without understanding that their homes are bookish. At fifteen they will be much more aware of their surroundings and the part their homes play in conditioning the judgment of others. The effect may be to turn them on to reading or to turn them off. You never can tell.

Then, you may have to become acquainted with many kinds of print that you have not encountered before; the teenage novel, for instance, is a recent phenomenon. Be careful not to scorn any kind of reading matter freely chosen and brought home. If you read some of it, don't be shocked by its explicitness about family life and the world of the streets, or by its seeming unliterariness. The conventions of most teenage literature derive from the dialogue of television plays—serials, interviews and comedy. The action is carried by the speech of the characters, swiftly, often vociferously, even violently. The tendency of adults to decry the repetitive sameness of this material, in a series like *Topliners* for example, has to be set against the teenager's disinclination to read any story where you have to wait for something to happen. Inexperienced readers are generally unwilling to engage with slow-moving introverted narrative. They need action, twice a page if possible, short chapters and cliff-hangers, the firm resolution of dilemmas and as little ambiguity as possible. The trouble is, both parents and teachers have too restricted an acquaintance with the bulk reading of teenagers because they don't greatly enjoy the small amount of it that they see and read. But any fourteen-year-old who is reading magazine stories is still a reader, a modern one.

A very percipient author, Robert Leeson, who knows these fourteen-year-olds well and writes for them with tact and skill, says that if teenagers tire of books they once took pleasure in, it 'may sometimes be the result of an unconscious feeling that the books are holding them back when they want to feel their way forward'. He knows that to win over those who are about to give up reading, an author has to be clear without being so simple in his style that the reader thinks he is defined as being slow-witted. The writer has to be precise and absolutely straightforward, the most demanding kind of writing as Orwell and Hemingway knew. Like them, Leeson knows that to engage the inexperienced reader the author has to 'get on with it', so that character emerges in action and speech and not in description or in the literary 'showing' that is now more fashionable than plain telling. Good storytellers are the source of all good literature. But sometimes, especially in English lessons where the teacher is too locked in a specialist approach to the subject, the young are made less enthusiastic than they might be because they encounter the ancients when they need the moderns—the telly-in-the-book. So if you see the book of the film lying around, let it be. Don't be deterred by those who call this kind of literature 'second class'.

Books in hard covers have little attraction for the occasional reader. A paperback is a teenage cult object: the more lurid the cover the greater the appeal. But this also means that books are possessed, like records and fancy socks, subject to the same change of mood as hairstyles, and part of the search for an identity that is both singular and social. These are difficult ideas for adults who grew up treating books with 'respect' that meant careful handling and attention. But if you want your fourteen-year-old to go on reading, you may have to tolerate kinds of literature of which you are naturally suspicious, both in its appearance and content and in the way it is used. Most difficult of all to swallow is the idea that to be encouraging you may have to draw back a little rather than to become more involved, so that even the most casual reader can feel he has a style and taste to be developed as his own.

Those who have studied the problems of the half-hearted teenage reader pin their faith on one particular strategy to help him: to accept positively all that he reads as reading. This means that a wide range of printed material will 'count' as significant. The essential nub of the problem remains: to put the right book into the right hands at the right time, and to do this, teachers and parents have to help each other again. Teachers face the acute form of their pupils' disinclination, so that they now have to read a great deal more of what is generally available, whatever its quality. They understand too the demands made by teenagers for stories that carry a new kind of conviction about social reality, notably in matters of sex and racism, language and class. The school story is set in the mixed comprehensive where most children go. The hero must have a credible identity, the heroine likewise and a truly equal share of whatever action is in progress. Parents do well to know some of this literature, to tolerate it, and not interfere unless they think that their child spends too long lying on his bed reading horror comics. Even then the comics may not have to be suppressed, but the rest of the reader's life may need to be examined.

When you are invited to discuss his work with his teachers, find out how much reading is expected of your child at school and of what kind. Even if the queue of waiting parents builds up behind you, suggest that you would like the English teachers to discuss with you what is read in class. You will probably find that you will enjoy *Una of Grub Street*, *Sounder*, *Joby*, *The Third Class Genie*, and be able to talk about them in no condescending way when books like these are set for homework. One school I know invites the parents to a reading night when the class reading books are on display alongside other recommended books. Episodes are read to the parents and the contents discussed. The enthusiastic parents convert the sceptical. The teachers report a noticeable increase in the amount of reading done by the pupils. There are fewer complaints and requests for censorship because the parents have taken care to see that the books are available at home. If you have done something like this you may then have to play a waiting game to see if reading will eventually come into its own. If it doesn't, then perhaps something equally valuable to the adolescent takes its place or you have to ask for special help. One thing is certain, we shall not make indifferent readers keener by going on about how important reading is.

Two further points about school reading. You can help your youngster with reading set for homework, if he will let you. This takes tact and patience with a fourteen-year-old and there are no rules. But we know from research reports that teachers often set chapters of a textbook to be read at home and then assume that the reading has been both done and understood. The inexperienced reader usually avoids reading homework because he doesn't know how information is organized to form a concept such as 'transport', 'rainfall', 'the divine right of kings' or 'democracy'. He cannot link events with a generalization without intermediate discussion. If you are asked to help, try to begin where the reader is. Encourage him to guess what the answer might be, then help him to look for it in the way that you would if you needed to know, neither evading ('You'd better look it up for yourself. It's all different since my day') nor taking over ('Now then, let's have a good look at this, shall we?'). It's tough. But then so is all significant learning until you get the hang of it. When I can I try to encourage the reader to tell me what he is expected to know by the time he has done his set reading. If he says 'I don't know', I begin with, 'Well let's see what the writer thinks he has to tell us'. I don't read more than the set piece, but if I have been successful in helping him answer his question the reader reads on for himself.

If an episode in a novel or a short story is set for homework, you can help by saying that you think it is important to read the whole piece at a stretch. Not only addicted readers need to have their reading time unbroken; less experienced ones need time and a place to do it. Many readers can read on the wing, in buses, trains and in queues, but this activity is learned as part of a constant reading habit, and some youngsters need the encouragement at home that comes from not being interrupted as often as they are bound to be in school. You don't have to plunge the household into silence, but it is helpful for a reader to have a comfortable chair in a corner away from the television and a separate reading light.

I am naturally unwilling to suggest that the young are

sometimes put off reading for life at this stage in their school careers, but I think they can be. If the conflict between 'the books I have to read' and 'the books I want to read' becomes too acute, then the pupil may give up reading altogether, especially if his parents seem to have joined up with teachers who say 'he should read more worthwhile books'. Just as we are never really sure what will help a child to start to read with enthusiasm, we are not clear, except in individual cases, what makes them seem to avoid reading. The answer lies partly in the narrow range of books we have traditionally offered them in school, partly in an anxiety about the high degree of reading skill needed to cope with specialist materials in our society at large and partly in our denial, even when we never say anything, that reading can be fun. In the next fifty years the young will have to deal with subject matter that wasn't even in existence when their parents were adolescent, hence our feelings of inadequacy and a tendency to be over-serious about reading. We are bound to be tolerant when the young remove themselves from the reading scene for certain periods, of their experimental or eclectic choice of reading matter, of their disinclination to approve of our taste in books. We must have an eye to what their teachers are doing to encourage wide and even indiscriminate reading, and we must still help them to choose books adventurously on the rare occasions when they let us. Above all, they must not think we have washed our hands of them as readers. That way lies the real opting out, for good this time.

The lost adolescent

It is impossible to consider adolescents who cannot read or write as a single group with a common difficulty; the history of their schooldays is a singular drama for each one. They share certain assumptions, however, including the belief that they are inadequate people, different from all those to whom reading comes 'naturally'. They are convinced that, as they have failed to master the chief means of learning in school, teachers cannot like or admire them. They reproach themselves, but also cling to alibis for their failure. ('I was ill as a child.') Their parents' worry is an added burden and the scorn of their classmates may make them aggressive. They avoid all tasks that involve reading and they are surprised that many people choose to do for pleasure the things that cost them strenuous efforts. With great skill they evade the problem altogether, yet their only hope is to turn and face it.

To help a lost adolescent to read or write is a serious and rewarding undertaking, but it can never be plain sailing. Reading inadequacy at this stage never comes alone; it is the outward symptom of a number of ills, social and psychological as well as those of illiteracy. It would be foolish to hope that by teaching him to read we can cure every adolescent's other problems, but all non-readers should have individual attention, understanding and help to learn. Young people who leave school unable to read are very bitter about their teachers. They tell how easy it was to skip lessons, how teachers never had enough time or patience. Looking back, they say: 'She should have *made* me do it.' This is the root of the problem.

Inexperienced readers who think they are different from real readers have never felt themselves being fluent. They never take risks by trying to follow the plot of a story as they read on their own. Instead they practise some reading rituals that they believe in, even when they never yield results. If you watch adolescent non-readers you see them trying to get clues *about reading*, not about the sense of what is written on the page. They sound and blend letters with amazing expertise and arrive at single words, but never the meaning of a sentence or a paragraph. They act as if the teacher were a magician with a bag of gold who repays good reading behaviour (doing what you're told) with the secrets of how to do it. They confuse teaching and learning, hoping to have something done to them when, in fact, they have to be the active ones. They have to be encouraged to risk being successful. The most tragic sight in any special reading class is a group of students doing more and more exercises in what they have failed to accomplish for the past eight years. They are sustained only by the economic reality of 'you can't get a job if you can't read' and this grim threat does not let them enjoy their learning which they think cannot, must not, be fun or give any pleasure.

If you want to help a non-reading, barely literate, unwilling-to-read teenager, here are some things to check up on. What, *exactly*, can he do, and what can he not do? Try to be as specific as you can. Most people recognize the general state: 'he just can't read'. Experts administer tests and quote the results. But few people take the trouble to see the task from the reader's point of view and to be particular in their reporting about his actual manoeuvres in the face of print. What does he get right? How does he look at the page? Where is he looking? Does he guess or wait for you to tell him what it says? How does what he thinks it says compare with the text itself? Could he read the labels on packets in the store cupboard or the signs on the highway or in the Highway Code? Try to come as close as you can to the details and the fine-grain of his problem because you may have more opportunity to observe him than the teacher in the rarefied atmosphere of the reading class, and it is in everyday life that you will see any significant progress.

When you are making as many detailed observations as you can, try to help him to believe that he can learn to read in a way that will make it worth the work he will have to put into it. There is no point in shirking the issue: there has to be effort by the learner. But supporting adults can offer help that is constant, firm, directly related to his needs and based on an understanding of his ability as well as his difficulties.

Unfortunately, parents are less likely at this stage to be the most effective teachers of their non-reading children. They are too emotionally involved. If you are persuaded that you really must help, see if you can remember the time when your child's difficulties first appeared. This is not straight-forward because you may have ignored his early stumblings in the hope that they would disappear with practice. Perhaps you still believe that his teachers underestimate his general ability, or you may even deprecate his efforts. Do you catch yourself saying: 'He enjoys school; it's just reading that's the problem', or 'He's just like his father, not much of a reader, really'? Before you try to offer any kind of help, check your attitudes to his failure. If you are reproaching yourself, excusing yourself, angry, over-anxious, accusing the school or just railing against fate, you should know that these are normal states of mind and feeling in the circumstances, but not helpful to the young who are insecure enough already.

Try instead to talk with your teenager about his difficul-ties in a way that is as emotionally neutral as possible so that you can both assess what has to be done. Discover what he thinks is wrong and listen carefully to everything he says. Let the talk stretch over a week or so without you nagging about the problem or constantly raising it. A solution or agreed plan of action takes time. You both have to get further than his saying 'Reading just isn't *me*'. At no stage should you say, 'Well, never mind'. He has to realize he will have to get down to reading sometime, yet this must not begin as a threat. Adolescents are relieved when adults don't make excuses for them; they want real help. They will grumble about having to do the work, but they know when someone cares enough to make demands of them. The young are resilient; they can face the reality of their situation, but they need someone to have confidence in them. This time the non-reader must understand he is not to wait for another set of reading processes to be done *to* him, either at home or at school.

The next step is to discover what is happening at school. Before you consult the teachers, look at the reports that have been sent home for the past two years to find where the first hints were being given of his problem. You can see if you were not paying attention or if the school was soothing you. 'Is a helpful and co-operative member of the class' is no solution to 'Should take more care with written work'. Make sure you have enough time with whoever has an overall responsibility for your child's literacy in order to discover the exact nature and extent of his capabilities and his disability. You may be dismayed, but you have to know what his unaided reading and writing are really like. Try to discover what he can read fluently, even if it is a book he read in his infant school, because progress begins there. Difficult as it is to create a sense of urgency without a hint of panic, parents, teachers and pupils have to face squarely their joint responsibility. Each must move forward from agreement about what is possible.

If the teachers are co-operative and keen to help, you need not provide extra lessons out of school time. Every education authority is bound to make adequate provision for children with learning difficulties. Private reading clinics are not looked on with favour by teachers because the child should have reading help as closely related as possible to the rest of his learning. If you are offered an interview with a psychologist, accept it. Co-operative parents help specialists to act quickly. No one can change the pattern of his education without consulting you, so you need not worry about his being removed suddenly to a special school.

If your child is having extra reading lessons in school you should be told how these are organized. Some schools have a separate department (the term 'remedial' is falling out of use), others let pupils have coaching by withdrawing them from lessons. No pupil should miss a subject he enjoys; he would not do well in the reading lesson that supplants it. You should be able to discover if the special help given to your child is casual, clinical or collaborative. Casual reading lessons are given by any teacher who is free at a given time. It is better than nothing but not sustained enough or insightful enough to bring about a radical change in a serious reading problem. Clinical help or remediation is usually organized as if it were a medical exercise in intensive care. If it is given in a special room full of apparatus it can never shake off the hospital atmosphere that pervades it. The pupil is a patient, an emotional and social cripple suffering from illiteracy. Many children who haunt special reading rooms take the line of least resistance and stay there throughout their secondary school lives. Some have difficulties that run deeper than their inability to read, and long-staying pupils find it difficult to win their way back from the safety of simpler tasks, the slower pace, less effort and easier excuses for failure to the everyday reality of the normal classroom. Part of the problem is that what is true of the pupils is also true of the teachers. If you think your child has been in the remedial class far too long, you should say so.

The most desirable school provision for an unenthusiastic reader with special difficulties is help given by an expert reading teacher who works in the ordinary classroom along-side the subject teacher. As yet this is rare because most teachers expect to work alone with their class behind the closed doors of their own domain. But where numbers are falling and classes are smaller, some secondary schools are experimenting with new strategies so that slow-reading pupils can work with their classmates. A poor reader need not read aloud in class unless he wants to, but he can benefit immeasurably from lessons where the pupils are read to. He, more than anyone, needs to be kept in touch with the literature that is worth reading. It is a mistake to believe that because a pupil would be daunted if asked to read *David Copperfield* he cannot understand or discuss it when someone else reads it. Where teachers work in pairs in this way the pupil can keep his self-respect, see how to measure up to his peers, and still proceed at his own rate.

A useful compromise between the remedial department and special help in the ordinary classroom is a reading room, a comfortable place where teachers go to share reading with pupils who need to read in peace for a stretch of time outside the more strenuous atmosphere of the class. In the reading room that I know best, every teacher and pupil is a volunteer; they want to be there because one knows how to help and the other needs help. The stigma of failure has been removed from the pupils, and the teachers discover what makes reading difficult and how pupils can be given the kind of attention they need. One of these teaching provisions should be available for your child, together with a communication system that keeps you in touch with what is being done. You have the difficult task of encouraging the youngster to make the most of what he is offered in school and of providing the support he needs at home. Your scope may seem limited, but you may be able to do more that you think.

First of all, find out how the teachers assess your child's ability in reading (and writing too) in school, apart from what is written in reports sent home. They are not always the same. You may be told that he has a low reading age, poor word attack skills, a poor comprehension rating and very little 'word power'. The proposed remedy may be the exercises in a 'reading laboratory'. This means that to progress in the school's estimation he will have to increase his reading scores on special cards or exercises that are graded to indicate what a reader can do. He will probably be given practice in *surveying* the title, the subheadings, the first and last paragraphs of a text, asking *questions* about it, *reading* it, picking out the salient points (*reviewing*) and finally saying (*reciting*) what he thinks the text is about. This technique (called SQ3R), together with exercises in skimming and scanning a paragraph, is now widely promoted as helpful to slow readers who have difficulties with textbooks. More powerful claims are made for teaching the young from this specially graded material and for encouraging reading strategies of this kind. But no exercise, however well ordered, will have the effect of a genuine reading task that encourages the reader to learn what he wants to know as a result of his own initiative. Practice in reading skill must relate what is read to the real context of experience. Some exercises provided by reading experts for adolescents who need to learn how to initiate reading in response to their own intentions and purposes are the equivalent of running on the spot for pentathlon athletes. If your child is having reading lessons that do not involve real books and real learning, the effect may not be lasting.

Reading laboratories and special materials often make adolescent non-readers believe that this is what they have to master, and therein lies the deception, unwitting on the part of the teacher, but a deception nevertheless. No raised reading age, comprehension score or word power mark is of any use if the learner does not read by and for himself in the end. The skills that are exercised by reading cards and answering questions transfer to other reading only when the reader consciously grasps the nature of the process. If he is enjoying laboratory reading and having continuous success, make sure that he goes back to his ordinary classroom work as soon as possible. If he works with reading cards rather than books for more that six weeks you should ask what steps are being taken to hasten his progress to real reading materials. These laboratory snippets of prose are not long enough to help the learner to discover how to build up the sense of a passage as he goes on. He needs more text, not less, if he is still having difficulty, and I must say again that *narrative* is still the best kind of text for *all* beginners, early or late. Share a humorous book—jokes, *Private Eye* or the like—with your learner to combat the dreary seriousness of much of this pedestrian material.

The Bullock Report is quite emphatic: 'There is no mystique about remedial education, nor are its methods intrinsically different from those employed by successful teachers anywhere'. The teenager's own needs and difficulties dictate what is to happen. He must have continuous insightful help and the close partnership of class teacher, reading teacher and parent in order to preserve his self-respect on which all else depends.

Sometimes help comes from the peer group; a non-reader can call on his friends once he has stopped hiding his disability. A student teacher can help because she has a less crowded timetable and to help one child to learn is the best way to study what is involved in teaching. If either of these offers to read with your youngster do not turn away the help as unskilled. The young notice what older teachers have stopped seeing and they know how to ask the questions, how to be strict even, and how to talk naturally about the problem.

You should know what progress looks like. For a youngster who has never voluntarily looked at a book, or even picked one up, to do so is a step forward. Teachers know that they have begun to help when the pupil arrives for his lesson of his own accord and does not have to be sought. If the reading practice stops having an oral ritual of 'calling back' a few sentences and becomes a desire to find out what happens next in a story, the move is significant. As soon as the reader asks a question of his own about the text, he has begun to behave like a reader; if he disagrees with the author he is nearly a critic. When the words come out in meaningful groups instead of one by one, and the intonation changes from the halting move from one word to the next, you can rejoice. Best of all are the words 'Don't tell me, don't tell me,' or 'I'll read it' when you share something, or a spontaneous offer to read a notice or a paragraph in a newspaper. Poor readers should never be set to decipher 'new' text with no advance indication of what it is about. They should be praised when they read again for themselves something that once gave them trouble and now is a reminder of how fluent they have become. Fluency is a feeling, a knowing that you can make text mean without anxiety because you want to, even when you stumble or make mistakes. Anything that contributes to this is progress.

I wish I could be easily hopeful about adolescents who cannot read, but long experience of teaching them and teaching their teachers has made me aware how much stands in the way of their success. Their failure is ever with them; the task often seems beyond both teacher and pupil. The learner can't face reading on his own and so many teachers have tried to help. Some young people really do not want to learn to read if being unable to guarantees that they will have an adult's attention for an hour a week. One young man I knew learned to read within a month of leaving school after years of special lessons. From the diversity of my pupils' problems I am persuaded that most adolescents *can* read, if

only a little. They think they have to *identify* words by means
of a series of secret rules, when they need only *recognize* the
ones they already know. Anyone who can say 'give way' in
response to a traffic sign can learn to read—if he wants to
and is prepared to enjoy it. I know I can help a boy or a girl to
learn if I can read a story and he or she wants me not to stop
until it is finished. Whoever is prepared to read with help for
more than twenty minutes at a stretch, who queries what the
author says, who wants to talk about the contents of the
book, who reads a joke and laughs, all of these will win
through. The parent's role is to be reassuring but firm, to
insist that reading matters not as a sign of intelligence but as
a normal activity. You have to offer a model by sharing
books and newspapers and offering help with writing tasks.
No adolescent learns to read in a vacuum, with artificial
reading matter and no purpose of his own. He needs real
books, real intentions and real help and he ought to have all
of these.

I said that, in the early days of reading before children go
to school, the adult's obligation is to do those parts of the task
that the beginner cannot manage for himself. It is still true
for the adolescent. He has to begin again and learn to behave
like a reader. The rest will follow if you have patience and
books worth sharing.

Choosing Books for Fourteens

By the time they are fourteen many young people have had
some of the most memorable reading experiences of their
lives. Graham Greene is convinced that the stories one
reads before then are woven into the rest of one's existence. I
have been lucky to meet adults to whom I read *Tom's
Midnight Garden* in my school class when it appeared in 1958.

They tell how its haunting appeal, both sad and right, has echoed in them since then like an extra memory of childhood. In schools even now the rowdiest group of boys still shivers through *Black Jack* by Leon Garfield or thrills to the heroism of Rosemary Sutcliff's tales. The extra-bookish furnish their imaginations with L. M. Boston's stories of Green Knowe, or Russell Hoban's *The Mouse and his Child*. They find the counterpart of their growing awareness of the depth of experience in William Mayne's *A Game of Dark*. Books that move their readers and reverberate in their memories are good stories, well-crafted. They appeal to all children, not only to the experienced readers. *The Iron Man* is a modern myth of great power that I would willingly read with those whose literary experience has been thin or non-existent. The problem about the best of books for the young is that not all potential readers discover them. Some are actively dissuaded by parents who want them to read the classics—*David Copperfield, The Lord of the Rings, Alice in Wonderland, Gulliver's Travels*—as soon as possible. Sometimes those who find a teenage novel they enjoy also find a well-meaning adult interposing a point of view about it between them and the story. The fortunate readers are those who have had their best reading experiences confirmed by more of what makes reading appeal to them. The least indulged are those who have never discovered the kind of experience that leads to enthusiastic discussion of a favourite character: the rat in *Charlotte's Web*, for instance.

If the young read any of these books, and there are more like them, they are capable of entering into the experiences of the characters the better to understand their own. In agreeing to the author's terms for the narrative of events or ideas they respond in ways they did not know they were capable of, and so begin to define their own sense of values. Confident fourteen-year-olds read as well as most adults and often enjoy books more. They are still able to lose themselves in a story, still excited by discovery. The critical detachment of the examination years is in the future, if not really far off. A certain whole-hoggishness characterizes this kind of reading, and adults who long to read more than they do, look back to this time of their lives with a nostalgic wistfulness that makes them keen to save this experience for their children against what they see as the obstacles of the electronic media. Those who have never read in this way continue to feel they have missed out somewhere, so they too are anxious to prevent their children from doing so. Competent teenage readers read more of what they like and look forward to new kinds of books. Their teachers supply the books (or the lists of books) they ought to read. So what is there for other supporting adults to do? I have already said that they should be tolerant of what the young choose for themselves—even when soft pornography, love or horror stories appear on the scene. Parents do not have to abandon all responsibility if they believe some reading matter is actually harmful, but they should know that to trust the young to choose worthwhile reading matter and to discern when a book has no relevance to life is not a passive role—but a very positive one.

As they think that books for the young are an important source of influence, many deeply concerned adults want to exercise their potent authority as parents, teachers and critics by ensuring that authors and publishers take up the 'right' attitudes to race, sex and class in what they produce for the young. They alert everyone to the dangers of prejudice, explicit or implicit, and to the needs of minority or oppressed groups. Certainly, shifts of sensibility in our culture make the crude depicting of cannibals in comics, the unrestricted imperialism of Biggles or the stereotyping of girls in traditional female roles a matter for protest. Ideas of social responsibility are changing, and books are bound to reflect the evolution of these values. Likewise, we know that many potential readers do not find themselves at home in what they are given to read by those who, like teachers, can enforce their choice. Some teenagers will not open a book because they have a fairly clear idea that they will not like what they find inside it—characters with whom they have too little in common in life style or prospects. For all that, I suggest that when we are choosing books even for fourteen-year-olds, we should trust the skilled author who is concerned to illuminate children's lives rather than the over-prejudiced critic who simply looks for representations of them.

To help the young to grow in discernment it is not enough to make sure that they never read a book that depicts undesirable attitudes. Their prejudices, like their sense of humour, are socially learned, and the world outside the book will always exert the greater influence. We need to offer choices if we want to make discriminating readers, and then let young adults choose for themselves. We can encourage more discussion of what is read. Then the reader may come to know that he has to ask 'Is the author right?' if he is to grow in understanding, not only of what he reads but also of what he thinks.

Fourteen-year-olds begin to discover the complexity of life, that issues are never wholly clear-cut, that people are neither saints nor sinners. Anyone who has encountered Long John Silver in *Treasure Island* realizes the ambiguity of the attractive villain. Stories for the young now present more complex ways of looking at events that once seemed ordinary—having parents, for instance—and new experiences are matters of feeling as well as unexpected adventures. The young begin to discover the sub-text of what they read, the implications of the unspoken. If they encounter Jane Austen, for example, they have to learn to notice what she is *not* saying. So I offer again, without apology, the advice that appears elsewhere in this book. When readers take steps forward to meet new kinds of reading they also make tracks back to what they have enjoyed and to where they feel secure. Tolerate this regression, especially if it takes the form of a passion for adventure stories of the James Bond variety, and be patient with the muddling with magazines as they listen endlessly to pop music. Know that Agatha Christie is the teenagers' Enid Blyton. They will move on again.

To understand a teenager's reading you should look at his school texts to see what you make of them. Next you should read the classical novel (like *Tess of the D'Urbervilles*) and the Shakespeare play (*Twelfth Night*) that are set for examination at O-level. Then, read at your own level a new novel or a biography. Having done all of that you will understand what the competent fourteen-year-old is being asked to do. He needs, above all, confidence in his own ability to choose other, more restful, reading for himself. He could profitably encounter much of the good teenage fiction that is available instead of indifferent novels for adults. As for the less experienced reader, he will not reach this level unless his reading is more extended, so I suggest that he too should discover the diversity of the material that is now available. The non-starter, dependent as he is on the choices of others, should also have real books written for adolescents and not the teenage form of the reading scheme.

To promote the reading interests of any fourteen-year-old a helpful adult could profitably read books by any of the following authors: Aiken, Ashley, Arundel, Banks, Bawden, Beckman, Blume, Boston, Roy Brown, Cate, Cawley, Chambers, Christoper, Clarke, Cleary, Clewes, Corlett, Cormier, Cooper, Dahl, Darke, Dickinson, Dhondy, Fitz-hugh, Garfield, Garner, Guy, Glanville, Virginia Hamilton, Hardcastle, Hines, Hinton, Leeson, Le Guin, Lester, Lingard, Lively, Mark, Mayne, Needle, Paton Walsh, Pearce, Peyton, Price, Rowe Townsend, Sudbery, Sutcliff, Trease, Westall, Willard, Woodford, Zindel.

This list is by no means exhaustive. A helpful survey of the field is John Rowe Townsend's *Written for Children*. Authors of books for the young are constantly asked to explain why they choose to write books for this audience. Their replies, in books such as *Only Connect* edited by Sheila Egoff and others, *The Thorny Paradise* edited by Edward Blishen, and *The Cool Web* are certainly worth reading.

You will soon discover that the predominant theme in most of these writers is *time*, especially that moment in all our lives when we encounter the idea that time passes, innocence fades, and childhood is no more. The author of books for this age group moves from telling to sharing, and comes close to the reader by narrating in the first person. The reader discovers the complexity of the 'I' in the story. In reading about crises of identity in the hero or heroine and the problems of moral choice the reader now comes to understand that resolutions can be only partial. Some endings cannot be happy and be right.

Some publishers have influenced the provision of books for young adults by making a distinctive list. The Bodley Head has one. But the teenage novel is still a hybrid. Libraries and booksellers are not sure where to put these books. Critics argue whether readers should choose them in preference to books for real adults. But more and more teachers are discovering their usefulness in promoting the kind of reading that makes readers, especially amongst those whose school experience of reading has been scant or unpleasant. You may be surprised by some of the themes in these books, but remember, there are no 'safe' stories. Fairy tales make that clear. However much we may want to hide from the young that what goes wrong in life is often due to our own nature, we cannot do so. In adolescence, more than at any other time, narrative fiction takes the reader to the limit of his known experience and calls on his imagination to extend it. We have to encourage young competent readers to find writers they can trust to do this. Read Peggy Woodford's collection of stories *You can't keep out the darkness* and you will see how the contributors see their responsibilities to their readers who are on their way to all that literature has to offer.

I wish I could be sure about what helps to bring indifferent readers to books and keeps them reading. The advice usually offered is 'match the book to the reader' and those who have the opportunity to speak individually to the young do this well. I have seen a truculent disinclined fourteen-year-old swept off his feet by a folio volume of Italian paintings, another overwhelmed by the wealth of good information in a book about fishing. They had simply no idea that books were like that and meant for them. But to be the agent of this discovery is not always possible for parents whose children do not even want to try. The problem is to find the book that indicates that the giver values the reader. This is the only rule that works. I know I do not easily put a Mills and Boon romance, the kind read by thousands of teenage girls, into the hands of someone I am teaching to read, not because it is not what she needs; it probably is. To read one of these novelettes she has to find it as *her* choice, not mine. I am the person who is to treat her seriously as a reader, to give her confidence that she will move beyond this stereotyped unreality. 'You're supposed to make me read real books,' a pupil once told me. Asked what real books were, he said, 'The wars of Troy and that lot.' Although he had read very little he had grasped that some books counted as 'real' reading and others were set at a lower rate. I was to value him more highly. So we read Roger Lancelyn Green's *Heroes of Greece and Troy*. I have seen good teachers turn the wanderings of Odysseus into serials more gripping than anything on television. Once you have got the hesitant reader to reach out for what he really likes to read he will see his own choice as the first step on the way to greater reading successes. If your inexperienced reader prefers television to everything else, the book-on-the-box has most meaning. Until it was put on at the adult viewing time and they saw the early flying machines, comparatively few parents had heard of *Flambards* as a trilogy of novels by K. M. Peyton. *Flambards* raises the same issues as *The Mill on the Floss* which became much more accessible after the TV serial turned it into 'known' story. Good television grasps the core of a book; the book itself lets the reader sit at the centre to contemplate its implications, and this experience has to be learned. For every indifferent reader I wish there could be an adult who would know how to link a story to that part of the reader willing to try to read it. My students do this all year long. To the less experienced reader the approach is less direct, not simply 'Here, try this', but 'This is a story about a boy who has been kidnapped. What do you think would happen if you were in his place? What do you do?' Books like Anne Holm's *The Hostage* or K. M. Peyton's *Prove Yourself a Hero* feed into this discussion.

Many people take the problem of the 'reluctant reader' very seriously. In 1969 Aidan Chambers wrote a book with this title in which he suggested that authors should write about topics that appealed to teenagers. He went on to edit a series of such books called *Topliners*. Other series followed. Some, like Longmans *Knockouts* are carefully graded to give even the slowest and least experienced pupil a chance to engage with a real story which is written as well as possible within the short length that encourages a reader to finish a whole book. These special books embolden the timorous, and they also have a special use in encouraging young people who have learned English as their second language. I want to be sure, however, that the readers who enjoy these stories—and there are now a great many of them—do not feel that they can only stay at this level of reading, however successfully. The crucial point is this: readers need to know many books; each one becomes more significant as it joins the others that have been read before. Our chief task is to create this bulk of reading in the less experienced. If we can encourage reading with a partner, the effect is usually more lasting. Aidan Chambers was clear that he did not want *Topliners* to become 'a kind of literary remedial course. It could do, and should do, what any literature that is whole does: grow to satisfy writers and readers in increasingly multifarious ways, responding to its own history, to other arts, and to the needs of its own time.' I agree, so all supporting adults need to be better informed about the whole range of children's literature for this age group.

What now can we choose for the non-starter? Remember, he has been condemned to the non-books, the cards, the specially written series, the little books, for longer than anyone reading this page. The 'simple' book at his level of interest is still a non-book. If you have any reading time with someone who has 'remedial' lessons at school, let him choose and encourage him to be bold in his choice. Let him see what the full range of a library or a bookshop can be. Let him handle books of all kinds, not only those he can read. If you can, teach him to *browse*, to turn pages, just as we did for the very beginner. If you can help him to enjoy the *idea* of reading, or even persuade him that a fine book is worth a few more minutes of his time, you will have set him a little further on his way. Help him too with reading what is in the world around him, and depress, as far as you can, his feeling that reading is beyond him. My instinct is to make reading more special in as many ways as possible with these young people who are usually so aware of the usefulness of reading that they never discover its effectiveness as self-indulgence. Adult books have pictures and captions; newspapers are more scanned than read; you can skip pages and still follow a story. The really inexperienced reader doesn't know this, so he has to discover new forms of enjoyment that change his notion of what reading is, that it is not just getting the words right in an official form. So choose books that adults divert themselves with. The school will all too readily supply the hard tack of useful text. As for the really late beginner, see if you can share the reading job in such a way that he gradually takes on more of it. Do not offer a suitable book in a specially written series unless it is requested. Let school become the supplier of these. Choose instead all the funny books you can find. Begin with *The Piemakers* by Helen Cresswell, move to *The Worst Kids in the World* by Barbara Robinson, Betsy Byars' *The Eighteenth Emergency* and Paul Zindel's *My Darling, My Hamburger*. With all of these the persistent non-starters can be persuaded to try. *Mind Your Own Business* by Michael Rosen is within the scope of absolutely everyone who can cast an eye on a line of print. No one can read it and not get the message that reading can really be fun.

The fourteen-year-old wants to choose his reading for himself when he is out of school. We want him to become as competent and as sensitive as any good adult reader. We have to strengthen his strengths and assure him of our support. The rest will follow.

Questions at Fourteen or so

My daughter's school report says she 'underfunctions' and 'does not reach her potential' because she reads too little. What shall I do?

Clearly the teachers are wondering why your daughter does not do so well in class as they think she should. They have their reasons for thinking so and they could share these thoughts with you. They also want you to encourage your daughter to read more, but she may not want to. Find out what she willingly reads, extend it with new and more interesting material if she will accept it from you. Share your favourite reading with her. Encouragement helps more than criticism.

Are schools failing in their purpose if young people leave them unable to read and write?

It is difficult for bookish people to understand that school is not a congenial place for many young people at the present time. From schools of all kinds some pupils long to escape, and they often learn to read after they have left. Adults who learn to read believe that, even when they have had expert help, they have taught themselves, and could have done so earlier if they had wanted to. Blaming schools for inefficiency is no help to the literacy problem.

My youngster just doesn't read. She is not behind her classmates who do, but she spells badly, she can't write a decent letter and has very few informed ideas outside school work. I think she is a modern illiterate.

Note quite. I expect she reads more than you know about. As for writing, the number of occasions for significant personal writing declines each year. The non-writers are in something of the same case as the non-readers; they don't know what doing it well feels like. My experience is that when personal relationships demand more intimate communications than are possible on the family telephone then writing paper is more in demand. Meanwhile, see that every piece of official note-taking (forms and the like) that concerns the young lady is done by her.

What can I do to help my thirteen-year-old who is still reading very slowly and sounding out letters when she meets a new word?

Unfortunately, thirteen-year-olds no longer have the curiosity of a six-year-old about letters and writing. She is probably performing rituals in the hope of understanding the system of letter-and-sound relationships which she thinks has eluded her. In a very sensitive and helpful book, *Children's Minds*, Margaret Donaldson suggests that readers (even the very youngest) can be helped to understand that the relationship of letters and sounds is a series of *options*: *k*—the sound—can be written *c, k,* or *ck*. You should read with her when you can, showing her that she actually can go faster, take more chances and understand better.

Surely no literate parents would let their children reach the age of fourteen unable to read? Do non-readers not always come from a poor background?

When investigated, assumptions like these prove to be both unhelpful and wrong. At one point in the history of Europe nine-tenths of the population who were learning to read had illiterate parents. Even now, some children of highly literate parents reject reading entirely, a phenomenon which has complex social and psychological implications. Bold statements like this are judgments about social class, not about reading. But if there is a significant gap between the culture of the home and that of the school there will be difficulties for some children.

I have heard of the 'back to basics' movement. Why do not all teachers adopt it?

Do not be led into thinking that once upon a time everyone could read because there was a good, universal 'basic' teaching method. This is nostalgia, not history. Also, the present nature of literacy has no precedent. We need a learning and teaching collaboration that meets the aspirations of those who want and need modern literacy. There is no simple past standard of reading and writing to go back to, and to try is to be always disappointed.

A Lifetime's Pleasure; or the Lost Adolescent?

When she is doing homework my fourteen-year-old seems to spend a lot of time copying passages from books. It makes her handwriting fluent, but does it really help her to understand what she reads?

It all depends on *why* she is copying. Advanced students collect quotations from writers who say things well or express ideas clearly. Teachers often ask pupils to 'make notes', and unless this is demonstrated as a skill, the young have no other means of collecting information than taking passages from their reading. Thus, some material goes from one book to another without passing through the reader's head. If your daughter is answering questions, they may be framed in such a way as to demand some thought about the answers. To progress in understanding the reader has to learn to *question* the text, to *judge* the value of what the author says. The best intermediate operation between reading and writing is talk. Discuss the topic at some time, if she will let you.

At every stage in her school life my child has had extra reading lessons. She is used to them and has accepted the fact that she is a slow reader. Can she ever hope to get better?

To be really sure, I should have to know your daughter quite well. The question is too complicated for the answer to be a simple yes or no. The young learn best when they do for themselves and by themselves what they are learning, and teachers of slow readers should always be making themselves redundant. The reader must go it alone. Extra lessons are helpful up to the point where they breed a habit of dependance. Whatever happens now should be a weaning process. Help her to behave like an independent reader in any way you can.

What is cloze procedure?

Another kind of reading test more recently adopted for nationwide use. Words are omitted from a passage and the reader has to supply the missing words. The proportion of correctly guessed words indicates how well the reader has understood the passage. Some cloze tests are used to find out if children are learning less than they might do from school texts, not just because the content is difficult, but also because of the way the texts are written.

My family came to England from Cyprus ten years ago. My children now speak English fluently and we speak Greek at home. The teachers say the fourteen-year-old still has reading and writing problems. What should I do?

Be assured that bilingual children are good learners, often better than those who have never needed to acquire a second language. Perhaps the teacher makes too much fuss about reading aloud; your daughter may read very well when she reads for herself. Perhaps her books are too simple or too unrelated to her vocabulary. Let her have as many good English story books from the library as you can. If you know an English family well, talk with the parents and the children about what they read. Next, ask the teacher to be absolutely precise about the nature of the 'problems', especially the writing problems. If she can define them, she will be able to cure them and should do so. Should you feel that you are not able to understand the difficulties more exactly, find the nearest language centre in your area and ask the teacher in charge if you can discuss the matter with her. The progress of bilingual children is bound to seem slow to any teacher who does not understand how these children use language to learn. But now there are many who do, and who are very skilled in helping because they understand the positive aspects of bilingualism.

A Note about
Spelling and Writing

When our great-grandparents were learning to write they
had vigorous handwriting and spelling lessons, or so we
believe. Certainly very few of them were encouraged to write
what they wanted to say, to compose on their own behalf.
Instead they copied model sentences in order to acquire
marketable clerkly skills of fine penmanship and correct
orthography which were associated in the minds of their
employers with other virtues, such as punctuality, cleanli-
ness and obedience. Nowadays we want young people to
write in order to have their say, to sort out their thinking. We
persist, however, in confusing them, and ourselves, about
the relationships of reading, writing and spelling and we still
think that good spelling is evidence of ordered behaviour.
We also depress our young by insisting that the first state of
their writing, the initial draft, must be free from error—a
demand never made of professional writers. Think of all the
notes of acknowledgment you have read at the beginning of
books where the author thanks the typist. In nine times out
of ten that includes correcting the spelling mistakes, but no
one thinks the worse of the author for that.

I want to dispel the notion that reading automatically
makes a pupil's spelling better. It accustoms him to the sight
of words, yes, but when he writes for himself, he becomes
fluent because his fingers take over from his eyes. Spelling is
the consequence of the regularization of the written language
which was made necessary by the spread of printing.
Checking spelling is a kind of proof-reading. Some children
discover early how letters occur in groups; others profit from
having the letters pointed out to them. A few people never
make mistakes; some have trouble all their lives long. If we
help a child to be accurate we set him free to say what he
wants to say without shifting his attention from the meaning
he is concerned to express to the letters in the words he wants
to use. At fourteen a writer should be nearly automatic in

writing all familiar words. If he is not, you must know how to help him.

Spelling *is* important, if only because so many people who have the learner's fate in their hands say it is. As the writer's confidence in himself grows, so does his spelling improve with sympathetic encouragement. Teachers have been aware for a long time now that over-correcting children's written work can actually make spelling matters worse. The experts say that spelling 'should be part of the fabric of normal classroom experience neither dominating nor neglected'. Examiners know however that sometimes they are distracted from the ideas expressed by spelling errors and this is reflected in the mark they give. Here is part of a composition written by a fourteen-year-old who later became soundly competent:

> When I was at my grandfather's house he showed me his anshient possesions. He has a Nazi war helmit, two bronse medells and pictures he took from a solder's pocket. He says the proces of killing is not so terrable or ingenerious as people think for it is over in a minite.

When the writer's attention is focused on getting his ideas in order he is more concerned to get the words down than to get them right. Sometimes clerical errors increase as the young move into a more complex stage of thinking and finding the language to match. Then they need to write in two stages: the first draft sorts out the ideas, the order, the argument, while the second gives the writer a chance to edit or proof-read his work. Just as they need to *feel* the fluency of reading well, so the young have to experience the flow of producing text on a page for an audience to read. When they think of the reader's comfort, then they take trouble to correct the spelling. Whoever took in hand the piece we have quoted would explain to the writer that there are spelling rules, but they all have exceptions because in English the same sounds have different letter groups. The sound k can be written as k, c or ck. The learner discovers or is told our spelling system left us with a set of choices and the printers made decisions about some of them. Sometimes the sets of correspondence are easy to learn (the *cough, bough,* thou*g*ht complication is not so difficult as it seems) but the *-ible -able* ending is always a trap. No one can know all the individual patterns of relationship but most children can get the hang of the system. The writer manages some difficult things—*anshient* is a good try—and will soon master others. *Minute,* for example, is usually safe when the adjective meaning 'very small' has been discovered, written in the same way and pronounced differently.

Should parents make a fuss about spelling? Yes, if they have to do with what is being written, but not in all school homework and not every time. Do not expect a first shot at a new word to be exact if the word has never before passed along the fingers on to the page. Encourage the writer to use the word he wants to use rather than the less appropriate one which he can safely spell. The most significant help comes to shaky spellers in discussion with their friends. In school they are often allowed to work in pairs, helping each other in ways that the teacher, with a poised red pencil, never can. In this way they learn that spelling rules came from the grammar of the language and from the ways in which we set meaning down to be read so that the ambiguities of sounds can be sorted out at a glance. Pupils help each other to distinguish *beer, bier, bear* and *beard* in the same way as they never make mistakes in reading *said—heard,* and the two words we write as *lead.*

Learners can benefit from adult patience and from the support of their peers but in the end they need a strategy to help them to help themselves. In a pamphlet for teachers that other supporting adults could read with profit, Mike Torbe says this is what learners should do:

1. Look at the word: say it to yourself.
2. Trace it with your finger.
3. See if it looks the way it sounds. (The learner makes the decision for himself.)
4. Write the word and underline the part of it that looks as if it might give you trouble.

5. Shut your eyes and see if you can see the word in your head. If you can't, say the word again. Does the sound remind you of the way it looks?

6. If that doesn't work, look at it again. Say it in any way that will remind you of what it looks like. Say it the way you see it. Feb-roo-ary, Wed-nes-day.

7. Cover the word. Write it from memory. Try to see it in your head as you are writing.

8. Check it. See if you have got it right. Compare your version with the right one. Cover it. Try again.

The most common errors are: *approximations* (*medells* for *medals*) when the writer is using a rule he knows, in this case that 'l' at the end of a word is often doubled; *the wrong option for the sound* (an*sh*ient, because *sh* is known better than *ci*); *prefixes and suffixes*—English has muddled the double consonant (*possessions*) which depends on the origin of the word and the original prefix. Look at *misled*, *mishandled*, *misshapen*; note the strange place of 'e'—does it disappear, as in *write*: *writing* or stay as in *love*: *lovely*; count the actual number of letters. Some inexperienced writers stop short when they first try *accommodation* or *conservation*.

Other kinds of help come from letting the writer see the word written correctly, by helping him to associate it with another he knows—en*gine*—en*gin*eering, by encouraging him to keep a list, not a long one, of words he is inclined to misspell regularly, to ask about strange words he meets for the first time. If he can safely ask without being told 'you should know that' he will ask again.

Fourteen-year-olds write as much as twelve pages a week in school if they are on a course leading to examinations. If they are timid or hesitant writers, or think that they cannot write and spell, they may produce a reluctant twenty lines or so. As with their reading, early failure brings later inexperience. To learn to write is to write, and correct spelling is the consideration an author offers the first reader of his manuscript.

Epilogue

In the end, adults, however well-intentioned, have to retire from the scene and leave the young to those who really teach them to read, the gifted writers who choose them for their audience. We have said all along that our support is only temporary. If you have helped someone to move from the first halting steps with words on a page to confident fluency you will agree that nothing is more satisfying.

No child should fail to read and write. If you have run into difficulties beyond your understanding and the scope of this book, I must stand by all that I have said and lend an ear or a hand. My kind publishers, whose patience is endless, will act as go-between.

I owe much to all my colleagues and friends in the English Department at the Institute of Education in London, who, distinguished practitioners of literacy as they are, have given me time and support. For my students who uncover the difficulties of individual children, and for Judith Graham, Elizabeth Plackett, Viki Austerfield and Stephen Armstrong who worked with me on a reading problem for four years I have great admiration and gratitude. My children, who had their share of normal problems, lent me their books and willingly read mine.

Book Lists

In the lists which follow I have recommended as many books as space allows, but if you want to keep up to date with what is being published for children it is worth taking out a subscription to one of the specialized journals. You will not necessarily find them stocked by newsagents.

Books for Keeps Pat Triggs (Ed.) The School Bookshop Association, 1 Effingham Road, Lee, London SE12 8NZ
Books for Your Children Anne Wood and Carole Thomson (Eds.) 34 Harborne Road, Edgbaston, Birmingham B15 3AA
The Good Book Guide to Children's Books Elaine Moss (Editorial Adviser) 91 Great Russell Street, London WC1V 3PS
Growing Point Margery Fisher (Ed.) Ashton Manor, Northampton NN7 2JL
School Librarian Joan Murphy (Ed.) The School Library Association, Victoria House, 29–31 George Street, Oxford OX1 2AY
Signal Nancy Chambers (Ed.) The Thimble Press, Lockwood, Station Road, South Woodchester, Stroud, Gloucestershire GL5 5EQ

Some useful books about children's books which I have referred to in the text are:

Children's Minds Margaret Donaldson (Croom Helm/Fontana paperback)
The Cool Web Griselda Barton, Margaret Meek & Aidan Warlow (Eds.) (Bodley Head paperback)
Cushla and her Books Dorothy Butler (Hodder & Stoughton)
Involving Parents in Nursery & Infant Schools Barbara Tizard, Jo Mortimore & Bebb Burchell (Grant McIntyre)

Only Connect Sheila Egoff (Ed.) (O.U.P. paperback)
Reading: The Language Experience Approach Norah
  Goddard (Macmillan)
Reading: tests and assessment techniques Peter D. Pumfrey
  (Hodder & Stoughton)
Reversals Eileen Simpson (Gollancz)
Spelling: Caught or Taught Margaret Lee Peters
  (Routledge)
Teaching Spelling Mike Torbe (Ward Lock paperback)
The Thorny Paradise Edward Blishen (Ed.) (Kestrel)
Written for Children John Rowe Townsend (Penguin
  paperback)

Books before Five

You can start looking at pictures with children as early as
you like, but the baby should want to look at the picture
rather than at something else. Some books that children
enjoy at this stage remain their favourites throughout childhood, so do not think that they should 'grow out' of them.
Tell the story of the pictures but let the young reader join in
with his version and additions.

  You may find these useful:

Babies Need Books Dorothy Butler (Bodley Head)
Reading for Enjoyment with 0–6 Year Olds Dorothy Butler
  (Baker Book Services Ltd)

NURSERY RHYMES AND OTHER VERSE
Cakes and Custard Brian Alderson (Ed.), illus. Helen
  Oxenbury (Heinemann)
A Child's Garden of Verses Robert Louis
  Stevenson (many editions)

Come Hither Walter de la Mare (Ed.) (Kestrel/Puffin paperback)

Lavender's Blue Kathleen Lines (Ed.), illus. Harold Jones (O.U.P.)

Mother Goose Brian Wildsmith (O.U.P.)

The Mother Goose Treasury Raymond Briggs (Hamish Hamilton/Puffin paperback)

The Oxford Book of Poetry for Children Edward Blishen (Ed.) (O.U.P.)

JINGLES, NURSERY GAMES AND FINGER PLAYS
This Little Puffin Elizabeth Matterson (Ed.) (Puffin paperback)

A Nursery Companion Iona & Peter Opie (Eds.) (O.U.P.)

BOARD BOOKS (Bodley Head)
Animal Babies Robert Broomfield

Clothes Shirley Hughes

Farm Animals Betty Youngs

Flowers and *Fruit* David Hughes

Indoors and *Out-of-Doors* Maureen Roffey

Wheels and *Wild Animals* William Stobbs

TRADITIONAL RHYMES AND STORIES WITH PICTURES
Chicken Licken Kenneth McLeish (Longman)

Dame Wiggins of Lee Ferelith Eccles Williams (World's Work)

Drummer Hoff Barbara Emberley, illus. Ed Emberley (Bodley Head)

The Great Big Enormous Turnip Helen Oxenbury (Heinemann/Piccolo paperback)

The House That Jack Built Rodney Peppé (Kestrel/Lion paperback)

Humpty Dumpty Rodney Peppé (Kestrel)

Kevin the Kitten Terry Hall (Hart-Davis)

The Little Red Hen Janina Domanska (Hamish Hamilton)

The Old Woman and Her Pig Paul Galdone (Bodley Head)

The Owl and the Pussycat   Edward Lear, illus. Nicola
   Bayley (Cape)
Sing a Song of Sixpence   Mary Tozer   (World's Work)
The Story of the Three Bears   William Stobbs   (Bodley
   Head/Puffin paperback)
The Story of the Three Little Pigs   William Stobbs   (Bodley
   Head)
Ten Green Bottles   Susanna Gretz   (Kestrel)
The Three Billy Goats Gruff   Paul Galdone   (World's Work)
Tinker, Tailor, Soldier, Sailor   Bernard Lodge, illus.
   Maureen Roffey   (Bodley Head/Lion paperback)

ALPHABET BOOKS AND FIRST COUNTING BOOKS
ABC   Brian Wildsmith   (O.U.P.)
Anno's Alphabet   Mitsumasa Anno   (Bodley Head)
Anno's Counting Book   Mitsumasa Anno   (Bodley Head)
Helen Oxenbury's ABC of Things   Helen
   Oxenbury   (Heinemann)
A Kipling ABC   John Lockwood Kipling   (Macmillan)
The Most Amazing Counting Book   Robert
   Crowther   (Kestrel)
The Most Amazing Hide-and-Seek Alphabet Book   Robert
   Crowther   (Kestrel)
My Big Picture Word Book   Linda Hayward   (Collins)
A Number of Things   Helen Oxenbury   (Heinemann)
A Peaceable Kingdom: The Shaker Abecedarius   illus. Alice
   and Martin Provensen   (Kestrel/Puffin paperback)

PICTURE BOOKS
The Baby   John Burningham   (Cape)
Benjamin and the Box   Alan Baker   (Deutsch/Lion
   paperback)
The Blanket   John Burningham   (Cape)
The Cat in the Hat   Dr Seuss   (Collins)
Changes, Changes   Pat Hutchins   (Bodley Head)
The Dog   John Burningham   (Cape)
Dogger   Shirley Hughes   (Bodley Head/Lion paperback)
Each Peach Pear Plum   Janet & Allan
   Ahlberg   (Kestrel/Lion paperback)

Goodnight, Goodnight Eve Rice (Bodley Head/Puffin paperback)
Grandfather Jeannie Baker (Deutsch)
How Do I Put It On? Shigeo Watanabe, illus. Yasuo Ohtomo (Bodley Head/Puffin paperback)
In a House I Know Leila Berg, illus. John Walmsley (Methuen)
Little Tim stories Edward Ardizzone (O.U.P. and Bodley Head)
Mine's the Best Crosby Bonsall (World's Work)
Mr Gumpy's Outing John Burningham (Cape/Puffin paperback)
Mr Rabbit and the Lovely Present Charlotte Zolotow, illus. Maurice Sendak (Bodley Head/Puffin paperback)
My Cat Likes to Hide in Boxes Eve Sutton, illus. Lynley Dodd (Hamish Hamilton/Puffin paperback)
New Blue Shoes Eve Rice (Bodley Head/Puffin paperback)
The Rabbit John Burningham (Cape)
Rosie's Walk Pat Hutchins (Bodley Head/Puffin paperback)
The Seasons Brian Wildsmith (O.U.P.)
Spaceman, Spaceman Barbara Ireson (Carousel paperback)
The Tale of Peter Rabbit Beatrix Potter (Frederick Warne)
Tales of Oliver Pig Jean Van Leeuwen, illus. Arnold Lobel (Bodley Head/Corgi paperback)
The Tiger who came to Tea Judith Kerr (Collins/Lion paperback)
Titch Pat Hutchins (Bodley Head/Puffin paperback)
Truck Donald Crews (Bodley Head)
The Very Hungry Caterpillar Eric Carle (Hamish Hamilton/Puffin paperback)
Where The Wild Things Are Maurice Sendak (Bodley Head/Puffin paperback)
In the Night Kitchen Maurice Sendak (Bodley Head/Puffin paperback)

Outside Over There   Maurice Sendak   (Bodley Head)
Where's Spot?   Eric Hill   (Heinemann)
Whistle for Willie   Ezra Jack Keats   (Bodley Head/Puffin paperback)

Books from Five to Seven

In school, children have reading lessons. At other times they discover how many kinds of reading there are. If your child is just beginning, don't miss the fun and the experience offered by the books on the first list. Above all, try not to push your child ahead too fast. All five-year-olds profit from the books they enjoy and the stories they hear if reading is sharing pleasure with an adult and not just one long lesson.

You may find these useful:

Breakthrough to Literacy   David Mackay   (Longman)
Learning to Read with Picture Books   Jill Bennett   (A *Signal* publication)

BOOKS TO LOOK AT TOGETHER
Anno's Journey   Mitsumasa Anno   (Bodley Head)
Bodley Head Board Books   (listed in full on p. 230)
Collins Mini Pop-up Books
The Great Menagerie   Anon. verses by Anthea Bell, a reproduction of the antique pop-up book   (Kestrel)
Little Blue and Little Yellow   Leo Lionni   (Hodder & Stoughton)
The Most Amazing Hide-and-Seek Alphabet Book   Robert Crowther   (Kestrel)
The Snowman   Raymond Briggs   (Hamish Hamilton/Puffin paperback)

Truck Donald Crews (Bodley Head)
Up and Up Shirley Hughes (Bodley Head/Lion paperback)

BOOKS FOR THOSE STARTING TO READ
Each of the authors in this list has a number of other books worth looking at. All of these can be read to a child many times so that the child eventually can read alone.

Are You My Mother? P. D. Eastman (Collins)
Benjamin and the Box Alan Baker (Deutsch/Lion paperback)
The Big Sneeze H. E. Todd, illus. Val Biro (Hodder & Stoughton)
Cannonball Simp John Burningham (Cape/Puffin paperback)
Funny Bones Janet & Allan Ahlberg (Heinemann)
Happy Families Janet & Allan Ahlberg (Kestrel/Puffin paperback)
Harry the Dirty Dog Gene Zion, illus. Margaret Bloy Graham (Bodley Head/Puffin paperback)
Joseph's Yard Charles Keeping (O.U.P.)
Little Grey Rabbit's Washing Day Alison Uttley (Collins)
Look What I've Got Anthony Browne (Julia MacRae)
Magical Changes Graham Oakley (Macmillan)
Meg and Mog Helen Nicoll (Heinemann/Puffin paperback)
Mike Mulligan and His Steam Shovel Virginia Lee Burton (Faber/Puffin paperback)
Mine's The Best Crosby Bonsall (World's Work)
New Blue Shoes Eve Rice (Bodley Head/Puffin paperback)
Nini on Time Errol Lloyd (Bodley Head)
Not Now Bernard David McKee (Hutchinson)
PB Takes a Holiday Gerald Rose (Bodley Head)
Panda's Puzzle Michael Foreman (Hamish Hamilton)
The Tale of Thomas Mead Pat Hutchins (Bodley Head)
Tilly's House Faith Jaques (Heinemann/Lion paperback)

A Time to Laugh   Sara & Stephen Corrin (Eds.)   (Faber)
The Trouble with Jack   Shirley Hughes   (Bodley Head)
A Wet Monday   Dorothy Edwards   (Methuen)
What Did You Do In the Holiday?   Celia
   Berridge   (Deutsch)
A Winter Story   Max Bolliger, illus. Beatrix Schären
   (Kestrel)
Would You Rather   John Burningham   (Cape)

RHYMES AND POEMS
To learn the tune on the page and to discover that the sounds
of the words are related to how they are written, children
need verses that have rhythm and word play.

Lollipops   Brian Thompson   (Kestrel)
Matilda Jane   Jean & Roy Gerrard   (Gollancz)
Mother Goose Comes to Cable Street   Rosemary Stones &
   Andrew Mann   (Kestrel/Puffin paperback)
Mother Goose Treasury   Raymond Briggs   (Hamish
   Hamilton/Puffin paperback)
A Nursery Companion   Iona & Peter Opie (Eds.)
   (O.U.P.)
The Puffin Book of Magic Verse   Charles Causley
   (Ed.)   (Puffin paperback)
Roger Was a Razor Fish   Jill Bennett (Ed.)   (Bodley
   Head/Hippo paperback)
Sally Go Round the Sun   David Mackay   (Kestrel)

BOOKS FOR THE TOP END OF THE AGE RANGE
a) with text and pictures

A Child's Book of Manners   Fay Maschler   (Cape)
The Church Mouse   Graham Oakley   (Macmillan)
Come Away From the Water, Shirley   John
   Burningham   (Cape)
*How Tom Beat Captain Najork and His Hired
   Sportsmen*   Russell Hoban, illus. Quentin
   Blake   (Cape/Puffin paperback)

The Mouse and the Egg William Mayne, illus. Krystyna Turska (Julia MacRae/Lion paperback)
My Grandmother's Djinn Brian Robb (Deutsch)
Seven Years and a Day Colette O'Hare, illus. Beryl Cook (Collins)
The Sleeping Beauty Brothers Grimm (many editions)
Trick a Tracker Michael Foreman (Gollancz)
Tusk, Tusk David McKee (Hutchinson)
A Walk in the Park Anthony Browne (Hamish Hamilton)

b) more text and fewer pictures

The Big Brass Band Marjorie Darke (Kestrel)
Burglar Bill Janet & Allan Ahlberg (Heinemann/Lion paperback)
Clever Polly and the Stupid Wolf Catherine Storr (Faber/Puffin paperback)
The House That Sailed Away Pat Hutchins (Bodley Head/Lion paperback)
I'm Fed Up R. & A. Van der Meer (Hamish Hamilton)
Little Old Mrs Pepperpot Alf Prøysen (Hutchinson/Puffin paperback)
The Owl Who Was Afraid of the Dark Jill Tomlinson (Methuen/Puffin paperback)
Winnie the Pooh A. A. Milne (Methuen/Magnet paperback)

STORIES TO READ TO CHILDREN
Aesop Fables Patricia Crampton (re-teller) (Dent)
Chanticleer and The Fox Geoffrey Chaucer, illus. Barbara Cooney (Longman)
Just So Stories Rudyard Kipling (Macmillan/Piccolo paperback)
The Land of Green Ginger Noel Langley (Kestrel/Puffin paperback)

Little Pete Stories Leila Berg (Methuen/Puffin
  paperback)
My Naughty Little Sister Dorothy
  Edwards (Methuen/Puffin paperback)
Stories for Six Year Olds/Seven Year Olds Sara & Stephen
  Corrin (Faber/Puffin paperback)
The Wolf and the Seven Little Kids Brothers Grimm,
  translated by A. Rogers (Pelham books)
Worzel Gummidge Barbara Euphan Todd (Evans/Puffin
  paperback)

Books from Seven to Ten

A useful list is Jill Bennett's *Reaching Out* (A *Signal*
publication).

PICTURE BOOKS
Asterix the Gaul René Goscinny, illus. Albert
  Uderzo (Hodder & Stoughton/Knight paperback)
Joan of Arc a facsimile of 1897 edition Louis-Maurice
  Boutet de Monvel (Viking Press, New York,
  distributed by the Transatlantic Book Service, London)
Tintin in America Hergé (Methuen/Magnet paperback)

TRADITIONAL STORIES, FAIRY TALES & LEGENDS
Abbey Lubbers, Banshees & Boggarts Katharine
  Briggs (Kestrel)
Arabian Nights Amabel Williams-Ellis (Blackie)
English Fairy Tales illus. Edward Ardizzone (Deutsch)
Fables Arnold Lobel (Cape)
Fairy Tales of Gold Alan Garner (Collins)

King Arthur and His Knights of the Round Table   Roger
   Lancelyn Green   (Faber/Puffin paperback)
The Light Princess   George MacDonald, illus. Maurice
   Sendak   (Bodley Head)
Mazel and Shlimazel   Isaac Bashevis Singer, illus. Margot
   Zemach   (Cape)
Popular Folk Tales   Brothers Grimm, Brian Alderson
   (Ed.)   (Gollancz)
The Silent Playmate   Naomi Lewis (Ed.)   (Gollancz)

STORIES OF ALL KINDS
The Battle of Bubble and Squeak   Philippa
   Pearce   (Deutsch/Puffin paperback)
The Bee Rustlers   Jan Needle   (Collins)
The Best of Branestawm   Norman Hunter   (Bodley Head)
The Borrowers   Mary Norton   (Dent/Puffin paperback)
Charlotte's Web   E. B. White   (Hamish Hamilton/Puffin
   paperback)
The Children of Green Knowe   Lucy M. Boston
   (Faber/Puffin paperback)
The Fantastic Mr Fox   Roald Dahl   (Allen &
   Unwin/Puffin paperback)
Flat Stanley   Jeff Brown   (Methuen/Magnet paperback)
Gowie Corbie Plays Chicken   Gene Kemp   (Faber)
The Iron Man   Ted Hughes   (Faber)
Journey Into War   Margaret Donaldson   (Deutsch)
King Grisly-Beard   Brothers Grimm, illus. Maurice
   Sendak   (Bodley Head)
King of the Knockdown Gingers   Geraldine Kaye
   (Hodder & Stoughton/Hopscotch paperback)
The Kingdom of Carbonel   Barbara Sleigh
   (Longman/Puffin paperback)
The Land of Green Ginger   Noel Langley   (Kestrel/Puffin
   paperback)
The Little House in the Big Woods   Laura Ingalls
   Wilder   (Methuen/Puffin paperback)
Mouldy's Orphan   Gillian Avery   (Collins/Puffin
   paperback)

Mrs Pepperpot's Year Alf Prøysen (Hutchinson/Puffin paperback)

Nice Day Out? Dick Cate (Hamish Hamilton)

The Railway Children E. Nesbit (many editions)

Ramona and Her Mother Beverly Cleary (Hamish Hamilton/Puffin paperback)

The Robbers Nina Bawden (Gollancz)

The Runaway Gillian Cross (Methuen)

The Shrinking of Treehorn Florence Parry Heide (Kestrel/Puffin paperback)

Soumchi trans. by Amos Oz & Penelope Farmer, illus. Papas (Chatto)

The Stone Book Quartet Alan Garner (Collins/Lion paperback)

Tales of a Fourth Grade Nothing Judy Blume (Bodley Head/Piccolo paperback)

Thunder and Lightnings Jan Mark (Kestrel//Puffin paperback)

What Difference Does It Make Danny? Helen Young (Deutsch)

What the Neighbours Did Philippa Pearce (Kestrel/Puffin paperback)

POETRY BOOKS

Beastly Boys and Ghastly Girls William Cole (Methuen/Magnet paperback)

I Like This Poem Kaye Webb (Ed.) (Puffin paperback)

The Oxford Book of Children's Verse Iona & Peter Opie (O.U.P.)

Peacock Pie Walter de la Mare (Faber)

The Penguin Book of Salt-Sea Verse Charles Causley (Ed.) (Puffin paperback)

The Young Puffin Book of Verse Barbara Ireson (Ed.) (Puffin paperback)

NON-FICTION

The City of Gold Peter Dickinson (Gollancz)

Everest Charles Clarke (Sackett & Marshall)

The Guinness Book of Records   N. D. McWhirter
   (Ed.)   (Guinness)
The Iguanodon Mystery   William Edmonds   (Kestrel)
So You Want to be Prime Minister   Des Wilson
   (Kestrel/Peacock paperback)
Street Flowers   Richard Mabey   (Kestrel)
Tracks   Niko Tinbergen & E. A. R. Ennion   (O.U.P.)

Books for Eleven

Suddenly, there are hundreds of books for good readers, and
the problem is what to choose. As they gain experience, some
children range over everything they can find. Others stay
with what they know best. By now your children will choose
their own books if they know what they like. The late starters
need encouragement to be adventurous. No one should be
put off by other adults when they say things like 'Haven't
you read *The Wind in the Willows* yet?' As we grow older we
tend to forget exactly *when* we read the important books of
our childhood, but certain titles always seem to crop up
when children's books are talked about. Those in this first
list are often called 'classics'. You will find them all in
paperback editions. Don't force them into children's hands
without reading them again for yourself. They may not now
seem to be exactly what you remember reading. All of these
books need the reader to be fairly independent but it's quite
usual to give some help at the start.

The Adventures of Tom Sawyer   Mark Twain   (many
   editions)
Alice's Adventures in Wonderland   Lewis Carroll   (many
   editions)
Black Beauty   Anna Sewell   (many editions)

Charlotte's Web   E. B. White   (Hamish Hamilton/Puffin
   paperback)
A Christmas Carol   Charles Dickens   (many editions)
Heidi   Joanna Spyri   (many editions)
The Hobbit   J. R. R. Tolkien   (Allen & Unwin)
Jungle Book   Rudyard Kipling   (Macmillan/Piccolo
   paperback)
The Little House on the Prairie   Laura Ingalls
   Wilder   (Methuen/Puffin paperback)
Little Women   Louisa M. Alcott   (many editions)
Peter Pan   J. M. Barrie   (many editions)
The Princess and the Goblin   George
   MacDonald   (Scripture Union/Puffin paperback)
The Railway Children   E. Nesbit   (many editions)
Rewards and Fairies   Rudyard
   Kipling   (Macmillan/Piccolo paperback)
The Secret Garden   Frances Hodgson Burnett   (many
   editions)
Swallows and Amazons   Arthur Ransome   (Cape/Puffin
   paperback)
Treasure Island   R. L. Stevenson   (many editions)
We Didn't Mean to Go to Sea   Arthur
   Ransome   (Cape/Puffin paperback)
The Wheel on the School   Meindert de
   Jong   (Lutterworth/Puffin paperback)
The Wind in the Willows   Kenneth
   Grahame   (Methuen/Magnet paperback)

Most appropriate at this time are legends of heroes, an-
cient and modern. Superman and Batman are part of a very
old tradition in storytelling. Science fiction too begins to be
popular. Collections of stories are to be found in all the
paperback imprints. Here is a sample:

All But A Few   Joan Aiken   (Cape/Puffin paperback)
A Book of Heroes   William Mayne   (Hamish Hamilton)
A Book of Sea Legends   Michael Brown   (Hamish
   Hamilton/Puffin paperback)

The God Beneath the Sea   Edward Blishen & Leon
  Garfield   (Longman)
Heroes of Greece and Troy   Roger Lancelyn Green
  (Bodley Head/in two volumes in Puffin paperback)
The High Deeds of Finn Mac Cool   Rosemary Sutcliff
  (Bodley Head/Puffin paperback)
The Ice Warrior and Other Stories   Robin Chambers
  (Kestrel/Puffin paperback)
King Arthur and His Knights of the Round Table   Roger
  Lancelyn Green   (Faber/Puffin paperback)
Old Peter's Russian Tales   Arthur Ransome   (Puffin
  paperback)
Trillions   Nicholas Fisk   (Puffin paperback)
Warrior Scarlet   Rosemary Sutcliff   (O.U.P./Puffin
  paperback)

Many of the books recommended by selectors for this stage
are stories about the beginnings of the problems of growing up.
Some children read them eagerly and many adults read them
for the values and attitudes they convey. Others do not want to
confront their deepest fears in this way, so you have to be
tactful about recommendations and avoid too much interference. Any of the following would be 'a good read' and a
genuine literary experience for children of this age. Many of
them are recommended in school.

The Borrowers   Mary Norton   (Dent/Puffin paperback)
Carrie's War   Nina Bawden   (Gollancz/Puffin
  paperback)
The Children of Green Knowe   Lucy M. Boston
  (Faber/Puffin paperback)
The Chronicles of Narnia   C. S. Lewis   (Collins/Lion
  paperback)
A Dog so Small   Philippa Pearce   (Kestrel/Puffin
  paperback)
The Eighteenth Emergency   Betsy Byars   (Bodley
  Head/Puffin paperback)
A Few Fair Days   Jane Gardam   (Hamish Hamilton)

The Ghost of Thomas Kempe Penelope Lively
(Heinemann/Piccolo paperback)
I am David Anne Holm (Methuen/Magnet paperback)
The Incredible Adventures of Professor Branestawm Norman
Hunter (Bodley Head/Puffin paperback)
The Incredible Term of Tyke Tiler Gene Kemp
(Faber/Puffin paperback)
No Way of Telling Emma Smith (Bodley Head)
The Runaway Summer Nina Bawden (Gollancz/Puffin
paperback)
The Shadow-Cage and Other Tales of the Supernatural
Philippa Pearce (Kestrel/Puffin paperback)
The Silent Playmate Naomi Lewis (Ed.) (Gollancz)
The Stone Book Quartet Alan Garner (Collins/Lion
paperback)
Tom's Midnight Garden Philippa Pearce (O.U.P./Puffin
paperback)

LATE STARTERS
Some children miss a stage and still don't want to be seen
reading 'little' or 'baby' books when their contemporaries
have moved into longer stories or 'big' books. You can help a
late starter, or a reader who needs more experience, with
something funny or a tale that begins with the familiar and
becomes surprising.

The Adventures of Tintin Hergé (Methuen/Magnet
paperback)
Asterix the Gaul (and many others) René Goscinny, illus.
Albert Uderzo (Hodder & Stoughton/Knight
paperback)
A Boy and His Bike Richard Potts (Dobson/Puffin
paperback)
Dragonfall 5 (and sequels) Brian Earnshaw
(Methuen/Magnet paperback)
Fattypuffs and Thinifers André Maurois (Bodley
Head/Puffin paperback)

Flat Stanley Jeff Brown (Methuen/Magnet paperback)
The Shrinking of Treehorn Florence Parry Heide
  (Kestrel/Puffin paperback)
Some Swell Pup Matthew Margolis, illus. Maurice
  Sendak (Bodley Head/Puffin paperback)
What the Neighbours Did Philippa Pearce (Kestrel/Puffin
  paperback)

Books before Fifteen

By this time, no one can be sure which books the young will
enjoy and profit from. Many young readers will be as skilled
as adults; others will be finding their way to what they like;
some may be resting, looking to magazines and pop music
for contact with the culture of their generation.

There are many fine novels for teenagers. But this is the
time when the move to reading 'the classics' is featured in
school, and teachers are apt to expect young secondary
school pupils to take on a fair amount of independent
reading. Here are some novels that adults can provide for
readers who are looking for a more mature viewpoint in what
they read.

'CLASSICAL FAVOURITES' (Do not expect them all to be an
instant success. Some need a helpful introduction, from a TV
or radio adaptation or an enthusiast.)
The Adventures of Huckleberry Finn Mark Twain (many
  editions)
The Adventures of Sherlock Holmes A. Conan Doyle
  (J. Murray & Cape/Pan paperback)
Anne of Green Gables L. M. Montgomery
  (Harrap/Puffin paperback)
King Solomon's Mines H. Rider Haggard (many
  editions)

Lassie Come Home   Eric Knight   (Cassell/Puffin paperback)

The Lord of the Rings   J. R. R. Tolkien   (Allen & Unwin)

Lorna Doone   R. D. Blackmore   (many editions)

Moonfleet   J. Meade Falkner   (E. J. Arnold/Puffin paperback)

Our Exploits at West Poley   Thomas Hardy   (O.U.P. paperback)

Tarka the Otter   Henry Williamson   (Bodley Head/Puffin paperback)

The Thirty-Nine Steps   John Buchan   (many editions)

Tom Brown's Schooldays   Thomas Hughes   (many editions)

FINDING YOURSELF IN A BOOK

Every list goes quickly out of date, and none more so than those with a strong contemporary flavour and appeal. Nowadays we are specially concerned with the lives of girls, for example, and the nature of our multicultural society. Books for young adults seem quickly to lose touch with what most concerns teenagers—the world they are about to enter and the roles they will expect to play. For writers, the move from childhood to adulthood offers a rich vein of experience to be explored, especially in the awakening of a young person's realization that life is neither simple nor straightforward.

Most of the authors whose books appear in this list have written many other books. All are involved in the production of fiction for teenagers, either in the 'realistic' way or as particular 'secondary worlds' or allegories. The step from these books to adult literature is a short one.

The Basketball Game   Julius Lester   (Peacock paperback)

Black Jack   Leon Garfield   (Kestrel/Puffin paperback)

The Blue Hawk   Peter Dickinson   (Gollancz/Puffin paperback)

A Boy in your Situation Charles Hannam (Deutsch)

Breaktime Aidan Chambers (Bodley Head)

The Chocolate War Robert Cormier (Gollancz/Lion paperback)

The Clearance Joan Lingard (Hamish Hamilton/ Beaver paperback)

The Dark is Rising Susan Cooper (Bodley Head/ Puffin paperback)

Dear Hill Gwynneth A. Jones (Macmillan)

Devil by the Sea Nina Bawden (Gollancz)

The Devil on the Road Robert Westall (Macmillan)

The Diary of Anne Frank Anne Frank (Hutchinson/Pan paperback)

East End at Your Feet Farrukh Dhondy (Collins/Topliner paperback)

The Ennead Jan Mark (Kestrel/Puffin Plus paperback)

Flambards K. M. Peyton (O.U.P./Puffin paperback)

The Friends Rosa Guy (Gollancz/Puffin paperback)

A Game of Dark William Mayne (Hamish Hamilton)

The Ghost on the Hill John Gordon (Kestrel/Peacock paperback)

The Gods in Winter Patricia Miles (Hamish Hamilton)

Goldengrove Jill Paton Walsh (Bodley Head paperback)

The Guns of Darkness Anne Schlee (Macmillan)

The Hostage Anne Holm (Methuen)

The Intruder John Rowe Townsend (O.U.P./Peacock paperback)

The Iron Tsar Geoffrey Trease (Macmillan/Piccolo paperback)

It William Mayne (Hamish Hamilton/Puffin paperback)

Jack Holborn Leon Garfield (Kestrel/Puffin paperback)

Kestrel for a Knave (Kes) Barry Hines (Michael Joseph/Penguin paperback)

The *Mantlemass* novels Barbara Willard (Kestrel/Puffin paperback)

The Mark of the Horse Lord Rosemary Sutcliff (O.U.P.)

Midnight is a Place   Joan Aiken   (Cape/Puffin paperback)

A Most Beautiful Day   Isaac Bashevis Singer   (Julia MacRae)

The Mouse and His Child   Russell Hoban   (Faber/Puffin paperback)

My Darling, My Hamburger   Paul Zindel   (Bodley Head/Lion paperback)

My Father, Sun-Sun Johnson   Everard Palmer (Deutsch)

My Mate, Shofiq   Jan Needle   (Deutsch/Lion paperback)

Nobody's Family is Going to Change   Louise Fitzhugh   (Gollancz/Lion paperback)

One More River   Lynne Reid Banks   (Vallentine, Mitchell/Peacock paperback)

The Pigman   Paul Zindel   (Bodley Head/Lion paperback)

Please Don't Go   Peggy Woodford   (Bodley Head)

Prove Yourself a Hero   K. M. Peyton   (O.U.P./Puffin Plus paperback)

Red Shift   Alan Garner   (Collins/Lion paperback)

A Saturday in Pudney   Roy Brown   (Abelard-Schuman)

Scarf Jack   P. J. Kavanagh   (Bodley Head/Puffin paperback)

Silver's Revenge   Robert Leeson   (Collins)

The Slave Dancer   Paula Fox   (Cape/Pan paperback)

The Summer After the Funeral   Jane Gardam   (Hamish Hamilton/Peacock paperback)

The Third Class Genie   Robert Leeson   (Collins/Lion paperback)

Tulku   Peter Dickinson   (Gollancz)

A Very Long Way from Anywhere Else   Ursula Le Guin (Gollancz/Peacock paperback)

The Warden's Niece   Gillian Avery   (Bodley Head paperback)

The Waterfall Box   John Gordon   (Kestrel)

Watership Down   Richard Adams   (Kestrel/Puffin paperback)

The Wizard of Earthsea   Ursula Le Guin (Gollancz/Peacock paperback)

The Wirrun Trilogy   Patricia Wrightson   (Hutchinson)
You can't keep out the darkness   Peggy Woodford (Ed.)
    (Bodley Head)
Your Friend, Rebecca   Linda Hoy   (Bodley Head—a
    Paperback Original)

FOR THOSE STILL PUZZLED WHERE TO START
Some adolescents are still uncertain about reading. They
avoid it whenever they can, yet their teachers and parents
constantly urge them to do it. The books that are written for
inexperienced readers often fail to show what real readers
enjoy about reading. Instead, they simplify sentences, plots
and ideas and so leave tentative readers with the idea that
they are not with real books, only reading books.

If you want to find something that will encourage someone
who is not enthusiastic about reading, look for something
practical that will enlarge the scope of the non-reader's
interests (hobbies, and sports are good starting places), or
find something funny that confirms reading as a pleasure
without strings attached.

These are only samples. Consult a good library for more.

Berry's Book of How It Works   Roland Berry
    (Black/Puffin paperback)
Come to Mecca   Farrukh Dhondy   (Collins/Lion
    paperback)
Cooking is a Way Round the World   Fay Maschler
    (Kestrel/Puffin paperback)
Cops and Robbers   Janet & Allan Ahlberg
    (Heinemann/Lion paperback)
Light Verse for Children   Gavin Ewart (Ed.)   (Batsford)
The Making of a Gymnast: Karen Kelsall Story   Jean
    Boulogne   (Robson)
Scramble Cycle   E. & R. Radlaver   (Franklin
    Watts/Target paperback)
You Tell Me   Roger McGough & Michael Rosen
    (Kestrel/Puffin paperback)

INDEX

Index

Index

social awareness, 212
social background, 58
songs, 22, 33, 43–4
Sounder, 199
sounding out, teaching method,
    26, 42, 69, 72, 74–5, 120, 146,
    147
speech *see* language
spelling, 41–2, 120–1, 181–2,
    223–6; reform of, 72–4
Spelling: Caught or Taught, 181
SQ3R, teaching method, 207
Squirrel Wife, The, 138
stages of reading, 24, 103, 104–5
Stone Book Quartet, The, 157, 174
stories, making up, 38–9, 48,
    69–70, 87, 91, 92, 125, 131
Stories for Seven Year Olds, 99
Stories for Six Year Olds, 99
Storr, Catherine, 135
Street Flowers, 144
Sutcliff, Rosemary, 174, 211
symbols, in language, 37; in play,
    36–7

Tale of Jemima Puddleduck, The, 105
Tale of Peter Rabbit, The, 50
talk, importance of, 52, 80, 191,
    204, 221
teachers, aims, 26; approaches to
    teaching, 64–9, 123, 125–7;
    attitudes, 10, 24, 64, 117, 119,
    158–9; as partners, 9, 61, 62,
    85–6, 87, 91, 119, 131, 168
teaching, approaches, 25, 69–78;
    methods, 61, 72–3, 74–8,
    116–17, 208; special, 129–30,
    206; *and see* remedial
Teaching Spelling, 181
television, 41, 52, 92–3, 106, 143,
    160, 164, 176, 216; how
    much?, 182
Tess of the D'Urbervilles, 214
tests, 150; kinds, 118–19, 184,
    221–2
text, 25, 164
thinking, 11, 18, 35
Third Class Genie, The, 199

Thirty-Nine Steps, The, 172
This Little Puffin, 43
Thompson, Brian, 72
Thorny Paradise, The, 214
Tiger who came to tea, The, 51
Time to Laugh, A, 101
time, for reading, 50, 54, 80, 160,
    182; length of, 29, 108
Tinbergen, Niko, 144
Tintin, 108, 134
Todd, Barbara Euphan, 99
Tolkien, J. R. R., 37, 138, 154,
    178
Tom's Midnight Garden, 210
Topsy and Tim, 100
Torbe, Mike, 181, 225
Townsend, John Rowe, 214
Tracks, 144
tradition, oral, 34
traditional tales, 52, 65, 98, 122,
    137–8
Treasure Island, 177, 213
Treasure Seekers, The, 177
Truck, 102
Twain, Mark, 154
typeface, size of, 46, 101–2

Una of Grub Street, 199
Underground, 178

vertical grouping, 104
Very Hungry Caterpillar, The, 45
vocabulary, 100, 191; sight
    vocabulary, 61, 76

Warrior Scarlet, 174
Water Babies, The, 172
Wet Monday, A, 102
What did you do in the holiday?, 97
Where the Wild Things Are, 49, 97,
    102
Whistle for Willie, 97
White, E. B., 153
Wider Heritage, A, 185
Wilson, Des, 143
Wind in the Willows, The, 148
Winnie the Pooh, 99
Wizard of Earthsea, The, 173

254